RENOVATION
OF THE HEART

PUTTING ON THE CHARACTER
OF CHRIST

BESTSELLING AUTHOR OF *THE DIVINE CONSPIRACY*
DALLAS WILLARD

NAVPRESS

A NavPress resource published in alliance
with Tyndale House Publishers, Inc.

NavPress is the publishing ministry of The Navigators, an international Christian organization and leader in personal spiritual development. NavPress is committed to helping people grow spiritually and enjoy lives of meaning and hope through personal and group resources that are biblically rooted, culturally relevant, and highly practical.

For more information, visit www.NavPress.com.

Renovation of the Heart: Putting On the Character of Christ

Copyright © 2002, 2012 by Dallas Willard. All rights reserved.

A NavPress resource published in alliance with Tyndale House Publishers, Inc.

NAVPRESS and the NAVPRESS logo are registered trademarks of NavPress, The Navigators, Colorado Springs, CO. *TYNDALE* is a registered trademark of Tyndale House Publishers, Inc. Absence of ® in connection with marks of NavPress or other parties does not indicate an absence of registration of those marks.

Cover design by Dan Jamison
Cover illustration by Dan Jamison
Creative Team: Sue Geiman, Don Simpson, Amy Spencer, Pat Reinheimer

Unless otherwise indicated, all Scripture quotations are taken from the New American Standard Bible,® copyright © 1960, 1962, 1963, 1968, 1971, 1972, 1973, 1975, 1977 by The Lockman Foundation. Used by permission. The author's paraphrases and translations are marked as PAR. Scripture quotations marked NIV are taken from the Holy Bible, *New International Version,*® *NIV.*® Copyright © 1973, 1978, 1984 by Biblica, Inc.® Used by permission. All rights reserved worldwide. Scripture quotations marked NRSV are taken from the New Revised Standard Version Bible, copyright © 1989, Division of Christian Education of the National Council of the Churches of Christ in the United States of America. Used by permission. All rights reserved. Scripture quotations marked AMP are taken from the *Amplified New Testament,* copyright © 1954, 1958 by The Lockman Foundation. Used by permission. Scripture quotations marked KJV are taken from the *Holy Bible,* King James Version.

Some of the anecdotal illustrations in this book are true to life and are included with the permission of the persons involved. All other illustrations are composites of real situations, and any resemblance to people living or dead is coincidental.

For information about special discounts for bulk purchases, please contact Tyndale House Publishers at csresponse@tyndale.com or call 800-323-9400.

Library of Congress Cataloging-in-Publication Data

Willard, Dallas, 1935-
  Renovation of the heart : putting on the character of Christ / Dallas
Willard.
    p. cm.
Includes bibliographical references.
  ISBN 1-57683-296-1
  1. Spiritual formation. I. Title.
  BV4511 .W535 2002
  248.4—dc21

                                           2002002119

ISBN 978-1-57683-296-7 (hardback)
ISBN 978-1-61521-632-1 (paperback)

Printed in the United States of America

22 21 20 19
17 16 15 14 13

To L. Duane Willard,
who was big when I was small
and always made a place for me,
and whom I dearly love and treasure

CONTENTS

ACKNOWLEDGMENTS

My thanks, as always, to the many persons who have helped me along the way. To my family, above all, and especially to Bill Heatley, who read the entire manuscript and gave many insights and suggestions; and to John S. Willard, who typed a lot of it and who also made numerous penetrating comments. James Bryan Smith suggested helpful revisions for the earlier chapters as Todd Hunter did for the whole book. The book really wouldn't have made it into existence without the encouragement and excellent editorial direction of Don Simpson, or without the help in managing my life from Jane Lakes Willard, Becky Heatley, Jan Johnson, and Keith Matthews.

PRELUDE

Those who drink of the water that I will give them will never
again be thirsty. The water that I will give will become in
them a spring of water gushing up to eternal life.

JESUS OF NAZARETH (JOHN 4:14, PAR)

When we open ourselves to the writings of the New Testament, when we absorb our minds and hearts in one of the Gospels, for example, or in letters such as Ephesians or 1 Peter, the overwhelming impression that comes upon us is that we are looking into another world and another life.

It is a divine world and a divine life. It is life in the "kingdom of the heavens." Yet it is a world and a life that ordinary people have entered and are entering even now. It is a world that seems open to us and beckons us to enter. We feel its call.

The amazing promises to those who give their life to this new world through their confidence in Jesus leap out at us from the page.

For example, we read Jesus' own words, that those who give themselves to him will receive a "living water," the Spirit of God Himself, that will keep them from ever again being thirsty—being driven and ruled by unsatisfied desires—and that this "water" will become a well or spring of such water "gushing up to eternal life" (John 4:14, PAR). Indeed, it will even become "rivers of living water" flowing from the center of the believer's life to a thirsty world (John 7:38).

Or we read Paul's prayer that believers would "know the love of Christ that surpasses knowledge, so that they may be filled with all the fullness of God . . . by the power at work within us, that is able to accomplish abundantly far more than all we can ask or imagine" (Ephesians 3:19-20, PAR).

Or Peter's words about how those who love and trust Jesus "rejoice with an indescribable and glorious joy" (1 Peter 1:8, NRSV), with "genuine mutual love" pouring from their hearts (1:22), ridding themselves of "all malice, and all guile, insincerity, envy, and all slander" (2:1, NRSV), silencing scoffers at the Way of Christ by simply doing what is right (2:15), and casting all their anxieties upon God because he cares for us (5:7).

The vision is clear, and no one open to it can mistake what it means. But while all is clear and desirable, we must admit that, in many historical periods as well as today, Christians generally only find their way into this divine life slowly and with great difficulty, if at all.

I believe one reason why so many people do in fact *fail* to immerse themselves in the words of the New Testament, and neglect or even avoid them, is that the life they see there is so unlike what they know from their own experience. This is true even though they may be quite faithful to their church in the ways prescribed and really do have Jesus Christ as their only hope. Therefore the clear New Testament presentation of the life we are unmistakably offered in Christ only discourages them or makes them hopeless.

Why should this be so? Surely the life God holds out to us in Jesus was not meant to be an unsolvable puzzle! And that only leaves us with the explanation that, for all our good intentions and strenuous methods, *we do not approach and receive that life in the right way*. We do not comprehend and convey the wisdom of Jesus and the Bible about the human being and about its redemption by grace from the destructive powers that have come to occupy it in all of its primary dimensions.

It really isn't true that where there is a will there is automatically a way, though of course will is crucial. There is also needed an understanding of exactly what needs to be done and how it can be accomplished: of the instruments for the realization of that life and the order of their use.

Spiritual formation in Christ is an orderly process. Although God can triumph in disorder, that is not his choice. And instead of focusing upon what God *can* do, we must humble ourselves to accept the ways he *has chosen* to work with us. These are clearly laid out in the Bible, and especially in the words and person of Jesus.

He invites us to leave our burdensome ways of heavy labor—especially the "religious" ones—and step into the yoke of training with him. This is a way of gentleness and lowliness, a way of soul rest. It is a way of inner transformation that proves pulling his load and carrying his burden *with him* to be a life that is easy and light (Matthew 11:28-30). The perceived distance and difficulty of entering fully into the divine world and its life is due entirely to *our failure to understand that "the way in" is the way of pervasive inner transformation and to our failure to take the small steps that quietly and certainly lead to it.*

This is a hopeful, life-saving insight. For the individual it means that all of the hindrances to our putting off the old person and putting on the new one *can be removed or mastered*. And that will enable us to walk increasingly in the wholeness, holiness, and power of the kingdom of the heavens. No one need live in spiritual and personal defeat. A life of victory over sin and circumstance is accessible to all.

For our Christian groups and their leaders, it means that there is a simple, straightforward way in which congregations of Jesus' people can, without exception, fulfill his call to be an *ecclesia*, his "called out" ones: a touch point between heaven and earth, where the healing of the Cross and the Resurrection can save the lost and grow the saved into the fullness of human beings in Christ. No special facilities, programs, talents, or techniques are required. *It doesn't even require a budget.* Just faithfulness to the process of spiritual formation in Christlikeness exposed in the Scriptures and in the lives of his "peculiar people" through the ages (Titus 2:14, KJV).

INTRODUCING SPIRITUAL FORMATION

The "Beyond Within" and The Way of Jesus

Watch over your heart with all diligence,
for from it flow the springs of life.
PROVERBS 4:23

We live from our heart.

The part of us that drives and organizes our life is not the physical. This remains true even if we deny it. You have a spirit within you and it has been formed. It has taken on a specific character. I have a spirit and it has been formed. This is true of everyone.

The human spirit is an inescapable, fundamental aspect of every human being; and it takes on whichever character it has from the experiences and the choices that we have lived through or made in our past. That is what it means for it to be "formed."

Our life and how we find the world now and in the future is, almost totally, a simple result of what we have become in the depths of our being—in our spirit, will, or heart. From there we see our world and interpret reality. From there we make our choices, break forth into action, try to change our world. We live from our depths—most of which we do not understand.

"Do you mean," some will say, "that the individual and collective disasters that fill the human scene are not imposed upon us from without? That they do not just *happen* to us?"

Yes. That is what I mean. In today's world, famine, war, and epidemic are almost totally the outcome of human choices, which are expressions of the human spirit. Though various qualifications and explanations are appropriate, that is in general true.

Individual disasters, too, very largely follow upon human choices, our own or those of others. And whether or not they do in a particular case, the situations in which we find ourselves are never as important as our responses to them, which come from our "spiritual" side. A carefully cultivated heart will, assisted by the grace of God, foresee, forestall, or transform most of the painful situations before which others stand like helpless children saying "Why?"

The Bible is full of wisdom on these matters. That is why we call major books of the Old Testament "wisdom literature." Jesus sums it all up in his teachings. He is the power and the wisdom of God (1 Corinthians 1:24). For example, he tells us, "Seek first the kingdom and God's righteousness, and all else shall be provided to you" (Matthew 6:33, PAR). And "Everyone who hears these words of mine and does them is like a wise man who built his house upon rock. The rain fell and the streams rose and the winds blew and beat upon the house. But it did not collapse, for it was built on rock" (Matthew 7:24-25, PAR).

Accordingly, the greatest need you and I have — the greatest need of collective humanity — is *renovation of our heart*. That spiritual place within us from which outlook, choices, and actions come has been formed by a world away from God. Now it must be transformed.

Indeed, the only hope of humanity lies in the fact that, as our spiritual dimension has been *formed,* so it also can be *transformed.* Now and throughout the ages this has been acknowledged by everyone who has thought deeply about our condition — from Moses, Solomon, Socrates, and Spinoza, to Marx, Nietzsche, Freud, Oprah, and current feminists and environmentalists. We, very rightly, continually preach this possibility and necessity from our pulpits. Disagreements have only to do with *what* in our spirit needs to be changed and *how* that change can be brought about.

☙ THE REVOLUTION OF JESUS ❧

AND ON THESE TWO points lies the inescapable relevance of Jesus to human life. About two thousand years ago he gathered his little group of friends and trainees on the Galilean hillsides and sent them out to "teach all nations" — that is, to make students (apprentices) to him from all ethnic groups. His objective is eventually to bring all of human life on earth under the direction of his wisdom, goodness, and power, as part of God's eternal plan for the universe.

We must make no mistake about it. In thus sending out his trainees, he set afoot a *perpetual world revolution:* one that is still in process and will continue until God's will is done on earth as it is in heaven. As this revolution culminates, all the forces of evil known to mankind will be defeated and the goodness of God will be known, accepted, and joyously conformed to in every aspect of human life.[1] He has chosen to accomplish this with and, in part, through his students.

It is even now true, as angelic seraphim proclaimed to Isaiah in his vision, that "the whole earth is full of His glory," the glory of the holy Lord of hosts (Isaiah 6:3). But the day is yet to come when "the earth will be filled with the *knowledge* of the glory of the LORD, as the waters cover the sea" (Habakkuk 2:14, emphasis added).

The revolution of Jesus is in the first place and continuously a revolution of the human heart or spirit. It did not and does not proceed by means of the formation of social institutions and laws, the outer forms of our existence, intending that these would then impose a good order of life upon people who come under their power. Rather, his is a revolution of *character,* which proceeds by changing people from the inside through ongoing personal relationship to God in Christ and to one another. It is one that changes their ideas, beliefs, feelings, and habits of choice, as well as their bodily tendencies and social relations. It penetrates to the deepest layers of their soul. External, social arrangements may be useful to this end, but they are not the end, nor are they a fundamental part of the means.

On the other hand, from those divinely renovated depths of the person, social structures will naturally be transformed so that "justice roll[s] down like waters and righteousness like an ever-flowing stream" (Amos 5:24). Such streams *cannot* flow through corrupted souls. Conversely, a renovated "within" will not cooperate with public streams of unrighteousness. It will block them—or die trying. It is the only thing that can do so.

T. S. Eliot once described the current human endeavor as that of finding a system of order so perfect that we will not have to be good. The Way of Jesus tells us, by contrast, that any number of systems—not all, to be sure—will work well if we are genuinely good. And we are then free to seek the better and the best.

This impotence of "systems" is a main reason why Jesus did not send his students out to start governments or even churches as we know them today, which always strongly convey some elements of a human system. They were, instead, to establish beachheads of his person, word, and power in the midst of a failing and futile humanity. They were to bring the presence of the kingdom and its King into every corner of human life simply by fully living in the kingdom with him.

Those who received him as their living Lord and constant instructor would be "God's chosen ones, holy and beloved" (Colossians 3:12, NRSV) and would learn how to "be blameless and harmless, children of God, faultless in the midst of a twisted and misguided generation, from within which they shine as lights in the world, lifting up a word of life" (Philippians 2:15-16, PAR).

Churches—thinking now of local assemblies of such people—would naturally be the result. Churches are not the kingdom of God, but are primary and inevitable expressions, outposts, and instrumentalities of the presence of the kingdom among us. They are "societies" of Jesus, springing up in Jerusalem, in Judea, in Samaria, and to the furthest points on earth (Acts 1:8), as the reality of Christ is brought to bear on ordinary human life. This is an ongoing process, not yet completed today: "And this gospel of the kingdom shall be preached in the whole world for a witness to all nations, and then the end shall come" (Matthew 24:14).

THE HUMAN "WITHIN"

THROUGH THE PRESENCE OF his kingdom, Jesus answers the deepest needs of human personality for righteousness, provision, and purpose. If we set him aside, we still face the unavoidable questions: What makes our lives go as they do? What could make them go as they ought? Inability to find adequate answers leaves us rudderless in the flood of events around us and at the mercy of whatever ideas and forces come to bear upon us. And that, basically, is the human situation. You can see it day by day all around you.

However, thoughtful people through the ages have tried to answer these questions, and they have with one accord found, as already stated, that what matters most for how life goes and ought to go is what we are on the "inside." Things good and bad will happen to us, of course. But what our life amounts to, at least for those who reach full age, is largely, if not entirely, a matter of what we become within. This "within" is the arena of spiritual formation and, later, transformation.

Within are our thoughts, feelings, intentions—and their deeper sources, whatever those may be. The life we live out in our moments, hours, days, and years wells up from a hidden depth. What is in our "heart" matters more than anything else for who we become and what becomes of us. "You're here in my arms," the old song says, "but where is your heart?" That is what really matters, not just for individual relationships, but also for life as a whole.

The author Oscar Wilde once remarked that by the age of forty everyone has the face they deserve. This is a truly profound, if painful, truth. But it really applies to the "within" expressed by the face—to the heart and also the soul, and not to the face merely as one surface area of the body. Otherwise it would not much matter.

Now, right on the conscious surface of our "world within" lie some of our thoughts, feelings, intentions, and plans. These are the ones we are aware of. They may be fairly obvious to others as well as to ourselves. In terms of them we consciously approach our world and our actions within it.

But these surface aspects are also a good indication of the general nature of the unconscious "spiritual depth within," of what sorts of things make it up. But the thoughts, feelings, and intentions we are aware of are, after all, only a small part of the ones that are really there in our depths; and they often are not the ones most revealing of who we actually are and why we do what we do.

What we really think, how we really feel, and what we really would do in circumstances foreseen and unforeseen may be totally unknown to ourselves or to others familiar with us. We may pass one another—even pass ourselves, if you can imagine that—like "ships in the night." We do it all the time.

The hidden dimension of each human life is not visible to others, nor is it fully graspable even by ourselves. We usually know very little about the things that move in our own soul, the deepest level of our life, or what is driving it. Our "within" is astonishingly complex and subtle—even devious. It takes on a life of its own. Only God knows our depths, who we are, and what we would do.

Thus the psalmist cries out for God's help in dealing with—himself! "Search me, O God." "Let the meditations of my heart be acceptable to you." "Renew in me a right spirit." At a certain point my own "beyond that is within" (my heart) has been formed and I am then at its mercy. Only God can save me.

❧ THE "SPIRITUAL" ASPECT OF MAN ❧

I HAVE ALREADY SPOKEN of the hidden world of the self as our *spiritual* side. The language of "spiritual," "spirit," and "spirituality" has become increasingly common today, and it cannot be avoided. But it is often unclear in meaning, and this can be dangerous. It can lead us down paths of confusion and destruction. "Spiritual" is not automatically "good." We must be very careful with this language. Nevertheless, in the sense of "spiritual," which means only "nonphysical," the hidden or inner world of the human self is indeed spiritual.

Interestingly, for all our fine advances in scientific knowledge, the proud product of human thought, they tell us *nothing* about the inner life of the human being. The same is true for all the fields of study that try to base themselves upon such knowledge. At most the sciences can indicate some fascinating and important correlations between our inner life and events in the physical and social world running alongside it.

This is because the subject matter of the sciences is, precisely, the outer, physical, measurable, publicly perceptible world: roughly, the world of "the five senses," as we often say. In its nature the physical is a totally different type of reality from the spiritual side of the human being, which remains "hidden" in a way the physical world never can be. This is by now an old story, but often repressed or forgotten. Science misses the heart.

Paradoxically, the "spiritual" side of us—though it is not perceivable by the senses and though we can never fully grasp it in any way—is never entirely out of our mind. It always stands in the margin of our consciousness, if not the center. It is really the only thing that is celebrated (or degraded) in the arts, in biography and history, and in most of our popular writings in magazines and the like. Their emphasis is continually upon what people think and feel, on what they might or should do and why, and on what kind of character they have. Human beings "gossip" about nothing else, and now much of what is called "news" is really just gossip.

But that only emphasizes how we are constantly aware of the spiritual side of life. We know immediately that it is what really matters. We pay more attention to it—in ourselves and others—than to anything else. And there is a deep, if often perverted, wisdom in this. For *the spiritual simply is our life,* no matter what grand theories we may hold or what we may say when trying to be "intellectual," "well informed," and "up-to-date."

This insuppressible interest explains why, in recent decades and in many ways, the spiritual, in the inclusive human sense, has repeatedly thrust itself to the forefront of our awareness. From the cultural and artistic uprisings of the sixties to the environmentalisms and countless "spiritualities" of the nineties— from pop-culture new age to the postmodernisms of the academy—the swelling protest from the human depths has recently been shouting at us that the physical and public side of the human universe cannot sustain our existence. "Man shall not live by bread alone." We would do well to listen, no matter who is talking.

Those are, of course, words from Jesus. And his way is truly the way of the heart, or spirit. If we would walk with him, we must walk with him at that interior level. There are very few who really do not understand this about him. He saves us by realistic restoration of our heart to God and then by dwelling there with his Father through the distinctively divine Spirit. The heart thus renovated and inhabited is the only real hope of humanity on earth.

The statement that "Man shall not live by bread alone" was adapted by Jesus from the history of the Jewish experience with God. Jesus was, among other things, the most profound and powerful expression of that experience. But it was also given new and profound meaning by his death and resurrection. Through them he established a radically new order of life on earth within the kingdom of God. It was free of any specific ethnic or cultural form. All human beings can now live the life of the renovated heart by nourishing ourselves constantly on his personal presence—now here in our world, beyond his death and ours.

Contrary to what many say today, our deliverance (salvation) does not arise out of the murky human depths from which our natural life springs—whether that includes an "oversoul" or "collective unconsciousness" or not. But Jesus moves into and through those very depths, whatever they contain, to bring us home to God. There, too, he is Master. The spiritual renovation and the "spirituality" that comes from Jesus is nothing less than an invasion of natural human reality by a supernatural life "from above."

❧ SPIRITUALITY AND SPIRITUAL FORMATION AS *MERELY HUMAN* ❧

IN SHARP CONTRAST, SPIRITUALITY and spiritual formation are often understood today as entirely human matters. The "beyond that is within" is thought to be a human dimension or power that, if we only manage it rightly, will transform our life into divine life. Or at least it will deliver us from the chaos and brokenness of human existence—at a minimum, perhaps, from life-destroying addictions, such as to alcohol, work, sex, drugs, or violence. We are engulfed by books, programs, and seminars that rest upon this assumption.

Thus, for example, one now hears "spirituality" described as "our relationship to whatever is most important in our life." Or perhaps as "the process of becoming a positive and creative person." These are words taken from contemporary writings, and they represent deep currents of human thought and culture.[2]

Certainly we do not intend to deride any good thing, and we are thankful for whatever truly helps human beings in their desperate life upon the earth. Nothing else would be compatible with the spirit of Jesus. The constant love of God is extended to every human being who ever lives, sometimes in places and postures that God himself would not prefer, but still with some good effect. But whether or not a spirituality adequate to human need and producing genuine renovation of the heart can be a matter of mere human abilities is a question of fact. To be mistaken about it will have consequences of the most serious nature.

In any case, we may be sure of this: the formation and, later, transformation of the inner life of man, from which our outer existence flows, is an inescapable human problem. *Spiritual formation, without regard to any specifically religious context or tradition, is the* process *by which the human spirit or will is given a definite "form" or character.* It is a process that happens to everyone. The most despicable as well as the most admirable of persons have had a spiritual formation. Terrorists as well as saints are the outcome of spiritual formation. Their spirits or hearts have been formed. Period.

We each become a certain kind of person in the depths of our being, gaining a specific type of character. And that is the outcome of a process of spiritual formation as understood in general human terms that apply to everyone, whether they want it or not. Fortunate or blessed are those who are able to find or are given a path of life that will form their spirit and inner world in a way that is truly strong and good and directed Godward.

The shaping and reshaping of the inner life is, accordingly, a problem that has been around as long as humanity itself; and the earliest records of human thought bear eloquent witness to the human struggle to solve it[3]— but with very limited success, one would have to say.

True, some points in human history have shown more success in the elevation of the human spirit than others. But the low points far exceed the high points, and the average is discouragingly low. Societies the world around are currently in desperate straits trying to produce people who are merely capable of coping with their life on earth in a nondestructive manner. This is as true of North America and Europe as it is of the rest of the world, though the struggle takes superficially different forms in various areas. In spiritual matters there really is no "Third World." It's all Third World.

❧ REACHING BEYOND THE MERELY HUMAN ❧

SO SPIRITUAL TRANSFORMATION, THE renovation of the human heart, is an inescapable human problem with no human solution. We take no satisfaction in pointing this out. It is something that can be learned from a survey of world history, world cultures, and past and present efforts to deal with human life by religion, education, law, and medicine. And this observation unfortunately stands firm when we take into consideration the many techniques that are taught in the various psychologies and competing spiritualities of our own day.

Genuine transformation of the whole person into the goodness and power seen in Jesus and his "Abba" Father—the only transformation adequate to the human self—remains the necessary goal of human life. But it lies beyond the reach of programs of inner transformation that draw *merely* on the human spirit—even when the human spirit is itself treated as ultimately divine.

The reality of all this is currently veiled from view by the very low level of spiritual life seen in Christianity as now placed before the general public. That low level explains why there are at present so many psychologies and spiritualities contesting the field—often led or dominated by ex-Christians who have abandoned recognized forms of Christianity as hopeless or even harmful.

Recently, however, a widespread and intense interest in spiritual formation, under that very name, has arisen among many groups of Christians and their leaders. Why is that? It is mainly due to a realization—confirmed now by many thorough and careful studies, as well as overwhelming anecdotal evidence—that, in its current and recent public forms, Christianity has not been imparting effectual answers to the vital questions of human existence. At least not to wide ranges of self-identifying Christians, and obviously not to nonChristians. And spiritual formation has now presented itself as a hopeful possibility for responding to the crying, unmet need of the human soul. The hope springs once again for a response to the need that is both deeply rooted in Christian traditions and powerfully relevant to circumstances of contemporary life.

✎ GOD MOVES FORWARD ✎

GOD PERIODICALLY MOVES UPON his people and in their surrounding culture to achieve his everlasting purposes for that tiny stretch of cosmic time we call "human history." This usually happens in ways that no one but he could have planned or foreseen and in ways that lie far beyond our control or comprehension.

We discover, usually after the fact, that a pervasive and powerful shift has occurred. It may happen to the individual, to the group, or to an entire culture. Old ways of doing things cease to be effective, though they may have been very powerful in the past. There arises a very real danger that we will set ourselves in opposition to what God truly is doing now and aims to do in the future. Often we miss the opportunity to act with God in the now. We fail to find, quickly enough, new wineskins for the new wine.

Such a new move of God was what happened in the emergence of the Hebrew people from Egypt "when the time was right" and again in their entry into and emergence from Babylonian exile. Again, we see it in the emergence of a "Christian" people within Jewish culture, and then the emergence of a nonethnic "body of Christ" from the Jewish church.

Since then, the pervasive and powerful movement of God has happened again and again during the sojourn of Christ in his people on the earth: the overwhelming of classical paganism, the emergence of the monastic form of Christian devotion, the Cistercian, Franciscan, and Devotio Moderna transformations within monasticism, the Protestant Reformation, Pietism, Wesleyan and American revivalism, and many other such movements of less historical effect, such as the twentieth-century charismatic countercultural upsurges ("Jesus People," and so on). The rise and outworkings of such movements are clearly the result of God's hand in our midst.

And God is still moving. The quest for spiritual formation (really, as indicated, spiritual *trans*formation) is in fact an age-old and worldwide one. It is rooted in the deep personal and even biological need for goodness that haunts humanity. It has taken many forms and has now resurfaced at the beginning of the twenty-first century to meet our present situation. This is, I am sure, part of an incoming tide of God's life that would lift our lives today for our voyage into eternity. Our hearts cry out, "Lord, I want to be a Christian in my heart."

So this quest, currently so deeply felt, is at once new and very old, both very promising and full of danger, illuminative of our lacks and failures and bursting with grace, an expression of the eternal quest of God for man and of man's ineradicable need for God. This contemporary quest for spiritual formation is essential to the life of God in his people as they presently move toward the fulfillment of his purposes for today and beyond.

Viewed sociologically and historically, as well as spiritually, the new impulse is an aspect of the dissolution of Protestant denominationalism as we have known it and of the emergence of a new—but also an old—identity for Christians: crossing all denominational lines and national and natural boundaries.

It is now generally recognized that the question, "Am I a Christian?" can no longer be answered in any significant manner by citing denominational, ethnic, or national names or symbols. There are now 33,800 different Christian denominations on earth.[4] Clearly, an adequate answer must go deeper than our religious associations. It must refer to what we are in our heart—before God, in the depths of our being, always the focal point of *Christian* spiritual formation.

Such an answer has always been required "before God." Who can deny it? But that has not always been recognized and given adequate emphasis among us—especially not in the recent past—although we are increasingly doing so today. This change is an extremely good thing and a highly promising departure from the recent past of Christians worldwide.

DISTINCTIVELY CHRISTIAN SPIRITUAL FORMATION

WE CAN SAY, IN a preliminary manner, that *spiritual formation for the Christian basically refers to the Spirit-driven process of forming the inner world of the human self in such a way that it becomes like the inner being of Christ himself.*[5] In what follows we must carefully examine what this means for today. But we can say at the outset that, in the degree to which spiritual formation in Christ is successful, the outer life of the individual becomes a natural expression or outflow of the character and teachings of Jesus.

Christian spiritual formation is focused entirely on Jesus. Its goal is an obedience or conformity to Christ that arises out of an inner transformation accomplished through purposive interaction with the grace of God in Christ.

Obedience is an essential outcome of Christian spiritual formation (John 13:34-35; 14:21).

External manifestation of "Christlikeness" is not, however, the focus of the process; and when it is made the main emphasis, the process will certainly be defeated, falling into deadening legalisms and pointless parochialism. That is what has happened so often in the past, and this fact is a major barrier to wholeheartedly embracing Christian spiritual formation in the present. We know now that peculiar modes of dress, behavior, and organization just are not the point.

"Externalism," as we might call it, was even a danger in New Testament times. But "That Christ be formed within you," is the eternal watchword of Christian spiritual formation (Galatians 4:19, PAR). This word is fortified by the deep moral and spiritual insight that, while "the letter of the law kills, the spirit gives life" (2 Corinthians 3:6, PAR).

To illustrate briefly, Jesus' teachings in the Sermon on the Mount (Matthew 5–7) refer to various wrong behaviors: acting out anger, looking to lust, heartless divorce, verbal manipulation, returning evil for evil, and so forth.[6] But, as abundant experience teaches, to strive merely to *act* in conformity with his expressions of what living in the kingdom of God from the heart is like is to attempt the impossible. And it will also lead to doing things that are obviously wrong and even ridiculous—such as self-castration as a presumed act of devotion to Christ, which unfortunately has repeatedly occurred in Christian history.

The "outward" interpretation of spiritual formation, emphasizing specific *acts* as it does, will merely increase "the 'righteousness' of the scribe and Pharisee." It will not, as we must, "go beyond it" (Matthew 5:20, PAR) to achieve genuine transformation of *who I am* through and through—Christ's man or woman, living richly in his kingdom.

A Way of Grace and Rest

THE INSTRUMENTALITIES OF *CHRISTIAN* spiritual formation therefore involve much more than human effort and actions under our control. Well-informed human effort certainly is indispensable, for spiritual formation is no passive process. But Christlikeness of the inner being is not a human attainment. It is, finally, a gift of grace.

Though we must act, the resources for spiritual formation extend far beyond the human. They come from the interactive presence of the Holy Spirit in the lives of those who place their confidence in Christ. They also come from the spiritual treasures—people, events, traditions, teachings—stored in the body of Christ's people on earth, past and present.

Therefore we must understand that spiritual formation is not only formation *of* the spirit or inner being of the individual, though that is both the process and the outcome. It is also formation *by* the Spirit of God and by the spiritual riches of Christ's continuing incarnation in his people—including, most prominently, the treasures of his written and spoken word and the amazing personalities of those in whom he has most fully lived.

Spiritual formation is, in practice, the way of rest for the weary and overloaded, of the easy yoke and the light burden (Matthew 11:28-30), of cleaning the inside of the cup and the dish (Matthew 23:26), of the good tree that cannot bear bad fruit (Luke 6:43). And it is the path along which God's commandments are found to be not "heavy," not "burdensome" (1 John 5:3).

It is the way of those learning as disciples or apprentices of Jesus "to do all things that I have commanded you," within the context of his "I have been given say over everything in heaven and earth" and "Look, I am with you every minute" (see Matthew 28:18,20).

But—I reemphasize, because it is so important—the primary "learning" here is *not* about how to act, just as the primary wrongness or problem in human life is not what we do. Often what human beings do is so horrible that we can be excused, perhaps, for thinking that all that matters is stopping it. But this is an evasion of the real horror: the heart from which the terrible actions come. In both cases, it is *who we are* in our thoughts, feelings, dispositions, and choices—in the inner life—that counts. Profound transformation there is the only thing that can definitively conquer outward evil.

It is very hard to keep this straight. Failure to do so is a primary cause of failure to grow spiritually. Love, we hear, is patient and kind (1 Corinthians 13:4). Then we mistakenly try to *be* loving by *acting* patiently and kindly— and quickly fail. We should always do the best we can in action, of course; but little progress is to be made in that arena until we advance in love itself— the genuine inner readiness and longing to secure the good of others. Until we make significant progress there, our patience and kindness will be shallow and short-lived at best.

It is love itself—not loving behavior, or even the wish or intent to love—that has the power to "always protect, always trust, always hope, put up with anything, and never quit" (1 Corinthians 13:7-8, PAR). Merely trying to act lovingly will lead to despair and to the defeat of love. It will make us angry and hopeless.

But taking love itself—God's kind of love—into the depths of our being through spiritual formation will, by contrast, enable us to act lovingly to an extent that will be surprising even to ourselves, at first. And this love will then become a constant source of joy and refreshment to ourselves and others. Indeed it will be, according to the promise, "a well of water springing up to eternal life" (John 4:14)—not an additional burden to carry through life, as "acting lovingly" surely would be.

∽ THE PRESENT OPPORTUNITY ∾

IN RENEWING THE LANGUAGE and reality of "spiritual formation" in our time and in opening afresh the way to the reality of it, the Spirit of God now calls his people to live from an adequate basis for character transformation, resulting in obedience to and abundance in Christ. This really is something different. The present moment is not an occasion to keep on doing the same things Christians have been doing in the recent past—except now "really meaning it." It is time to change our focus, individually and in our Christian groupings.

If we as Christ's people genuinely enter Christ's Way of the Heart, individuals will find a sure path toward becoming the persons they were meant to be: thoroughly good and godly persons, yet purged of arrogance, insensitivity, and self-sufficiency. Christian assemblies will become what they have been in many periods of the past and what the world desperately calls for today: incomparable schools of life—life that is eternal in quality now, as well as unending in quantity.

This is possible because the spirit and inner being of the human, as well as the process of its renovation in Christ, is an orderly realm where, even in the disorder of its brokenness, God has provided a methodical path of recovery. Grace does not rule out method, nor method grace. Grace thrives on method and method on grace.

Spiritual formation in Christ is therefore not a mysterious, irrational— possibly hysterical—process: something that strikes like lightening, whenever and wherever it will, if at all. Or something that is magically conferred upon us as we dwell in the midst of curious rituals and antique practices. Spiritual experiences (Paul on the Damascus road, and so on) do not constitute spiritual formation, though they could be a meaningful part thereof and sometimes are.

This, I freely admit, is contrary to a view of grace as passivity that is widely held now. But the God-ordained order of the soul under grace must be discovered, respected, and cooperated with, if its God-intended results for spiritual growth are to be attained.

Spiritual formation is something we human beings can and must undertake—as individuals and in fellowship with other apprentices of Jesus. While it is simultaneously a profound manifestation of God's gracious action through his Word and Spirit, it is also something we are responsible for before God and can set about achieving in a sensible, systematic manner.

The aim of this book is, accordingly, intensely practical. It aims to help those who are "seeking the kingdom of God and His righteousness" to find them and to fully live in them. It also hopes to be of help to leaders of groups that seriously intend to carry out all aspects of Christ's Great Commission by training people to do all things he said (Matthew 28:18-20).

Finally, it offers itself to any seeking person — whether explicitly identified as Christian or not — as an avenue to the goodness in God, for which the heart by nature longs. It would be a guide for all who intensely desire to attain the inner life of Jesus Christ himself, allowing him to

> Be of sin the double cure,
> Save from wrath and make me pure.[7]

Matters for Thought and Discussion

1. How do you understand Jesus' promise about the "water" he gives and about our never thirsting again (John 4:14)? What does it mean for you practically? For others you know?

2. Can you describe in some detail the spiritual (nonphysical) side of you? And how that side of you affects your actions and life? Try extending your description to the spiritual side of a saint (such as Mother Teresa of Calcutta) and of a committed terrorist.

3. Do you agree or disagree with the idea that Jesus and his apprentices intend perpetual world revolution through character transformation?

4. Can it be true that "spiritual" does not automatically mean "something good"?

5. Compare "spiritual formation" as a merely human reality and project with distinctively Christian spiritual formation.

6. What are some of the issues that have driven the recent widespread interest in spiritual formation, both in the broader society and among Christians?

7. What dangers lie in an "outward" or "external" interpretation of spiritual formation? How is this related to legalism?

8. Does the recent emergence of spiritual formation offer a genuinely new opportunity for advancing the cause of Christ and blessing human life in our time?

2

THE HEART IN THE SYSTEM OF HUMAN LIFE

A certain expert stood up to check [Jesus] out, saying: "Teacher, what shall I do to receive eternal life?"

Jesus responded, "What does the law say? How do you read it?"

And he answered: "YOU SHALL LOVE THE LORD YOUR GOD WITH ALL YOUR HEART, AND WITH ALL YOUR SOUL, AND WITH ALL YOUR STRENGTH, AND WITH ALL YOUR MIND; AND YOUR NEIGHBOR AS YOURSELF."

And Jesus said, "Well, there you have your answer. Do that and you will live."

LUKE 10:25-28 (PAR)

❧ CARE REQUIRES UNDERSTANDING ❧

Understanding is the basis of care. What you would take care of you must first understand, whether it be a petunia or a nation. If you would care for your spiritual core—your heart or will—you must understand it. That is, you must understand your spirit. (I will try to clarify terms such as "heart," "will," and "spirit" below.)

If you would form your heart in godliness or assist others in that process, you must understand what the heart is and what it does, and especially its place in the overall system of human life.

Some years ago *The Reader's Digest* ran, at intervals, helpful articles on the various parts of the body: the ear, the lungs, the foot, the stomach, and so forth. The aim was to put readers in better position to care for their physical health.

The titles were always similar: "Hi, I'm Joe's Liver" (or lung, or foot, and so on). The properties and structure of the liver or other organ would be described, and its role in the body as a whole explained. Then there would be some discussion of how to keep that particular body part in good condition and to assist it in its function.

Now we might have titled this chapter, "Hi, I'm Joe's Heart" — in the spiritual sense of "heart." Its aim is to explain the nature of the heart (spirit, or will) and its function in the person as a whole. In order to do this we will take a look at the whole person and distinguish the various aspects, including the heart, which compose us.

☙ THE CONTEMPORARY BATTLE OVER HUMAN NATURE ❧

THIS IS NOT AN EASY task under any circumstances. But it is made triply difficult by the fact that *the nature of the person* is, today, a battlefield of conflicting academic, scientific, artistic, religious, legal, and political viewpoints.

Now I must at this point implore the reader to stay with me for the next few paragraphs and not to regard what is discussed in them as merely academic. We must understand that in today's "Western culture" the "academic" is never "merely." It is the academic that today governs the idea systems of our world and opposes traditional views of human nature — specifically, the Judeo-Christian or biblical understanding of human life.

Today you will hear many presumably learned people say that there is no such thing as human nature, or that human beings do not have a nature. Now, there is a long historical development back of this view, which we cannot deal with here, and it is not entirely without an important point. But that point is mis-made in the statement that human beings do not have a nature. It then becomes a part of the unchecked political and moral rage against identity that characterizes modern life. This is a rage predicated upon the idea that identity restricts freedom. If I am a human being, as opposed to, say, a brussels sprout or a squirrel, that places a restriction upon what I can do, what I ought to do, or what should be done to me.

Now, this embattled state of human nature tells us at least two things:

First, it tells us that the issue of human nature is of great importance — too important for us to leave alone. We must deal with it if we are to have anything useful to say about spiritual formation and about the spiritual life that Jesus brings. Otherwise what we say will have no relation to the concrete existence of real human beings, and this, unfortunately, is all too often the case in speaking of the "spiritual."

Second, it tells us that the confusion now publicly prevailing over the makeup of the human being may not be due to its inherent obscurity. Rather, it may be due to the fact that it is a field where strongly armed prejudices — assumptions about what must be the case, "don't bother me with facts" —

prevent even well-intended people from seeing what, at least in basic outline, is fairly obvious, simple, and straightforward.

We especially have in mind opinions to the effect that a human being is purely physical, just an animal—basically, just the human brain. Or the opinion that human beings are, as such, good, or not to be forced to do anything they don't want to do. Or the opinion that human beings do not actually have a nature and that all classifications of them—male/female, black/white, and so on—are "social constructions" with no reality apart from the judgments and motivations of social groups or cultures. At present, governmental and social institutions are heavily invested in such opinions favoring the social construction of the human being.

This current state of affairs may prevent otherwise thoughtful people from seeing the value of what has traditionally been regarded as the best of "common sense" about life and of what has been preserved in the wisdom traditions of most cultures—especially in two of the greatest world sources of wisdom about the human self, the Judeo-Christian and the Greek, the biblical and the classical.

Now, when we set aside contemporary prejudices and carefully examine these two great sources, I believe it will become clear that "heart," "spirit," and "will" (or their equivalents) are words that refer to one and the same thing, the same fundamental component of the person. But they do so under different aspects. "Will" refers to that component's power to initiate, to create, to bring about what did not exist before. "Spirit" refers to its fundamental nature as distinct and independent from physical reality. And "heart" refers to its position in the human being, as the center or core to which every other component of the self owes its proper functioning. But it is the same dimension of the human being that has all these features.

With this preliminary understanding, let us begin our exploration of "Joe's heart" by thinking about how it functions in a life that is in fairly good order.

◈ THE HEART DIRECTS THE LIFE ◈

THOSE WITH A WELL-KEPT heart are persons who are prepared for and capable of responding to the situations of life in ways that are good and right. Their will functions as it should, to choose what is good and avoid what is evil, and the other components of their nature cooperate to that end. They need not be "perfect"; but what all people manage in at least a few times and areas of life, they manage in life as a whole.

Now, in order to see what this means and why it is so, we must be clear about what the "heart" or "spirit" is *within the human system* and how it can effectively govern our lives for good.

The human heart, will, or spirit is the executive center of a human life. The heart is where decisions and choices are made for the whole person. That is its function.

This does not mean that the whole person actually does only what the heart directs, any more than a whole organization actually does precisely what the chief executive officer (CEO) directs. That would be ideal, perhaps (and again, perhaps not); but as any CEO or person in a management position—or even the head of a family—knows, the system rarely goes as it is directed, and never perfectly so. Many factors are always at work in the decisions and actions that actually occur. The individual, like the group, is often divided into incoherent fragments. "Like a city that is broken into and without walls is a man who has no control over his spirit" (Proverbs 25:28).

Still, the ideal is there because of the necessities imposed by real life—"a house divided cannot stand," and so on—and only to the degree that we come close to that ideal are our lives well directed or even coherent. In a world deeply infected with evil and "stuff" that just happens, the usual case is that the individual does not consistently do what his or her own heart says is good and right, and all too often it is the same with groups of all kinds.

And how rare to find a group that consistently functions well for the good it envisions. In fact, the group usually exhibits the divided hearts and lives of its members even more strikingly than does the individual alone. That is because of its larger scope and greater complexity. When successful, spiritual formation (or, really, reformation) unites the divided heart and life of the individual. That person can then bring remarkable harmony into the groups where he or she participates.

◈ THE SIX BASIC ASPECTS OF A HUMAN LIFE ◈

NOW, WHEN WE TAKE a closer look at the whole person, we find that there are six basic aspects in our lives as individual human beings—six things inseparable from every human life. These together and in interplay make up "human nature."

1. Thought (images, concepts, judgments, inferences)
2. Feeling (sensation, emotion)
3. Choice (will, decision, character)
4. Body (action, interaction with the physical world)
5. Social context (personal and structural relations to others)
6. Soul (the factor that integrates all of the above to form one life)

Simply put, every human being thinks (has a thought life), feels, chooses, interacts with his or her body and its social context, and (more or less) integrates all of the foregoing as parts of one life. These are the essential factors in a human being, and nothing essential to human life falls outside of them. The ideal of the spiritual life in the Christian understanding is one where all of the essential parts of the human self are effectively organized around God, as they are restored and sustained by him.

Spiritual formation in Christ is the process *leading to that ideal end, and its result is love of God with* all *of the heart, soul, mind, and strength, and of the neighbor as oneself.* The human self is then fully integrated under God.

The salvation or deliverance of the believer in Christ is essentially holistic or whole-life. David the psalmist, speaking of his own experience but prophetically expressing the understanding of Jesus the Messiah, said, "I bless the LORD who gives me counsel; in the night also my heart instructs me. I keep the LORD always before me; because he is at my right hand, I shall not be moved. Therefore my heart is glad, and my soul rejoices; my body also rests secure" (Psalm 16:7-9, NRSV).

Note how many aspects of the self are explicitly involved in this passage: the mind, the will, the feelings, the soul, and the body. A major part of understanding spiritual formation in the Christian traditions is to follow closely the way the biblical writings repeatedly and emphatically focus on the various essential dimensions of the human being and their role in life as a whole.

THE HUMAN SELF IS *NOT* MYSTERIOUS!

AND HERE I MUST implore the reader to bear with me again, and not to take what I say here as merely academic. The human self, as I have already said, is not "mysterious" in any sense not equally applicable to every other thing that exists. To understand *anything,* of course, some intelligent attention and methodical inquiry is required. What is not mysterious also may not be obvious. And some subject matters are more difficult to penetrate than others. But God has created all things in such a way that they are inherently intelligible.

They have parts, these parts have properties, which in turn make possible relationships between the parts to form larger wholes, which in turn have properties that make possible relationships between larger wholes, that form still larger wholes, and so on. This basic structure of created reality applies to everything from an atom or grain of salt to the solar system or the galaxy, from a thought or a feeling to a whole person or a social unit.

Ultimately, of course, the very existence of anything is mysterious in the sense that it rests on the mystery of God. What explains everything else, God himself, must be, in an important sense, unexplainable—though not necessarily completely unknowable. But as to *what* the human being is, it is simply a whole of a certain kind, consisting of parts with properties and functions that give rise to the properties and functions of whole persons. These, in turn, make possible the relationships persons have to the natural and social worlds and—beyond all these, if they are fully alive as spiritual beings—to the kingdom of God. That is what makes up human nature.

And the subject of our study in approaching human life—the "unit of analysis" for our study—is *the whole person in its social and spiritual context.* The six "aspects," as we have called them, are distinct ranges of abilities, or things all human beings—but not squirrels or brussels sprouts—can and must do: We can and must feel, think, choose, act, and be acted upon through our body. We must enter or lack personal relations and integrate each of these aspects of our being with all the others. This latter task is the work of the *soul,* as already noted, which is the deepest level of unity (or disunity) in a person's life and the most inclusive object of redemption.

Each aspect or dimension of the person will be a source of weakness or strength to the whole person, depending upon the condition it is in, and the condition it is in will depend, finally, upon the heart. A person who is *prepared* and *capable* of responding to the situations of life in ways that are "good and right" is a person whose soul is in order, under the direction of a well-kept heart, in turn under the direction of God. We can better see what this means if we keep in mind what each dimension of the human being does. (We will be brief at this point and will return for a fuller treatment of each dimension in later chapters.)

A Brief Initial Survey of the Six Human Dimensions

THOUGHT
Thought brings things before our minds in various ways (including perception and imagination) and enables us to consider them in various respects and trace out their interrelationships with one another. Thought is that which enables our will (or spirit) to range far beyond the immediate boundaries of our environment and the perceptions of our senses. Through it our consciousness reaches into the depths of the universe, past, present, and future, by reasoning and scientific thinking, by imagination and art—and also by divine revelation, which comes to us mainly in the form of thought.

FEELING
Feeling inclines us toward or away from things that come before our minds in thought. It involves a tone that is pleasant or painful, along with an attraction or repulsion with respect to the existence or possession of what is

thought of. How we feel about food, automobiles, relationships, positions, and hundreds of other things illustrates this point.

Notice that feeling and thought always go together. They are interdependent and are never found apart. There is no feeling without something being before the mind in thought and no thought without some positive or negative feeling toward what is contemplated. What we call "indifference" is never a total absence of feeling, positive and negative, but simply an unusually low degree of feeling, usually negative.

The connection between thought and feeling is so intimate that the "mind" is usually treated as consisting of thought and feeling *together.* I shall do so here. Of course the mind thus understood—or understood in any way you like—is a quite complicated aspect of the person, with numerous subdivisions built into both thought and feeling. In the ruined soul, the mind becomes a fearful wilderness and a wild intermixture of thought and feeling, manifested in willful stupidities, blatant inconsistencies, and confusions, often to the point of obsession, madness, or possession. This condition of mind is what characterizes our world apart from God. Satan, "the prince of this world" (John 12:31; 14:30), holds sway over it.

WILL (SPIRIT, HEART)

Volition, or choice, is the exercise of will, the capacity of the person to *originate* things and events that would not otherwise be or occur. By "originate" here we mean to include two of the things most prized in human life: freedom and creativity. These are really two aspects of the same thing when properly understood, which is *power to do what is good*—or evil.

The power in question belongs to individuals alone. Nothing *makes* them originate the good (or evil) they do. It is possible for them to not do it. Or to do it. Although a free action has many conditions, those conditions do not an action make. If it is *our* act, there must be added to those conditions the inner and always unforced "yes" or "no" by which the person responds to the situation. This response is our unique contribution to reality. It is ours, it is *us,* as nothing else is.

Without the inner "yes" there is no sin, for only that "yes" (or "no") is *just us.* The *thought* of sin is not sin and is not even a temptation. Temptation is the thought plus the inclination to sin—possibly manifested by lingering over the thought or seeking it out. But sin itself is when we inwardly say "yes" to the temptation, when we *would* do the deed, even though we do not actually do it. Similar distinctions must be drawn with reference to doing what is good and right. These distinctions with reference to volition or choice will turn out to be very important later in our discussions.

Now we need to be very clear on this point: the capacity for volition, and the acts of willing in which it is exercised, form the *spirit* in man. In this narrow and focused sense, the "spiritual" is not just the nonphysical, as we explained it earlier, but it is the central core of the nonphysical part in man. In us there is much that is not physical that also is not "spirit"—that is, not of the will.

There is, then, a spirit in man—a spirit that is *his* spirit. It is this that is the *human* spirit. And if we are to understand spiritual formation, we must understand what the spirit of the human being is. Spirit is, in general, that which is self-initiating and self-sustaining. Only God is purely spiritual, pure creative will and character. Only he can truly say, "I AM THAT I AM" (Exodus 3:14, KJV).

He is, in his fundamental and overall nature, *unbodily, personal power.* Human beings have only some small element of spirit—unbodily, personal power—right at the *center* of who they are and who they become. It is, above all, this spirit (or will) that must be reached, cared for, and transformed in spiritual formation. The human will is primarily what must be given a godly nature and must then proceed to expand its godly governance over the entire personality.

Thus will or spirit is also, as we have noted, the *heart* in the human system: the *core* of its being. That is why we have the biblical teaching that human good and evil are matters of the heart. It is the heart (Mark 7:21) and spirit (John 4:23) that God looks at (1 Samuel 16:7; Isaiah 66:2) in relating to humankind, and in allowing us to relate to him (2 Chronicles 15:4,15; Jeremiah 29:13; Hebrews 11:6).

And just as thought and feeling are inseparable, so volition is closely intertwined with them. To choose, one must have some object or concept before the mind and some feeling for or against it. There is no choice that does not involve both thought and feeling. On the other hand, what we feel and think is (or can and should be) to a very large degree a matter of choice in competent adult persons, who will be very careful about what they allow their mind to dwell upon or what they allow themselves to feel. This is crucial to the practical methods of spiritual formation.

Unfortunately, the fact that feelings and thoughts are largely a matter of choice is not widely understood—especially as it concerns feelings. We speak of feelings as "passions," and that is a word that implies passivity. But we are in fact very active in inviting, allowing, and handling our "passions," as we shall see in a later chapter.

So once again: what we have before us in our study of spiritual formation is the whole person, and the various basic dimensions of the human self are not separable parts. They are aspects thoroughly intermingled with each other in their natures and in their actions.

Especially, on the present point, *human life as a whole does not run by will alone.* Far from it. Nevertheless, life *must* be organized by the will if it is to be organized at all. It can only be pulled together "from the inside." That is the function of the will or heart: to organize our life as a whole, and, indeed, to organize it around God. And of course life must be organized, and organized well, if one's existence is to be even fairly tolerable to one's self or those around. Every civilization of any type has recognized this. A great part of the disaster of contemporary life lies in the fact that it is organized around feelings. People nearly always act on their feelings, and think it only right. The will is then left at the mercy of circumstances that evoke feelings. Christian spiritual formation today must squarely confront this fact and overcome it.

BODY

The body is the focal point of our presence in the physical and social world. In union with it we come into existence, and we become the person we shall forever be. It is our primary energy source or "strength"—our personalized "power pack"—a place where we can even stand in defiance of God, at least for a while. And it is the point through which we are stimulated by the world beyond ourselves and where we find and are found by others.[1]

Human personal relations cannot be separated from the body; and, on the other hand, the body cannot be understood apart from human relations. It is essentially social. Therefore our bodies are forever a part of our identities as persons. I, for example, will forever be the son of Maymie Joyce Lindesmith and Albert Alexander Willard. My body came from God through them, and they provided a social and spiritual context that, more than anything else, makes me the person I am.

Equally importantly, it is the body *from which* we live. We have already said that we do not live by will alone. Thank goodness! Our choices, as they settle into character (to be explained later) are "farmed out" or "outsourced" to our body in its social context, where they then occur more or less "automatically," without our having to think about what we are doing.

And that is, in general, a very good thing. Just recall how cumbersome it is when we *have* to think about what we are doing—learning to skate, drive a car, speak a language. The very purpose of learning or training in some activity is to bring it under our direction without our having to think about it or make decisions regarding it. The body makes this possible. It has a "knowledge" of its own.

Of course this basically good and even glorious feature of the body—its capacity to "have a life of its own," as we might say—is also a major problem for, and a primary area of, spiritual formation. For, trained in a world of wrongness and evil, the body comes to act wrongly "before we think," and

35

has "motions of sin in its members," as Paul said, which may thwart the true intent of our spirit or will by leaping ahead of it.

"It is not me," he cries, "but sin that dwells in me!" (Romans 7:17, PAR). And "the flesh wants what is contrary to the spirit and the spirit what is contrary to the flesh. They are in opposition to each other, so that it is impossible for you to do what you really want" (Galatians 5:17, PAR).

But at the same time, this amazing capacity of the body means that it (like the other dimensions of human life) can be re-formed to become our ally in Christlikeness. Such a re-formation of the body is one major part of the process of spiritual formation, as we shall see. The body is not, in the biblical view, essentially evil; and, while it is infected with evil, it can be delivered. Spiritual formation is also and essentially a bodily process. It cannot succeed unless the body is also transformed.

Social Context

The human self requires rootedness in others. This is primarily an ontological matter—a matter of *being* what we are. It is not just a moral matter, a matter of what *ought* to be. And the moral aspect of it grows out of the ontological.[2]

The most fundamental "other" for the human is, of course, God himself. God is the ultimate social fact for the human being. That is why people in general think more often about God than about any other thing, even sex and death. But because *all* are to be rooted in God—and really are, whether they want it or not—our ties to one another cannot be isolated from our shared relationship to him, nor our relationship to him from our ties to one another. Our relations to others cannot be right unless we see those others in their relation to God. Through others he comes to us and we only *really* find others when we see them in him.

"If someone says 'I love God,' and hates his brother, he is a liar," John unapologetically said, "for the one who does not love his brother whom he has seen, cannot love God whom he has not seen" (1 John 4:20). We only live as we should when we are in a right relation to God and to other human beings—thus the two greatest commandments, as quoted at the head of this chapter. Accordingly, the infant who is not received in love by the mother and others is wounded for life and may even die. It must bond with its mother or *someone* in order to take on a self and a life. And rejection, no matter how old one is, is a sword thrust to the soul that has literally killed many. Western culture is, largely unbeknown to itself, a culture of rejection. This is one of the irresistible effects of what is called "modernity," and it deeply affects the concrete forms Christian institutions take in our time. It seeps into our souls and is a deadly enemy to spiritual formation in Christ.

The power of our personal relations to others is what gives them their incalculable importance for the formation of our spirit and our entire life — for good, or for ill. And of course our body is the focus of these relations, from its DNA to "looks" (how we look or appear, and how we look at and are looked at by others), from touching and working together to talking and praying together.

But being with others, our social dimension, is also inseparable from our *inner* thoughts, feelings, choices, and actions. Their existence and nature are not independent of our social setting. Our very relation to Christ, our Savior, teacher, and friend, is located in the social dimension, along with our place in his body on earth — his continuing incarnation, the church. Rightly understood, it is true that "there is no salvation outside the church" — just not this "church" or that "church."

SOUL

The soul is that dimension of the person that interrelates all of the other dimensions so that they form one life. It is like a meta-dimension or higher-level dimension because its direct field of play consists of the other dimensions (thought, body, and so on), and through them it reaches ever deeper into the person's vast environment of God and his creation. It has been said that each soul is a star in the spiritual universe — or so it was meant to be (Matthew 13:43). And there can be no doubt that this is the biblical view, understanding that "soul" here is a term that refers to the whole person through its most profound dimension.

Because the soul encompasses and "organizes" the whole person, it is frequently taken to *be* the person. We naturally treat persons as "souls." But of course the soul is not the person. It is, rather, the deepest part of the self in terms of overall operations; and like the body, it has the capacity to operate (and does, largely, operate) without conscious supervision.

The soul is somewhat like a computer that quietly runs a business or manufacturing operation and only comes to our attention when it malfunctions or requires some adaptation to new tasks. It can be significantly "reprogrammed," and this too is a major part of what goes into the spiritual formation (re-formation) of the person.

Because the soul is so inclusive and fundamental and to some degree independent of conscious direction, biblical and poetic language often addresses it in the third person. The psalmist asked, "Why are you in despair, O my soul? And why have you become disturbed within me? Hope in God, for I shall again praise Him for the help of His presence" (Psalm 42:5). The "rich fool" of Luke 12 said, "I will say to my soul, 'Soul, you have many goods laid up for many years to come; take your ease, eat, drink and be merry'" (verse 19). In his poem "The Chambered Nautilus," Oliver Wendell Holmes intoned, "Build thee more stately mansions, oh my soul, as the swift seasons roll."

But for all of the soul's vastness and independence, the tiny executive center of the person—that is, the spirit or will—can redirect and re-form the soul, with God's cooperation. It mainly does this by redirecting the body in spiritual disciplines and toward various other types of experiences under God.

∽ THE WHOLE PICTURE ∾

NOW, WITH ALL OF this said, it will be useful for our purposes to depict the entire human self by the following diagram:

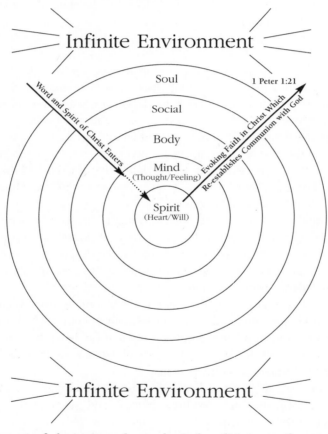

Diagrams of dynamic and nonphysical realities are of course always inadequate to what they depict, but they can nevertheless be helpful. They can convey important aspects of what we are trying to grasp.

Note that in this diagram the inner circles are not meant to *exclude* the outer ones, but to incorporate them in part: to be superimposed on them without exhausting them. But there is always more to what is represented by the outer circles than to what is represented by the inner.

Thus there is more to the mind than to the spirit (heart/will), though spirit intermingles with mind, and more to the body than to the mind, though mind intermingles with body, and so on. By making the soul the outer circle and interfacing it with an infinite environment, we indicate that it is the most inclusive dimension of the self, foundational to all others, but also that access to it *may* be achieved directly from sources entirely outside the person—from God, certainly, but possibly other forces as well, benign as well as dreadful.

The outer wall of the soul is perhaps like a permeable membrane in a biological organism, which is designed to allow passage of some but not all foreign objects. When that wall is broken, individuals are at the mercy of forces they cannot handle. The soul can be sustained intact and can function as it is supposed to only in the keeping of God. "Behold, all souls are Mine," says the Lord (Ezekiel 18:4).

INFLUENCE ON ACTION

BUT NOW WE TURN to action. Our actions *always* arise out of the *interplay* of the universal factors in human life: spirit, mind, body, social context, and soul. Action never comes from the movement of the will alone. Often—perhaps usually—what we do is not an outcome of deliberate choice and a mere act of will, but is more of a *relenting* to pressure on the will from one or more of the dimensions of the self. The understanding of this is necessary for the understanding and practice of spiritual formation, which is bound to fail if it focuses upon the will alone.

The inadequacy of good intentions alone to ensure proper action is marked by Jesus' words: "The spirit is willing but the flesh is weak." If the six dimensions are properly aligned with God and what is good—and therefore with each other—that "mere relenting" will be good, and our actions will simply be the good fruit of the good tree. If they are not so aligned, they will be the inevitable bad fruit of the bad tree.

We must clearly understand that there is a rigorous consistency in the human self and its actions. This is one of the things we are most inclined to deceive ourselves about. If I do evil, I am the kind of person who does evil; if I do good, I am the kind of person who does good (1 John 3:7-10). Actions are not impositions on who we are, but are expressions of who we are. They come out of our heart and the inner realities it supervises and interacts with.

Today one of the most common rationalizations of sin or folly is, "Oh, I just blew it." While there is some point to such a remark, it is not the one those who use it hope for. It does not exonerate them. While it may be true that there are other circumstances in which I would not have done the foolish or sinful thing I did, and while what I did may not represent me fully, "blowing it" *does* represent me fully. *I am the kind of person who "blows it."* "Blowing it" shows who I am as a person. I am, through and through, in my deepest self, the kind of person who "blows it"—hardly a lovely and promising thing to be.

Whatever my action is comes out of my whole person:

This diagram represents the human system on its own. The will or spirit, tiny power that it is, is very largely at the mercy of the forces playing upon it from the larger self and beyond. The God-intended function of the will is to reach out to God in trust. By standing in the correct relation to God through our will we can receive grace that will properly reorder the soul along with the other five components of the self.

In the life away from God, the order of dominance is:

Body

Soul

Mind (Thought/Feeling)

Spirit

God

This is the order in idolatry of all kinds, including that of those who worship "The Good Life," as it is often called.

"There are two Gods," Tolstoy once said. "There is the God that people generally believe in—A God *who has to serve them* (sometimes in very refined ways, say by merely giving them peace of mind). This God does not exist. But the God whom people forget—*the God whom we all have to serve*—exists, and is the prime cause of our existence and of all that we perceive."[3]

In the life under God, by contrast, the order of dominance is:

God

Spirit

Mind (Thought/Feeling)

Soul

Body

Here the body serves the soul; the soul, the mind; the mind, the spirit; and the spirit, God. Conversely, the life "from above" flows from God throughout the whole person, including the body and its social context.

The former order is characteristic of what Paul described as "the mind set on the flesh," which is "death" (Romans 8:6). The latter expresses "the mind set on the Spirit," which is "life and peace." For the individual away from God, "flesh" becomes, in practice, simply his or her body. Taking the body as our main concern makes it impossible to please God and at the same time ensures the utter futility of our life.

> For those who are according to [that is, who live life in terms of] the flesh [the natural human powers only] set their minds on the things of the flesh, but those who are according to the Spirit, the things of the Spirit. For the mind set on the flesh is death, but the mind set on the Spirit is life and peace, because the mind set on the flesh is hostile toward God; for it does not subject itself to the law of God, for it is not even able to do so. (Romans 8:5-7)

When the proper ordering of the human system under God is complete—which no doubt will never *fully* occur in this life because of the social dimension of the self and our finitude and the total spiritual environment surrounding us—then we have people who "love God with all their heart, and with all their soul, and with all their strength, and with all their mind; and their neighbor as themselves" (Luke 10:27, PAR; see also Mark 12:30-33). When we are like this, our whole life is an eternal one. Everything we do counts for eternity and is preserved there (Colossians 3:17).

The spirit must first come alive to and through God, of course. Otherwise we remain dead to him in trespasses and sins (Ephesians 2:1). But once the spirit comes alive in God, the lengthy processes of subduing all aspects of the self under God can begin. This is the process of spiritual formation viewed in its entirety.

It is the central point of this book that spiritual transformation only happens as each essential dimension of the human being is transformed to Christlikeness under the direction of a regenerate will interacting with constant overtures of grace from God. Such transformation is not the result of mere human effort and cannot be accomplished by putting pressure on the will (heart, spirit) alone.

ᴔ ISRAEL AND US ᴔ

AS IS SO OFTEN the case, there is an interesting and instructive parallel to the spiritual life of the individual in the historical events of the Old Testament. The descendants of Abraham became a distinct people in the furnace of Egyptian slavery. Though God was, as always, at work in the larger scene, the Israelites lived, so far as they knew, under total domination of a god-system focused in the Pharaoh. That is, in Egyptian slavery they were "dead" to the God of Abraham, Isaac, and Jacob. He meant nothing to them, had nothing to do with them—so far as they knew or cared.

At the proper time, he approached them through an outcast (Moses [Acts 7:37-40]), as he approaches us through an outcast (Jesus [Acts 7:52; Hebrews 13:12-14]). By an act of intervention into their deadness (Deuteronomy 11:1-7) he brought them (and later us) to a new life of interactive (covenant) relationship to him. This interactive, covenant relationship *is* eternal life (John 17:3). It is what it means to have been "born from above"—which Nicodemus, as a teacher in Israel, was supposed to have understood, but could not because he had only "the mind of the flesh" and so could think only in terms of "the natural" (see John 3:10).

But this eternal kind of life is not a passive life. Passivity was for the Israelites, and it is for us one of the greatest dangers and difficulties of our spiritual existence. The land promised to them was one of incredible goodness— "flowing with milk and honey," as it is repeatedly described. *But it still had to be conquered by careful, persistent, and intelligent human action, over a long period of time.*

In the beginning of the conquest of the Promised Land, the walls of Jericho *fell* down, to make clear God's presence and power. Welcome to the kingdom! But that never happened again. The Israelites had to take the remaining cities through hand-to-hand warfare, though always still with divine assistance.

What was then true of the Promised Land of the Israelites was then and is now true of individual human beings who come to God. The Israelites were saved or delivered by grace just as surely as we are. But in both cases "grace" means we are to be, and are enabled to be, active to a degree we have never been before. Paul's picture of grace is, "And God is able to make all grace abound to you, so that always having all sufficiency in everything, you may have an abundance for every good deed" (2 Corinthians 9:8).

We therefore live in "hot pursuit" of Jesus Christ. "My soul followeth hard after thee," the psalmist called out (63:8, KJV). And Paul's panting cry was, "That I may know Him, and the power of His resurrection and the fellowship of His sufferings, being conformed to His death" in order to participate in the life of his resurrection (Philippians 3:10-11). What are we to say of anyone who thinks they have something more important to do than that? The work of spiritual formation in Christlikeness is the work of claiming the land of milk and honey in which we are, individually and collectively, to dwell with God.

The old hymn rings out:

On Jordan's stormy banks I stand
and cast a wistful eye
To Canaan's fair and happy land,
where my possessions lie.

But the real Jordan, the spiritual "Jordan," is not physical death, as has usually been supposed. We need not and must not wait until we die to live in the land of milk and honey; and if we will only move to that land now, the passage in physical death will be but one more day in the endless life we have long since begun. That is exactly what Jesus meant when he said, "If anyone keeps my words he shall never see or taste death" (John 8:51, PAR).

✎ "HELTER SKELTER" ✎

THE MAN WHO PROSECUTED the infamous Manson family for their murders later wrote a book titled *Helter Skelter*. This phrase was taken from a song performed by a well-known rock music group. Manson used it to characterize the state of confusion in which he kept his followers, and himself as well. In a state of helter-skelter nothing makes sense, and everything makes as much sense as anything else. So, for example, when you cut someone's throat or stab them repeatedly and they die, you didn't really kill them and they didn't really die. That was Manson's teaching.

Aldous Huxley, in one of his retrospective writings, commented on how, among the associates of his youth, the endless talk of "meaninglessness" — the meaninglessness of life and therefore of everything in it — was merely an excuse to permit them to do whatever they wanted. Their life was organized (or, more properly, *disorganized*) around their feelings and wayward thoughts, with their will in tow.

But resolute action for the good requires that things make sense. You wouldn't want someone caught up in helter-skelter to work on your lawn mower or computer. Life makes sense only if you understand its basic components and how they interrelate to form the whole. Evil, on the other hand, thrives on confusion. God is not the author of confusion (1 Corinthians 14:33).

Frankly, our visible Christian world is not too far from helter-skelter with reference to its understanding of the makeup of the person and therefore of the spiritual life and spiritual formation. We need to access the fullness of biblical teachings on these matters. We suffer far too much from the influence of a surrounding culture that thrives on confusion. (And therefore its denial that human beings have a nature.) This may seem like a harsh thing to say about our "Christian world," and I am sorry to say it; but the issues here are too important to mince words.

Accordingly, much of what we do in Christian circles with very good intentions—hoping, we say, to see steady, significant growth in Christlikeness—simply makes no sense and leads nowhere so far as substantive spiritual formation is concerned.[4] What a brutal thing to say! But we need to recognize this, or show why it is not the case. In this chapter I hope we have taken significant first steps toward a clarity that can serve as a foundation for the effectual practice of Christian spiritual formation.

Matters for
Thought and Discussion

1. What is the relation between *caring* for something and *understanding* its nature? How does "The Contemporary Battle over Human Nature" affect our ability today to care for our own well-being and goodness?

2. What is the heart and what is its role in human life?

3. What are the six basic dimensions of the human being? Does the list leave anything out?

4. Relate the six dimensions to the Great Commandment (Luke 10:25-28) and to spiritual formation in Christ.

5. Explore the role feelings play in our current social and personal life. In media and popular arts. In church activities. Would you say you are (sometimes? never? always?) controlled by your feelings?

6. Do you agree or disagree with the explanation of *temptation* set forth in this chapter?

7. How does choice or volition depend upon thought and feeling? Why can't we just change our will? ("Human life does not run by will alone"!)

8. "Actions really do tell who we are." Agree? Disagree?

9. Is the comparison between Israel taking the Promised Land and our conquering by grace and action all the dimensions of our personality a valid one?

3

RADICAL EVIL
IN THE RUINED SOUL

*The Lord looks down from heaven on humankind to see if
there are any who are wise, who seek after God. They have
all gone astray, they are all alike perverse; there is
no one who does good, no, not one.*
PSALM 14:2-3 (PAR)

⮠ STARTING FROM RUIN ⮡

We must see the soul and the person in its ruined condition, with its malformed and dysfunctional mind, feelings, body, and social relations, before we can understand that it must be delivered and reformed and how that can be done. One of the greatest obstacles to effective spiritual formation in Christ today is simple failure to understand and acknowledge the reality of the human situation as it affects Christians and nonChristians alike. We must start from where we really are.

And here we recall that all people undergo a process of spiritual formation. Their spirit is formed, and with it their whole being. As I said earlier, spiritual formation is not something just for especially religious people. No one escapes. The most hardened criminal as well as the most devout of human beings have had a spiritual formation. They have become a certain kind of person.

You have had a spiritual formation and I have had one, and it is still ongoing. It is like education: everyone gets one—a good one or a bad one. We reemphasize that those are fortunate or blessed who are able to find or are given a path of life that forms their spirit and inner world in a way that is good.

In one of C. S. Lewis's more striking passages, he challenges us

to remember that the dullest and most uninteresting person you
talk to may one day be a creature which, if you saw it now, you

45

would be strongly tempted to worship, or else a horror and a corruption such as you now meet, if at all, only in a nightmare. . . . There are no *ordinary people*. You have never talked to a mere mortal. Nations, cultures, arts, civilizations—these are mortal, and their life is to ours as the life of a gnat. But it is immortals whom we joke with, work with, marry, snub, and exploit—immortal horrors or everlasting splendors.[1]

Strangely, it is precisely the intrinsic greatness of the person that makes it in its ruined condition "a horror and a corruption such as you now meet . . . only in a nightmare." If we were insignificant, our ruin would not be horrifying. G. K. Chesterton somewhere says that the hardest thing to accept in the Christian religion is the great value it places upon the individual soul. Still older Christian writers used to say that God has hidden the majesty of the human soul from us to prevent our being ruined by vanity.

This explains why even in its ruined condition a human being is regarded by God as something immensely worth saving. Sin does not make it worthless, but only lost. And in its lostness it is still capable of great strength, dignity, and heartbreaking beauty and goodness—enough so to hide from the unenlightened, or those who do not wish to understand, the horror it has become and is becoming.

✦ Evil Now a Non-Category ✦

BECAUSE IN OUR PRESENT thought world the horror is "hidden," "sin" as a condition of the human self is not available as a principle of explanation for those who are supposed to know why life goes as it does and to guide others. For example, why do around half of American marriages fail, or why do we have massive problems with substance addiction and with the "moral" failures of public leaders. Those who are supposed to know are lost in speculations about "causes," while the real sources of our failures lie in *choice* and the factors at work in it. *Choice is where sin dwells.*

Our social and psychological sciences stand helpless before the terrible things done by human beings, but the warpedness and *wrung*ness of the human will is something we cannot admit into "serious" conversation. We are like farmers who diligently plant crops but cannot admit the existence of weeds and insects and can only think to pour on more fertilizer. Similarly, the only solution we know to human problems today is "education."

And indeed education might be a good thing. Who can deny that? It could help. But what kind of education? And can we really think that if people only knew what is today generally understood to be the right thing to do, they would do it? Education as now understood—the actual social practice—*cannot* come to grips with the realities of the human self. It is not just a matter of "separation of church and state" and all that that has come to mean. Rather, education (the institution) has now adopted values, attitudes, and practices that make any rigorous understanding of the human self and life impossible.

❧ Soul Ruin Seen in a Church ❧

HERE IS A STORY ILLUSTRATING the profound corruption of the soul. It is a story about a church that would generally be regarded as successful or prosperous. Whether real or imagined, I leave you to ponder. In actuality you will find many churches that are a close fit to this description.

The church in question was founded out of conflict in another church. It called its first pastor, and things seemed to be going well until that pastor committed adultery and various improper financial acts. The congregation dismissed him, and a second pastor was appointed. He was very popular and the church grew, but he resigned after four years from stress, or a nervous breakdown, depending on whom you believed.

A third pastor came and was quite popular. Again, the church grew, but after a while he started giving himself salary raises, which the congregation did not knowingly approve. After ten years he left, started another church within ten miles of his former church, and took three hundred members with him.

A fourth pastor was called. Everything seemed fine. Then he had a sexual affair, which he eventually disclosed to his board and staff, expecting them to cover it up. In the midst of much lying and discord in the board and staff, the church seemed to go on as before. Of course the people in the community came to know about the affair anyway. A year or so later the pastor received a "call" from a larger church a two-hour drive away. He took the position, leaving behind a congregation, board, and staff full of strife and anger. This all happened in one congregation over a period of thirty-six years.

I use this story because, in the language of Peter, "judgment must begin at the house of God." It is there we see soul ruin at its greatest. If we can't simply do what is right there, where can we? The story also is illustrative of the extent to which sin, in a form everyone plainly recognizes as such, undermines even the efforts of Christ's own people to *be* his people. That is its power. Although the degree and details differ, the story of this church is—in spite of some very fine exceptions—all too common. (Leading Christian magazines now feature regular sections where the sad story is told month by month.)

I have also chosen the above story as an illustration because a major part of the response by Christians to manifest sin, in this case, was to cover it up.

This is not uncommon. No doubt it was "for the sake of the ministry," as is usually said. The "confessions" of the various pastors were often half-truths or less and were clearly matters of a formality which would, supposedly, allow the pastors and staff members to "get on with God's business." The exit of the last pastor left the church board and staff bitterly divided over issues of loyalty to the ex-pastor and over whether or not the truth of what had happened should be publicly stated.

A long period followed in which almost every meeting was filled with anger and tension and in which people retreated into their various camps, hardly speaking to each other. The words of James ring true: "Where you have envy and selfish ambition, there you find disorder and every evil practice" (James 3:16, NIV). Most Christians have never been in an intimate fellowship where the corrupted condition of the human soul did not in fact prevail—that is, in a fellowship in which they could assume that everyone would do what everyone knew to be right. And many people in our culture have, on the basis of their experiences, simply given up on the church—many of them in the name of God and righteousness.

In a period of a few weeks, some years back, three nationally known pastors in the Southern California area were publicly exposed for sexual sins. That is what is now called "news." But sex is far from being the only problem. The presence of vanity, egotism, hostility, fear, indifference, and downright meanness can be counted on among professing Christians. Their opposites *cannot* be counted on or simply assumed in the "standard" Christian group; and the rare individual who exemplifies them—genuine purity and humility, death to selfishness, freedom from rage and depression, and so on—will stand out in the group with all the obtrusiveness of a sore thumb. He or she will be a constant hindrance in group processes and will be personally conflicted by those processes, for he or she will not be living on the same terms as the others.

❧ AND BEYOND THE CHURCH ❧

NOW FOR THE REST of the verse from Peter: "If judgment first begins at the house of God, what shall be the outcome for those who give no heed to the gospel of God? And if it is difficult for the righteous to be saved, what will happen to the godless and rebellious" (1 Peter 4:17, PAR).

It really is a much worse situation outside the church than within. The daily news, courts, law offices, community, family, and educational and penal institutions provide a constant outpouring of wrongness and wrongdoing that wells up from the malformed human spirit, mind, soul, body, and social context.

Diogenes, the ancient Greek, lit a lantern and walked the streets of Athens at noonday looking for an honest man. He never found one, it is said. But as in the church, so in life generally, few are ready to deal with the realities of the deeper self, in themselves or in others. And those few are not exactly welcomed by others.

Socrates tried to deal with the realities of the souls of Athens and was killed for it. This is the customary fate of the "prophet." As Vance Havner used to say, Jesus was not crucified for saying "Behold the lilies of the field, how they toil not, neither do they spin," but for saying "Behold the Pharisees, how they steal."

≈ THE PROPHETIC WITNESS ≈

THE BIBLICAL, PROPHETIC ILLUMINATION of the human soul in its lostness is emphatic, starkly clear, and repeated over and over, from Moses and Samuel to Jesus, Paul, and John. The only path of spiritual transformation today still lies *through* this illumination. It must be gratefully and humbly accepted and applied, to oneself above all. When the prophet Jeremiah, for example, says, "The heart is more deceitful than all else and is desperately sick: Who can understand it?" we have to recognize from our heart that *we* are the ones spoken of, that, indeed, *I* am the one described. Only then is a foundation laid for spiritual formation into Christlikeness.

The initial move toward Christlikeness cannot be toward self-esteem, because of confusion about what self-esteem means, and because, realistically, I'm *not* okay and you're *not* okay. We're all in serious trouble. That must be our starting point. Self-esteem in such a situation will only breed self-deception and frustration—as is now increasingly recognized, by the way. For the realities of our soul will still be what they are and will still have the consequences for evil that they naturally do—regardless of what we or others may say to "pump ourselves up" and really, to conceal and deny who we are. A high opinion of ourselves will only make those consequences more difficult to deal with.

Denial—usually in some form of rationalization—is the primary device that humans use to deal with their own wrongness. It was the first thing out of the mouths of Adam and Eve after they sinned, and it continues up to the latest edition of the newspaper. The prophetic witness from God must throw itself against the massive weight of group and individual denial, often institutionalized and subtly built into our customary ways of speaking and interacting.

Jesus addressed leaders of his day in language that may seem harsh and pitiless to us, but that was the only possible way he could be of help to them, strongly self-defended as they were; and perhaps the same is true of us as well. "You Pharisees clean the outside of the dish, but your insides are full of greed and filth. How foolish of you! Isn't God as interested in your insides as your outside?" (Luke 11:39, PAR). And "if you wash a dish well on the inside, won't the outside come clean in the process?" (Matthew 23:26, PAR).

Jesus proceeds to point out how they love and vie for public recognition or "approval" (Luke 11:43) and how in doing so they are like graves, all nice and prettied up on the outside, but full of disgusting rot inside (verse 44; compare Matthew 23:27-28). They were unable to believe in Jesus because they sought to be honored by each other (John 5:44). They desired to be exalted. Spiritual transformation does not lie in this direction, for them or for us.

∽ PAUL'S SUMMARY ∾

OF COURSE THESE LEADERS had greater responsibilities and opportunities than ordinary people. But they were not, in general, more sinful. The condition addressed in them is the *human* condition, not the pharisaical condition. The Pharisee only makes the true human condition more obvious by all of his protestations of righteousness and his flamboyant religiosity. Paul systematizes the prophetic account of the human self and traces it to its root in his letter to the Romans:

> "THERE IS NONE RIGHTEOUS, NOT EVEN ONE; THERE IS NONE WHO UNDERSTANDS, THERE IS NONE WHO SEEKS FOR GOD; ALL HAVE TURNED ASIDE, TOGETHER THEY HAVE BECOME USELESS; THERE IS NONE WHO DOES GOOD, THERE IS NOT EVEN ONE."
>
> "THEIR THROAT IS AN OPEN GRAVE, WITH THEIR TONGUES THEY KEEP DECEIVING."
>
> "THE POISON OF ASPS IS UNDER THEIR LIPS";
>
> "WHOSE MOUTH IS FULL OF CURSING AND BITTERNESS";
>
> "THEIR FEET ARE SWIFT TO SHED BLOOD, DESTRUCTION AND MISERY ARE IN THEIR PATHS, AND THE PATH OF PEACE HAVE THEY NOT KNOWN."
>
> "THERE IS NO FEAR OF GOD BEFORE THEIR EYES." (Romans 3:10-18)

The very last statement from this collection of Old Testament diagnoses of the human condition goes to the core of the matter: "There is no fear of God before their eyes." Fear of God, the proverb tells us, is the beginning of wisdom (Proverbs 9:10). Although not the end or outcome of wisdom, to be sure, it *is* the indispensable beginning, I believe, and the principle part. One *begins* to get smart when he or she fears being crosswise of God: fear of not doing what he wants and not being as he requires.

Fear is the anticipation of harm. The intelligent person recognizes that his or her well-being lies in being in harmony with God and what God is doing in the "kingdom." God is not mean, but he is dangerous. It is the same with other great forces he has placed in reality. Electricity and nuclear power, for example, are not mean, but they are dangerous. One who does not, in a certain sense, "worry" about God, simply isn't smart. And that is the point of the verse.

❧ TRUE UNDERSTANDING ❧

"KNOWLEDGE OF THE HOLY One is understanding," Proverbs 9:10 concludes. "Knowledge" in biblical language never refers to what we today call "head knowledge," but always to *experiential involvement* with what is known—to actual engagement with it. Thus when Jesus defines the eternal life that he gives to his people as "that they might know thee, the only true God, and Jesus Christ, whom thou hast sent" (John 17:3, KJV), he is speaking of the grace of constant, close interaction with the Trinitarian being of God that Jesus brings into the lives of those who seek and find him.

This is only a deeper and fuller understanding of Proverbs 3:5-8: "Trust in the Lord with all your heart, and do not rely exclusively on your own understanding. In all your ways acknowledge him, and he will smooth your paths. Don't imagine you've got it all figured out. Be afraid of the Lord and avoid evil. It will heal your body and bring refreshment to your bones" (PAR).

Colossians 3:17 expresses the same basic fact, but now as the ultimate outcome of spiritual (trans)formation in Christ: "And whatever you do in word or deed, do all in the name of [in the place of, on behalf of] the Lord Jesus, giving thanks through Him to God the Father."

❧ NOT-GOD ❧

BUT ALL OF THIS, THE only sane and sound basis for human life, is precisely what is absent from the ruined heart. In Romans 1, Paul described the progressive departure from God that leads to life as we know and see it all around us—and, sadly, within us if we have not been thoroughly transformed by Christ. As we might expect from the passages already referred to, the slide into pervasive soul corruption begins with the heart (or will) deflecting the mind from God.

Human beings have always known there is a God and have had some degree of understanding of who he is and what he is like (Romans 1:19-20). Actually, they still do. But they were not pleased that he should have the place in the universe that he does have merely because he is who he is. And this is the key to understanding humanity's present condition. The first of the Ten Commandments deals with this inclination away from God (Exodus 20:2-3). As Augustine saw clearly, God being God offends human pride. If God is running the universe and has first claim on our lives, guess who *isn't* running the universe and does not get to have things as they please.

Philip Yancey tells us,

> The historian of Alcoholics Anonymous titled his work *Not-God* because, he said, that stands as the most important hurdle an addicted person must surmount: to acknowledge, deep in the soul, not being God. No mastery of manipulation and control, at which alcoholics excel, can overcome the root problem; rather, the alcoholic must recognize individual helplessness and fall back in the arms of the Higher Power. "First of all, we had to quit playing God," concluded the founders of AA; and then allow God himself to "play God" in the addict's life, which involves daily, even moment-by-moment, surrender.[2]

Denial and Its Effects

BUT IN TAKING ONESELF in practice (or humanity taking itself in practice) as God, the great world-historical force of *denial* comes into play. It is this that accounts for the perpetual human blindness to the obvious. We can never understand human affairs at any level without taking it into account. It alone explains why "the rulers of this age" (1 Corinthians 2:8, NRSV) do and are permitted to do the things they do—up to the crucifixion of "the Lord of glory" himself.

Denial of reality is a capacity inseparable from the human will as we know it, and it has its greatest power when it operates without being recognized as such. (Of course by "denial" we mean to include not only rejection of what is the case, but also affirmation of what is not the case.)

In a world apart from God, the power of denial is absolutely essential if life is to proceed. The will or spirit cannot—psychologically cannot—sustain itself for any length of time in the face of what it clearly acknowledges to be the case. Therefore it must deny and evade and delude itself. Paul's brilliant and inspired insight into the root of human evil—"There is no fear of God before their eyes"—must never be forgotten by those who would understand spiritual formation and would themselves be transformed into Christlikeness, or by those who simply want to be responsible leaders among humanity.

Now when the light of the fundamental truth and reality, God, is put out in the heart and the soul, the intellect becomes dysfunctional, trying to devise a "truth" that will be compatible with the basic falsehood that man is god; and the affections (feelings, emotions, even sensations) soon follow along on the path to chaos. "They became futile in their speculations," Paul continued, "and their foolish heart was darkened. Professing to be wise, they became fools." They pretended God was an animal—usually a monstrous animal or a human-like being—of some kind (Romans 1:21-23). But remember, the mind is now uprooted from reality. It is committed to the truth of a falsehood. "Garbage in, garbage out" is an *old* story, and then the strong desires, or "lusts" *(epithumiais),* plunge right into the garbage along with thought.

✎ SENSUALITY BECOMES CENTRAL ✎

THE HUMAN BODY BECOMES the primary area of pleasure for the person who does not live honestly and interactively with God, and also the primary source of terror, torture, and death. So it is an "obvious" thing to turn to for those who worship and serve "the creature rather than the Creator" (Romans 1:25, NRSV). And because bodily enjoyment is what they want, what they *choose* to pursue, God abandons them to their pursuit of every pleasurable sensation they can wring out of the body—primarily sexual, for that usually gives the greatest "kick," but bodily violence is a close second. This is the spiritual root of obsession with "sex and violence" in decadent societies, whether our own or those of other times and places.

"Free love," as it is euphemistically but falsely called, along with the various forms of perversion, are simply an extension of body worship (verses 26-27)—even the worship of breast, vagina, and penis witnessed to by both archeology and modern life (and the "abs" and "buns" of today). As logic teaches us, everything logically follows from a falsehood. If what is false is true, then everything is. So anything goes.

But then it turns out that sensuality *cannot* be satisfied. It is not self-limiting. That is partly because the effect of engaging in the practices of sensuality is to deaden feeling. Then awakens the relentless drive, the desperate need, simply *to feel,* to feel *something.* This drive is rooted in basic human nature, as we will discuss below. We have to have feeling, and it needs to be deep and sustained. But if we are not living the great drama of goodness in God's kingdom, sensuality through the body is all that is left under our "kingdom."

Paul observes to the Ephesians that

the Gentiles [those not knowing God] also walk, in the futility of their mind, being darkened in their understanding, excluded from the life of God, because of the ignorance that is in them, because of the hardness of their heart; and they, having become callous, have given themselves over to sensuality, for the practice of every kind of impurity with greediness. (Ephesians 4:17-19)

This is the natural progression in the flight from God.

The drive to self-gratification opens up into a life without boundaries, where nothing is forbidden—if one can "get away" with it. "Why?" is replaced with "Why not?" And because this is what these "gods" want—total license—God abandons them to a worthless or nonfunctional (*adokimon*) mind—that is, a mind that simply doesn't work. "As they did not see fit to center their knowledge upon God, God released them into the grip of a nonfunctional mind, to do what is indecent" (Romans 1:28, PAR).

The outcome is a humanity "filled with all unrighteousness, wickedness, greed, evil; full of envy, murder, strife, deceit, malice; they are gossips, slanderers, haters of God, insolent, arrogant, boastful, inventors of evil, disobedient to parents, without understanding, untrustworthy, unloving, unmerciful." And although they still know of the condemnation of God on such things, "they not only do the same, but also give hearty approval to those who practice them" (Romans 1:29-32).

❧ STILL TRUE TODAY ☙

IF YOU ARE A thoughtful and observant person you will probably recognize in this description the usual course of human affairs—thank God for any exceptions there may be! And if you find yourself substantially exempted from this picture, you can say thankfully, "There, but for the grace of God, go I."

Paul, at least, was not hopeful that things would get better as human history moved along. He was not a believer in "progress" as it has been humanly understood. In what seems to have been his last letter, perhaps the very last thing he wrote, he warned Timothy that

in the last days difficult times will come. For men will be lovers of self, lovers of money, boastful, arrogant, revilers, disobedient to parents, ungrateful, unholy, unloving, irreconcilable, malicious gossips, without self-control, brutal, haters of good, treacherous, reckless, conceited, lovers of pleasure rather than lovers of God; holding to a form of godliness, although they have denied its power. (2 Timothy 3:1-5)

One could be forgiven for thinking that this certainly looks like "now." Who does not recognize in these words the prevailing tone and texture of contemporary life? Who does not know that such behavior, if not approved outright, is excused or even justified by clever psychological, legal, and moral maneuvers, often reciting elevated "principles."

In fact this has been the end stage of every successful human society that has arisen on earth. Invariably, such a society begins to believe *it* is responsible for its success and prosperity and begins to worship itself and rebel against the understandings and practices that allowed it, under God, to be successful in the first place. "Jeshurun grew fat and kicked," the prophetic analysis states (Deuteronomy 32:15). The human decline into what was expressed in the words of Paul to Timothy is inevitable.

But underneath it all is the radical evil of the human heart—a heart that would make *me* God in place of God. The prophetic clarity still stands for all to read and test. Our human "righteousness" is like "filthy rags" (Isaiah 64:6, KJV). And over against this we hear intoned: "I, the LORD, search the heart, I test the mind, even to give to each man according to his ways, according to the results of his deeds" (Jeremiah 17:10).

❧ BEING LOST ❧

WITH THESE SOBERING VISTAS of the human heart and soul before us, we need now to rethink for our time what it means to be lost. For a ruined soul is a *lost* soul. What is a "lost soul"? Just someone God is mad at? When is a person lost? And is anyone lost today?

Considerable confusion on this topic has resulted from trying to think of being lost in terms of its *outcome*. Theologically, that outcome is hell—a most uncomfortable notion. Certainly, if you are lost in any sense there is little likelihood of your arriving where you want to be. But the condition of lostness is not the same as the outcome to which it leads. We're not lost because we are going to wind up in the wrong place. We are going to wind up in the wrong place because we are lost.

To be lost means to be *out of place,* to be omitted. "Gehenna," the term often used in the New Testament for the place of the lost, may usefully be thought of as the cosmic dump for the irretrievably useless. Think of what it would mean to find you have become irretrievably useless. Something that is lost is something that is not where it is supposed to be, and therefore it is not integrated into the life of the one to whom it belongs and to whom it is lost.

Think of what it means when the keys to your house or car are lost. They are useless to you, no matter how much you need them and desire to have them and no matter what fine keys they may be. And when we are lost to God, we are not where we are supposed to be in his world and hence are not caught up into his life. We are *not* "partakers of the divine nature," have *not* "escaped the corruption that is in the world" through lust (2 Peter 1:4, PAR).

We are our own god, and our god doesn't amount to much.

When we are lost to God, we are also lost to ourselves: we do not know where we are or how to get where we want to go. We may know we are lost or we may not. Many a driver is lost long before he knows he is—though rarely before his wife knows it. Many are lost before God but do not know it. They sincerely believe that they know where they are, where they are going, and how to get there; but in fact they do not, and they often find out too late. Disorientation to moral, personal, and divine reality, as well as to the physical, sometimes leads us across lines that *cannot* be recrossed. This is part of the tragic meaning of human time and action.

▬ "LOST" MEANS SELF-OBSESSION ▬

LOST PERSONS, IN CHRISTIAN terms, are precisely the ones who mistake their own person for God. They falsely identify, and cannot recognize, what is closest to them—themselves. Then, as we have noted, everything becomes delusional. Such a one really does think he is in charge of his life—though, admittedly, to manage it "successfully," he may have to bow outwardly to this or that person or power. But *he* is in charge (he believes), and he has no confidence in the one who really is God. As we have seen, such ones "do not see fit to center their knowledge upon God."

Their god, as Paul elsewhere wrote, is their "belly" (Philippians 3:19, KJV), the feeling center of the self. They are willing *slaves* of their feelings or appetites (Romans 16:18). They "want what they want when they want it," as the song says, and that is the ultimate fact about them. If they do not get it they become angry and depressed, and are a danger to themselves and others.

Edith Schaeffer, in one of her penetrating discussions of abortion, points out:

> The philosophy of living with an underlying motive of doing
> everything for one's own personal peace and comfort rapidly colors
> everything that might formerly have come under the headings of
> "right" and "wrong." This new way of thinking adds entirely new
> shades, often in blurring brushstrokes of paint that wipe out the
> existence of standards or cast them into a shadow that pushes
> them out of sight. If one's peace, comfort, way of life, convenience,
> reputation, opportunities, job, happiness, or even ease is threat-
> ened, "Just abort it." Abort what? Abort another life that is not yet
> born. Yes, but also abort the afflictions connected with having a
> handicapped child, and abort the burdens connected with caring
> for the old or invalid. Added swiftly are the now supposedly

thinkable attitudes of aborting a child's early security in his or her rights to have two parents and a family life; aborting a wife's need for having her husband be someone to trust and lean upon; aborting the husband's need for having a companion and friend as well as a feminine mate; aborting any responsibility to carry through a job started.[3]

Thus self-idolatry rearranges the entire spiritual and moral landscape. It sees the whole universe with different eyes. If it is not abortion that is at the center, it will be something else; but the fundamental pride of putting oneself at the center of the universe is the hinge upon which the entire world of the ruined self turns.

John Calvin said that "the surest source of destruction to men is to obey themselves."[4] Yet self-obedience seems the only reasonable path for nearly everyone: "So blindly do we all rush in the direction of self-love, that every one thinks he has a good reason for exalting himself and despising all others in comparison."[5] What an exquisite eye for detail Calvin had! He would find today's scene very familiar.

Dietrich Bonhoeffer's words capture the scene: "Whereas the primal relationship of man to man is a giving one, in the state of sin it is purely demanding. Every man exists in a state of complete voluntary isolation; each man lives his own life, instead of all living the same God-life."[6] Well, of course. Each is a god unto himself.

❧ HELL ❧

THUS NO ONE CHOOSES in the abstract to go to hell or even to be the kind of person who belongs there. But their orientation toward self leads them to become the kind of person for whom away-from-God is the only place for which they are suited. It is a place they would, in the end, choose for themselves, rather than come to humble themselves before God and accept who he is. Whether or not God's will is infinitely flexible, the human will is not. There are limits beyond which it cannot bend back, cannot turn or repent.

One should seriously inquire if to live in a world permeated with God and the knowledge of God is something they themselves truly desire. If not, they can be assured that God will excuse them from his presence. They will find their place in the "outer darkness" of which Jesus spoke. But the fundamental fact about them will not be that they are there, but that they have become people so locked into their own self-worship and denial of God that *they cannot want God*.

A well-known minister of other years used to ask rhetorically, "You say you will accept God when you want to?" And then he would add, "How do you know you will be able to want to when you think you will?" *The ultimately lost person is the person who cannot want God.* Who cannot want God to be God. Multitudes of such people pass by every day, and pass into eternity. The reason they do not find God is that they do not want him or, at least, do not want *him* to be God. Wanting God to be God is very different from wanting God to help me.

☙ INSULTING OUR PRIDE ❧

IS IT INSULTING TO suggest that someone is or may be lost? That his or her soul is ruined? There are so many fine-looking people all about us! Well, is it insulting to say, in appropriate circumstances, that someone has a physical disease that may be fatal, when you know it to be true? Perhaps treatment depends upon coming to know it. Say it is cancer or diabetes or AIDS? No doubt, in our hypersensitive, egotistical age, that could be insulting to some people. But that merely illustrates the delusional human condition that has been described earlier. If I am god, people shouldn't say such things to *me*.

Lostness is a factual condition of the self, of the ruined soul. You either have it or not, just as you either have or do not have a certain physical disease that can kill you. If you have that condition of lostness, you *may* not know it. Indeed, it is most likely you will not know it, because it is inherently a condition of self-blindness. You need treatment nevertheless, if you are not to be lost forever; and being informed of your condition and what to do about it can help you find relief. Should I say nothing to you merely because you might find it insulting? I must think more highly of you than that. The reality of evil in the human heart is not something to be ignored or treated lightly.

☙ CAN'T FACE UP TO EVIL ❧

WHEN THE FLOODTIDES OF evil break across the television screen or wash the pages of print media in what is now called "news," people roll their eyes helplessly and say, "Why?" They never say "Why?" when something good happens. But they would if they ever faced up to the reality of the ruined soul. However, they simply cannot deal with the actual content of the human heart, mind, body, social context, and soul. In "intellectual" circles (and don't we all live there now?) evil, like sin, is a non-category. It is impolite and politically incorrect to speak seriously of it, even if it involves flying airliners loaded with innocent victims into skyscrapers.

Some years ago a leading media personality had a high-level conference in Aspen, Colorado, on the topic of evil. (Shouldn't that meeting have been held elsewhere? South Los Angeles or Soweto?) The outcome was that one or two participants out of a large group thought that there was such a thing as evil. But most were either noncommittal on the point or certain that evil did not exist at all. When you heard their comments it was clear that they simply could not conceptualize the evil to be seen flourishing abundantly around them in the twentieth century. One of the most glaring evidences of the bankruptcy of contemporary ethical thinking is that it cannot deal with evil. A recent proposal to found a field of "Evil Studies" within academia will not be enthusiastically received.[7]

We should be very sure that the ruined soul is not one who has missed a few more or less important theological points and will flunk a theological examination at the end of life. Hell is not an "oops!" or a slip. One does not miss heaven by a hair, but *by constant effort to avoid and escape God.* "Outer darkness" is for one who, everything said, wants it, whose entire orientation has slowly and firmly set itself against God and therefore against how the universe actually is. It is for those who are disastrously in error about their own life and their place before God and man.[8] The ruined soul must be willing to hear of and recognize its own ruin before it can find how to enter a different path, the path of eternal life that naturally leads into spiritual formation in Christlikeness.

Spiritual formation is not something that may, or may not, be added to the gift of eternal life as an *option.* Rather, it is the path that the eternal kind of life "from above" naturally takes. It is the path one must be on if his or hers is to be an eternal kind of life.

It is not a project of "life enhancement," where the "life" in question is the usual life of "normal" human beings—that is, life apart from God. It is, rather, the process of developing a different kind of life, the life of God himself, sustained by God as a new reality in those who have confidence that Jesus is the anointed One, the Son of God. "Believing in him we have life in his name" (John 20:31, PAR). Those "in Christ"—that is, caught up in his life, in what he is doing, by the inward gift of birth from above— "are of a new making (*ktisis*). The 'old stuff' no longer matters. It is the new that counts" (2 Corinthians 5:17, PAR). Here in this new creation is the radical goodness that alone can thoroughly renovate the heart.

⤜ THE NECESSITY OF REMORSE ⤛

TO PROSECUTORS AND JUDGES in our court system, as well as to people in ordinary situations of life, it still matters greatly whether wrongdoers show signs of remorse or seem to be truly sorry for what they have done.

Why is that? It is because genuine remorse tells us something very deep about the individual. The person who can harm others and feel no remorse is, indeed, a different kind of person from the one who is sorry. There is little hope for genuine change in one who is without remorse, without the *anguish* of regret.

Much of what is called Christian profession today involves no remorse or sorrow at all over who one is or even for what one has done. There is little awareness of being lost or of a radical evil in our hearts, bodies, and souls—which we *must* get away from and from which only God can deliver us. To manifest such awareness today would be regarded—and certainly by most Christians as well—as psychologically sick. It is common today to hear Christians talk of their "brokenness." But when you listen closely, you may discover that they are talking about their *wounds*, the things they have suffered, not about the evil that is in them.

Few today have discovered that they have been disastrously wrong and that they cannot change or escape the consequences of it on their own. There is little sense of "Woe is me! for I am undone; because I am a man of unclean lips, and I dwell in the midst of a people of unclean lips: for my eyes have seen the King, the LORD of hosts" (Isaiah 6:5, KJV).

Yet, *without this realization of our utter ruin* and without the genuine revisioning and redirecting of our lives, which that bitter realization naturally gives rise to, *no clear path to inner transformation can be found.* It is psychologically and spiritually impossible. We will steadfastly remain on the throne of our universe, so far as we are concerned, perhaps trying to "use a little God" here and there. This will grow clearer as we look into the radical goodness of the renovated self.

Matters for
Thought and Discussion

1. Do you accept the idea that human beings apart from God are *ruined*? How would you describe that ruin? What does it mean in practical, day-to-day terms?

2. Do you see how the ruin in question is the result of the "spiritual formation" people receive in the natural course of human life on earth?

3. What is your sense of how *evil* functions (or does not function) among "informed" people today as a legitimate category of explanation of events around us?

4. In helping people to find Christ and follow through with spiritual formation in him, can we start with self-esteem? Why or why not? Is there a grain of truth in the self-esteem approach to life? If so, what is it? (See paragraphs 4–6 of this chapter for a suggestion.)

5. Where can you see evidence of soul-ruin in our wider world and in the "church visible"?

6. State briefly Paul's summary of the prophetic witness about the human condition.

7. How is *pride* (being god) at the basis of human ruin?

8. Why does *sensuality* come to play such a major role in human ruin?

9. Apply Paul's discussion of moral corruption in "the last days" to the world we now live in. Use one edition of a leading daily newspaper or weekly news magazine to do this.

4

RADICAL GOODNESS
RESTORED TO THE SOUL

*And such were some of you; but you were washed, but you
were sanctified, but you were justified in the name of
the Lord Jesus Christ, and in the Spirit of our God.*
1 CORINTHIANS 6:11

One of the amazing things about the human being is that it is capable of restoration, and indeed of a restoration that makes it somehow more magnificent because it has been ruined. This is a hopeful but strange thought. How it is so should become clear as we proceed. But for now we want to see clearly what goes on within the person who is "unruined," as we might say. In particular, we must see what is the basic shift (given regeneration and forgiveness) that can lead to the reordering of the six universal dimensions of the human self in subordination to God.

The key to understanding the overall reordering is provided by what we learned about the human ruin in the previous chapter. John Calvin, once again, remarked, "For as the surest source of destruction to men is to obey themselves, so the only haven of safety is to have no other will, no other wisdom, than to follow the Lord wherever he leads. Let this, then, be the first step, to abandon ourselves, and devote the whole energy of our minds to the service of God." With these words he simply restated the basic point of view of Christ's people through the ages.[1]

Calvin continued to explain:

By service, I mean not only that which consists in verbal obedience, but that by which the mind, divested of its own carnal feelings, implicitly obeys the call of the Spirit of God. This transformation (which Paul calls *the renewing of the mind,* Romans 12:2; Ephesians 4:23), though it is the first entrance of life, was unknown to all the philosophers. They give the government of man to reason alone. . . . But Christian philosophy bids her give place, and yield complete submission to the Holy Spirit, so that the man himself no longer lives, but Christ lives and reigns in him (Galatians 2:20).[2]

❧ SELF-DENIAL ❧

IT IS SUCH AN overall transformation of personality that Calvin captured under the heading "self-denial," a term he used to summarize the entire Christian life.[3] "Self-denial" must never be confused with self-*rejection;* nor is it to be thought of as a painful and strenuous *act,* perhaps repeated from time to time against great internal resistance. It is, rather, an overall, settled condition of life in the kingdom of God, better described as "death to self." In this and in this alone lies the key to the soul's restoration. *Christian spiritual formation rests on this indispensable foundation of death to self and cannot proceed except insofar as that foundation is being firmly laid and sustained.*

But what is this "self-denial" or "death to self," which goes hand in hand with restoration of the soul and eventually the whole person? At first it sounds like some dreadfully negative thing that aims to annihilate us. And frankly, from the point of view of the ruined soul, self-denial is and will always be every bit as brutal as it seems to most people on first approach. The ruined life is not to be enhanced but replaced. We must simply *lose* our life — that *ruined* life about which most people complain so much anyway. "Those who have found their life (soul) shall lose it," Jesus said, "while those who have lost their life (soul) for my sake shall find it" (Matthew 10:39, PAR). And again, "Whoever aims to save their life shall lose it, but whoever loses their life for my sake shall find it. For what have you gained by possessing the entire world if in the process you forfeit your life (soul) — lose yourself. What would you trade your very soul for?" (Matthew 16:25-26, PAR; also Mark 8:35-36; Luke 9:24-25).

We must always remember, in hearing these words of Jesus about the worth of the soul, that the art of the great teacher is to put things in ways you will remember even if you don't yet understand them. In that way you can keep working on them (and they on you) until you *do* understand them. Jesus is the master teacher of the human race, and he teaches accordingly.

And we have, I think, an intuitive sense that he is right about the worth of the soul. A German soldier fighting in the trenches along France's Marne river in World War I, where one million soldiers died on the Western front in 1914, wrote home: "What is the good of escaping all the bullets and shells if my soul is injured." Some losses are so great that nothing on earth can make recompense for them.

✑ LOSING OUR LIFE TO FIND IT ✑

WHEN JESUS SAYS WE must lose our lives if we are to find them, he is teaching, on the negative side, that we must not make ourselves and our "survival" the ultimate point of reference in our world—must not, in effect, treat ourselves as God should be treated, or treat ourselves *as* God. Thus Paul shockingly said, "Covetousness is idolatry" (Colossians 3:5, PAR). Isn't that somewhat exaggerated? No. Covetousness is self-idolatry, for it makes *my* desires paramount. It means I *would* take what I want if I could. To defeat covetousness we learn to rejoice that others enjoy the benefits they do.

To make my desires paramount is what Paul again described as having a "flesh mind" or "mind of the flesh," which is a state of death (Romans 8:6). Such a mind "sows to one's own flesh"—invests only in one's natural self—and "out of that flesh reaps corruption" (Galatians 6:8, PAR). "Corruption" or "coming apart" is the natural end of the flesh. "Flesh" can only be preserved by being caught up within the higher life of the kingdom of God and thus "losing" the life peculiar to it.

In other words, when Jesus says that those who find their life or soul shall lose it, he is pointing out that those who think they are in control of their life—"I am the master of my fate: I am the captain of my soul," as the poet William Ernest Henley said—will find that they definitely are not in control: they are totally at the mercy of forces beyond them, and even within them. They are on a sure course to disintegration and powerlessness, of *lostness* both to themselves and to God. They must surrender.

By contrast, if they give up the project of being the ultimate point of reference in their life—of doing only what they want, of "sowing to the flesh" or to the natural aims and abilities of a human being—there can be hope. If they *in that sense* lose their life in favor of God's life, or for the sake of Jesus and what he is doing on earth—remember the ongoing world revolution he is now conducting—then their soul (life) will be preserved and thus given back to them.

✑ DOING WHAT YOU WANT—GOD'S WAY ✑

WHAT DOES THAT MEAN? It means that they will then for the first time be able to do what they want to do. Of course they will be able to steal, lie, and murder all they want—which will be none at all. But they will also be able to be truthful and transparent and helpful and sacrificially loving, with joy—and they will want to be. Their life will be in this way caught up in God's life. They will want the good and be able to do it, the only true human freedom. The mind set on the spiritual is in that sense "life and peace" (Romans 8:6), because it lives from God and, "sowing into the spirit, out of the spirit reaps the eternal kind of life" (Galatians 6:8, PAR).

So—and this is of utmost importance to those who would enter Christian spiritual formation—life as normally understood, where the object is securing myself, promoting myself, indulging myself, is to be set aside.

"Can I still *think* about such things?" you may ask. Yes, you can. But you increasingly won't. And when you do, as formation in Christlikeness progresses, they simply won't matter. In fact, they will seem ridiculous and uninteresting. Jesus' words on not being anxious about what will happen to you and his admonitions to consider the flowers and birds (Luke 12:13-34) will seem obviously sane and right, whereas they previously sounded obviously crazy and wrong, or "out of touch with reality."

☙ TAKING THE CROSS ❧

THE SAME PARADOXICAL TONE applies to his teaching about who can be his disciple or apprentice. This too is put in very shocking language: "If you come to me," he said, "and do not prefer me over (do not 'hate') your own father, mother, wife, children, brothers and sisters—yes, and your very own life (soul)—you cannot be my apprentice" (Luke 14:26, PAR).

And then he uses an absolutely shocking image—one all too familiar to his hearers, but rather hard for us fully to appreciate today. It was that of a man carrying on his back the lumber that would be used to kill him when he arrived at the place of execution. "Whoever does not come after me carrying his own cross cannot be my apprentice" (verse 27, PAR).

The cross is an instrument of death, of "losing your life." The teaching here is exactly the same as in the statements about losing and finding our lives. It is one of comparative costs, as the verses that follow in Luke 14 show. Those who are not genuinely convinced that the only real bargain in life is surrendering ourselves to Jesus and his cause, abandoning all that we love to him and for him, *cannot* learn the other lessons Jesus has to teach us. They cannot proceed to anything like total spiritual transformation. Not that he will not let us, but that we simply cannot succeed. If I tell you that you cannot drive an automobile unless you can see, I am not saying I will not let you, but that you cannot succeed even if I do.

Still, from within the life that remains "lost" to God, the teaching of the Cross and of abandoning all that is "first" in ordinary human life seems repulsive and impossible. And it has often been disastrously misinterpreted, resulting in the destruction, not the renovation, of the human heart and life. It remains a dangerous half-truth if left to stand on its own. It is a negation that in practice can only rest on an affirmation.

◆ THE TRUE MEANING OF THE CROSS AND "COUNTING THE COSTS" ◆

ONE OF THE GREAT dangers in the process of spiritual formation is that self-denial and death to self will be taken as but one more technique or "job" for those who wish to save their life (soul). Self-denial will then externalize itself in overt practices of group identity that may seem very sacrificial, but can leave the "mind of the flesh" in full control. We see this, for example, in many who wear what they regard as plain clothing or who abstain from certain foods.

A well-known Methodist evangelist of other years, Sam Jones, used to say that a dancing foot and a praying knee do not grow on the same leg. This might prove to be a fairly good empirical generalization. It may be that as a matter of fact few prayerfully bent knees are on legs with a dancing foot at the end. Still, just *not* dancing would hardly prove that you had abandoned your life to God.

Practices of "mortification" can become exercises in more self-righteousness. How often this has happened! This dreary and deadly "self-denial," which is all too commonly associated with religion, can be avoided only if the primary fact of our inner being is a loving vision of Jesus and his kingdom. This is where correctly counting the cost comes in. Then outward manifestation of self-denial, or the absence thereof, will matter little, as it did for him.

The impression gained by most who hear about "counting the cost" of following Jesus is one of how terrible and painful that cost is. But to count the cost is to take into consideration both the losses and the gains of all possible courses of action, to see which is most beneficial. This done, Jesus knew, the trials of apprenticeship (discipleship) would appear to be the only reasonable path. As has been said, "He is not a fool who gives up what he cannot keep for the sake of what he can never lose." The cost of *non*-discipleship would then be seen for what it is—unbearable. That is why one would become able to sustain cheerfully the *much smaller* "cost of discipleship" to him.

◆ THE CROSS AND THE CALL TO THE GREATER LIFE ◆

THUS IN JESUS' OWN ministry he came proclaiming access to the kingdom of God: to God's present care and supervision, available to all through confidence in himself. "Repent, for life in the kingdom of the heavens is now available to you," was what he said. And his presence, actions, and teachings manifested and explained the kingdom. He made "disciples" by presenting them with the kingdom and introducing them into it by reaching their hearts, changing their vision of reality and their intentions for life.

Consider one of his "parables of the kingdom": "The kingdom of the heavens is like a treasure hidden in a field, which a man found and concealed it. He was ecstatic. He sold everything he had and bought the field" (Matthew 13:44, PAR).

Imagine that you discovered gold or oil in a certain property and no one else knew about it. Can you see yourself being sad and feeling deprived for having to gather all your resources and "sacrifice" them in order to buy that property? Hardly! Now you know what it is like to deny yourself, take up your cross, and follow Jesus!

Some pain is included, no doubt, because the old attachments are still there in our hearts and lives. They never all disappear at once. And we may experience some uncertainty from time to time, especially at the start. But the progress of spiritual formation will soon take care of that.

The new vision becomes an attachment and takes on an ever greater reality as we progress; and that, in turn, pushes the old attachments toward the exits of our lives—which we then are *not* sad to see go. Indeed we are happy about it. We come to want to *not* want what we now want, and to want to *not* think of what now lives before our mind; and we come to want to be made willing for what we are *not now* really willing.

So the self-denial of Matthew 16:24 and elsewhere in the Gospels is always the surrender of a lesser, dying self for a greater eternal one—the person God intended in creating you. Confidence in this is the occasion of "greatly rejoicing, with joy unspeakable and full of glory" (1 Peter 1:8, PAR). Jesus does not deny us personal fulfillment, but shows us the only true way to it. In him we "find our life." He would keep us from selling our birthright as creatures in God's image—a birthright of genuine goodness, sufficiency, and power for which we are fitted by nature—for a mere bowl of soup (Genesis 25:30-31): perhaps a little illicit sex, money, reputation, power, self-righteousness, and so forth—"the pleasures of sin for a season"—or for the mere promise or possibility of such.

The "cross" we must take is laid upon all obsessive and partial desires, so that the broad reach of *agape* love can integrate for us a whole and eternal life with God and man. Jesus was not some harsh ascetic who practiced or imposed pain for its own sake. He did not choose death because it was good in itself, but "for the joy that was set before him, he endured the cross and despised the shame" (Hebrews 12:2, PAR).

To take him as our master means that we trust his way is right and, as he himself did, always look to the larger good under God. Like him we keep on entrusting ourselves to the One who judges righteously (1 Peter 2:23). This is "losing our life and thereby saving it" in the manner Jesus taught.

⤳ PERFECT JOY ⤴

IN CHAPTER 8 OF *The Little Flowers of St. Francis of Assisi,* Francis gives his friend Leo a teaching about what "perfect joy" is. They are trudging through the snow from Perugia to the home of their group at St. Mary of the Angeles. For their brotherhood to give a great example of holiness and edification in all lands would *not* be perfect joy, Francis says. Nor would a great ministry of healing and raising the dead. Nor would possession of all languages and all science, nor all understanding of prophecy and Scripture, and insight into the secrets of every soul. Nor would even the conversion of all unbelievers to faith in Christ!

By this point brother Leo is amazed, and he begs Francis to teach him "wherein is perfect joy." The reply is that if, when they come to their quarters—dirty, wet, and exhausted from hunger—they are rejected, repeatedly rebuffed, and finally driven away by force, then "if we accept such injustice, such cruelty, and such contempt with patience, without being ruffled and without murmuring," and "if we bear all these injuries with patience and joy, thinking of the sufferings of our Blessed Lord, which we would share out of love for Him, write, O Brother Leo, that here, finally, is perfect joy."

⤳ THE CENTRALITY OF GIVING ⤴

GIVING AND FORGIVING ARE of course central to the divinely restructured life, as we take on the character truly suited to the human soul. Even from his strictly humanistic perspective, Erich Fromm rightly said, "The most widespread misunderstanding is that which assumes that giving is 'giving up' something, being deprived of, sacrificing. People whose main orientation is a non-productive one feel giving as an impoverishment. . . ; the virtue of giving, to them, lies in the very act of acceptance of sacrifice."[4]

This certainly fits in with the purely negative understanding of self-denial discussed above. In fact, it has become a part of our ethical culture. But, Fromm continued:

> For the productive character giving has an entirely different meaning. Giving is the highest expression of potency. In the very act of giving I experience my strength, my wealth, my power. The experience of heightened vitality fills me with joy. I experience myself as overflowing, spending, alive, hence as joyous. Giving is more joyous than receiving, not because it is a deprivation, but because in the act of giving lies the expression of my aliveness.[5]

∾ SUPPORTED ON THE KINGDOM ∾

BUT THIS UNDERSTANDING OF the goodness of giving—and hence of not making oneself the absolute point of reference—must be supported. In laying down my life I must experience much more than "my strength, my wealth, my power." There must be a realism to it. Otherwise one is in danger of falling into the same kind of cheery falseness that characterizes so much current talk of self-esteem. The necessary support for giving and forgiving is abundantly supplied by Jesus through the reality of the kingdom of God that he brings into our lives. He makes this available to us in response to our confidence in Him.

Only with this in support can we live in Jesus' teaching, "Give, and it will be given to you; good measure, pressed down, shaken together, running over, they will pour into your lap" (Luke 6:38). For there will be periods of time when, from the human point of view, our lap is empty: when we experience cross and tomb, but resurrection is not yet. We must then know with assurance the reality in Paul's words that "God loves a cheerful giver" and that he "is able to make all grace abound to you, that always having all sufficiency in everything, you may have an abundance for every good deed" (2 Corinthians 9:7-8).

Jesus' resurrected presence with us, along with his teaching, assures us of God's care for all who let him be God and let him care for them. "Do not be afraid, little flock, for your Father has chosen gladly to give you the kingdom" (Luke 12:32). It is love of God, admiration and confidence in his greatness and goodness, and the regular experience of his care that free us from the burden of "looking out for ourselves."

What remarkable changes this introduces into our day-to-day life! Personally, at the beginning of my day—often before arising—I commit my day to the Lord's care. Usually I do this while meditatively praying through the Lord's Prayer, and possibly the twenty-third Psalm as well. Then I meet everything that happens as sent or at least permitted by God. I meet it resting in the hand of his care. This helps me to "do all things without grumbling or disputing" (Philippians 2:14), because I have already "placed God in charge" and am trusting him to manage them for my good. I no longer have to manage the weather, airplanes, and other people.

∾ PULLING THE WHOLE SELF TOGETHER ∾

EXPERIENCE-BASED CONFIDENCE IN God's loving care allows all six dimensions of the human self progressively to come into harmony with each other and enables us to be generous in every respect to those around us. Only love of God frames and supports love of neighbor, giving it right direction and the power to carry out its aim of goodness within the kingdom. And love of

God and neighbor gradually pulls the entire structure of the person into proper alignment.

Without such support in God, talk of "giving being the highest expression of potency," and so on, will quickly degenerate into empty words, bravado, self-deception, hypocrisy—or even more self-deification, as in much of the "human potential" and new age movements today. It will be totally me-centered and thus will perpetuate the soul's ruin rather than its renovation. A great deal of attraction of the new age outlook and practice is its insistence that "I am God."

❧ DEAD TO SELF ❧

IN THE CLEAR AND forceful vision of Jesus and his kingdom, as our personality becomes progressively more reorganized around God and his eternal life, self-denial moves beyond more or less frequent acts to settled disposition and character.

At the first we must very self-consciously deny ourselves—reject the preeminence of what we want, when and as we want it—and we must look to quite specific motions of God's grace in and around us to guide and strengthen us in our occasions of self-denial. We will also need a wise and constant use of disciplines for the spiritual life. This is because, from where we start, the substance of our selves, formed in a world against God, is ready to act otherwise in all of its dimensions, especially in the social and the bodily. Our very habits of thinking, feeling, and willing are wrongly poised. We shall say more about this later, and about how we can and must work with God in the process of spiritual (trans)formation.

But there will come a time in the experience of the apprentice of Jesus where it is appropriate to speak of our being dead to self. There is no one way this comes to us, I think, and the language here must be handled carefully. It has been the source of much misunderstanding and harm in the past. But the fact that it represents is a fundamental, indispensable element in the renovation of the heart, soul, and life. Being dead to self is the condition where the mere fact that I do not get what I want does not surprise or offend me and has no control over me. Faithful servants of God know the secret, and many have left their testimony. George Mueller of Bristol, England, said, "There was a day when I died: died to George Mueller, his opinions, preferences, tastes and will; died to the world, its approval or censure; died to the approval or blame even of my brethren or friends, and since then, I have studied only to show myself 'approved unto God.'" Small wonder that one said of Mueller that he "had the twenty-third psalm written in his face."[6]

We often speak of those who sleep soundly as being "dead to the world."

By that we mean that what is happening around them does not disturb them, that they are unconscious of it and are doing nothing with reference to it. There is an important lesson here, though not a precise parallel.

The one who is dead to self will certainly not even notice some things that others would—for example, things such as social slights, verbal put-downs and innuendos, or physical discomforts. But many other rebuffs to "the dear self," as the philosopher Immanuel Kant called it, will be noticed still, often quite clearly. However, if we are dead to self to any significant degree, these rebuffs will not take control of us, not even to the point of disturbing our feelings or peace of mind. We will, as St. Francis of Assisi said, "wear the world like a loose garment, which touches us in a few places and there lightly."

Does this mean that the person who is dead to self is without feeling? Does Christ commend the famous "apathy" of the Stoic or the Buddhist elimination of desire? Far from it. The issue is not just feeling or desire, but right feeling or desire, or being controlled by feeling and desire. Apprentices of Jesus will be deeply disturbed about many things and will passionately desire many things, but they will be largely indifferent to the fulfillment of their own desires as such. Merely getting their way has no significance for them, does not disturb them.

They know that "God causes all things to work together for good to those who love God, to those who are called according to His purpose" (Romans 8:28). They do not have to look out for themselves because God—and not they—is in charge of their life. They appropriately look after things that concern them, but they do not worry about outcomes that merely affect adversely their own desires and feelings. They are free to focus their efforts on the service of God and others and the furthering of good generally, and to be as passionate about such things as may be appropriate to such efforts.

❧ SOME SENSITIVITY TO SELF WILL REMAIN ❧

DO THOSE PERSONS WHO are dead to self, who easily and regularly deny their self, have any mere sensitivity to self left? I think we will never be totally above such sensitivity. There is no reason we should be. Mere sensitivity to self is not itself wrong or sinful, so long as we do not welcome it or allow it to "take over" our actions and lives. (Recall the distinctions earlier drawn between the "thought of sin," inclination, or temptation, and sin itself.)

When I was a child I enjoyed shooting out an occasional street light or popping a stray cat with a BB gun. I confess that I am now completely dead to any attraction these activities once held for me. I have no feeling for them at all.

As I grew older, however, I became quite vain and dependent upon what others thought and said about me. A major part of my spiritual struggle in my late teens and early twenties was with vanity. I wanted praise. In time, by God's grace I became substantially—not totally—delivered, through meditation on Scripture, general studies, solitude, prayer, service to others, and just "experience," along with the movements of grace in my heart and soul. Perhaps I am rarely governed by vanity now—others, of course, must be the judge of that—but it is still something I frequently feel. And I know that it could be something that controls my feelings and behavior were I to let it or were God to abandon me to it.

The advice found in Thomas à Kempis is very good as an antidote to improper sensitivity:

> Choose evermore rather to have less than more.
> Seek ever the lower place and to be under all.
> Desire ever to pray that the will of God be all and wholly done.
> So, such a one enters the land of peace and quiet.[7]

If this plan were followed and were sufficiently accompanied by the movements of God's Spirit within us, we might make substantial progress toward what John Wesley described as the "Character of a Methodist":

> His one desire, is the one design of his life, namely, "not to do his own will, but the will of Him that sent him." His one intention at all times and in all things is, not to please himself, but Him whom his soul loveth. He has a single eye. And because "his eye is single, his whole body is full of light." Indeed, where the loving eye of the soul is continually fixed upon God, there can be no darkness at all, "but the whole is light; as when the bright shining of a candle doth enlighten the house." God then reigns alone. All that is in the soul is holiness to the Lord. There is not a motion in his heart, but is according to His will. Every thought that arises points to Him, and is in obedience to the law of Christ.[8]

This may be a bit more than many people could find credible for this life, but it is clearly the direction in which we can and should be moving as apprentices of Jesus. What we surely can say is that those who are dead to self are not controlled in thought, feeling, or action by self-exaltation or by the will to have their own way, but are easily controlled by love of God and neighbor. They still have some sensitivity to self-will, no doubt, and are never totally beyond the possibility of falling under subjugation to it. Only a proper discipline and grace will prevent this from actually happening. But they no longer are locked in a struggle with it.

⁂ STANDING FOR THE RIGHT WITHOUT EGOTISM ⁂

ONE OF THE REAL sources of difficulty here is confusion of our desire for what is good and right to prevail with our desire to have our own way. One often sees the effects of this confusion in controversies in families, in churches, or between religious and political groups.

In such cases, very important values are often at stake, and people are passionately committed to one side or another. That is as it should be. But more often than not, the contempt and anger for others that emerges in the conflict is nothing but a manifestation of the will to have my way.

Families, churches, communities, and sovereign nations become embroiled in deadly conflicts that would immediately disappear or be resolvable but for the relentless will to have my/our way. Very likely the First World War—with horrific worldwide consequences that reverberate to this day—was entirely due to this human tendency. A significant part of the business of police, courts, and hospitals is the result of the drive of mere self-will and has no genuine bearing on the good of individuals and groups, much less on the glory of God.

"Unless a grain of wheat falls into the earth and dies," Jesus said, "it remains by itself alone; but if it dies, it bears much fruit. He who loves his life [soul] loses it; and he who hates his life in this world shall keep it to life eternal" (John 12:24-25).

This is a law of human life, partly visible at the level of purely human understanding (remember Erich Fromm) and fully demonstrated in the life of Jesus and that of his people throughout the ages, for all to see. *It is the controlling principle of the renovated heart and the restored soul. Its radical goodness progressively subverts and replaces the radical evil in the fallen human heart, mind, body, soul, and social and other environment.*

⁂ BEYOND ANGER, RETALIATION, AND UNFORGIVENESS ⁂

TO ACCEPT, WITH CONFIDENCE in God, that I do not immediately have to have my way releases me from the great pressure that anger, unforgiveness, and the "need" to retaliate imposes upon my life. This by itself is a huge transformation of the landscape of our life. It removes the root and source of by far the greater part of human evil we have to deal with in our world.[9]

Thus Paul directed the Christians in Thessalonica to "see that no one repays another with evil for evil, but always seek after that which is good for one another and for all men" (1 Thessalonians 5:15). Jesus commanded not to "resist him who is evil; but whoever slaps you on your right cheek, turn to him the other also" (Matthew 5:39, PAR). And Peter calls us to follow Jesus in "not returning evil for evil, or insult for insult, but giving a blessing instead; for you were called for the very purpose that you might inherit a blessing" (1 Peter 3:9).

These remarkable teachings and examples, which do so much to immediately transform life, all presuppose that one has laid down the burden of having one's own way. You can't begin to even understand them, much less follow them, except from a posture of self-denial firmly supported upon confidence, and this based, in turn, in a strong experience of God's all-sufficient presence in your life.

But to step with Jesus into the path of self-denial immediately breaks the iron-clad grip of sin over human personality and opens the way to a fuller and ever fuller restoration of radical goodness to the soul. It accesses incredible, supernatural strength for life. Because we must be active agents in this progression "from strength to strength" (Psalm 84:7), it is crucial that we now seek to understand the three main components of any process of spiritual transformation.

Matters for Thought and Discussion

1. What do you think of John Calvin's understanding of human ruin and deliverance? (See paragraphs 2 through 4 of this chapter.)

2. What do you believe Jesus means when he speaks of the necessity of *losing* our soul or life and finding it again in him? (As with most of these "thought" questions, try to be as concrete and practical as possible in responding.)

3. Why can I not be Jesus' apprentice (disciple) if I do not take my cross and follow him?

4. What is it to "count the costs"? What are the gains as well as expenses?

5. Does St. Francis's teaching about *perfect joy* apply to you? Imagine some ways it might apply (what might actually happen) in your real-world context.

6. Why is *giving* so central to the restoration of the soul? How does giving depend on the reality of the kingdom?

7. Is being "dead to self" a realistic goal of growth in Christ? Is it the same as being nothing? Is it "healthy"?

8. How would you describe one who is dead to self—again, in real-life, practical terms?

9. Can *we* avoid *egotism* (pride of will) in standing for what is right and good? How would we do that—beyond anger?

SPIRITUAL CHANGE

The Reliable Pattern

But we all, with unveiled face beholding as in a mirror the glory of the Lord, are being transformed into the same image from glory to glory, just as from the Lord, the Spirit.
2 CORINTHIANS 3:18

We have looked, now, at the basic dimensions of the human self and at the central principle of its dysfunctionality and corruption (that is, self-worship), as well as at the foundation of its renovation (that is, self-denial). Spiritual formation in Christ is the process by which one moves and is moved from self-worship to Christ-centered self-denial as a general condition of life in God's present and eternal kingdom.

The next logical step in a practical treatment of spiritual formation might seem to be the provision of detailed instructions on how to move from a life of self-adulation to one of self-denial, dealing with each of the dimensions of the human being in turn. And we plan to do just that. But *before* it can be effectively done in our contemporary context, we must clear up a few more preliminary matters.

❧ TRANSFORMATION INTO CHRISTLIKENESS IS POSSIBLE ❧

FIRST OF ALL, WE must be clear that such a transition as is envisioned in Christian spiritual formation can actually happen, and can actually happen to *us*. This, today, is not obvious.

What we see around us today of the "usual" Christian life could easily make us think that spiritual transformation is simply impossible. It is now common for Christian leaders themselves to complain about how little real-life difference there is between professing, or even actual Christians, on the one hand, and nonChristians on the other. Although there is much talk about "changing lives" in Christian circles, the reality is very rare, and certainly much less common than the talk.

The "failures" of prominent Christian leaders themselves, already referred to, might cause us to think genuine spiritual formation in Christlikeness to be impossible for "real human beings." How is it, exactly, that a man or woman can respectably serve Christ for many years and then morally disintegrate? And the failures that become known are few compared to the ones that remain relatively unknown and are even accepted among Christians.

Recently, I learned that one of the most prominent leaders in an important segment of Christian life "blew up," became uncontrollably angry, when someone questioned him about the quality of his work. This was embarrassing, but it is accepted (if not acceptable) behavior; and in this case, it was the one who was questioning him who was chastised. That is in fact a familiar pattern in both Christian and nonChristian "power structures." But what are we to say about the spiritual formation of that leader? Has something been omitted? Or is he really the best we can do?

The same questions arise with reference to lay figures in areas of life such as politics, business, entertainment, or education, who show the same failures of character while openly identifying themselves as Christians. It is unpleasant to dwell on such cases, but they must be squarely faced.

Of course the effects of such failures depend on the circumstances, on how widely the failure becomes known, and on various other factors. In another case a pastor became enraged at something a subordinate did during a Sunday morning service. Immediately after the service he found that subordinate and gave him a merciless tongue-lashing. With his lapel mike still on! His diatribe was broadcast over the entire church plant and campus—in all the Sunday school rooms and the parking lot. Soon thereafter he "received the Lord's call" to another church. But what about the spiritual formation of this leader? Is that the best we can do? And is he not still really like *that* in his new position?

Malfeasance with money is less acceptable than anger, and sexual misconduct is less tolerated still. But is the inner condition (the heart) all that different in these cases—before God?

The sad thing when a leader (or any individual) "fails" is not just what he or she *did*, but the heart and life and whole person who is revealed by the act. What is sad is who these leaders have been *all along*, what their inner life has been like, and no doubt also how they have suffered during all the years before they "did it" or were found out. What kind of persons have they been, and what, really, has been their relation to God?

Real spiritual need and change, as we have emphasized, is on the inside, in the hidden area of the life that God sees and that we cannot even see in ourselves without his help. Indeed, in the early stages of spiritual development we could not endure seeing our inner life as it really is. The possibility of denial and self-deception is something God has made accessible to us, in part to protect us until we begin to seek him. Like the face of the mythical Medusa, our true condition away from God would turn us to stone if we ever fully confronted it. It would drive us mad. He has to help us come to terms with it in ways that will not destroy us outright.

Without the gentle though rigorous process of inner transformation, initiated and sustained by the graceful presence of God in our world and in our soul, the change of personality and life clearly announced and spelled out in the Bible, and explained and illustrated throughout Christian history, *is* impossible. We not only admit it, but also insist upon it. But on the other hand, the result of the effort to change our behavior *without* inner transformation is precisely what we see in the current shallowness of Western Christianity that is so widely lamented and in the notorious failures of Christian leaders.

"MISERABLE SINNER" CHRISTIANITY

BUT WE MUST ALSO recognize a second factor that leads many to think that spiritual formation to Christlikeness is impossible. This is the widely held view that the low level of spiritual living among professing Christians is to be regarded as "only natural," only what is to be expected—lamentable as that may be. According to this view, human nature, flesh, life, and its world are all essentially vile, rotten, and worthless, and *especially* on the inside. Mother Teresa of Calcutta and Hitler, as examples, were equally vile in their hearts, this view would say. But for various constraints from God and the situation in which God had placed her, Mother Teresa could have behaved just as wickedly throughout her life as Hitler did.

This outlook, which has sometimes been referred to as "miserable sinner" Christianity, feeds on a number of misunderstandings. One is that the ungodly condition of the human heart and life described in the Bible (recall the references in chapter 2) is essential to human beings *as such*, and therefore remains true until we pass from this life and take a new form. (That of angels, perhaps. See Luke 20:36.) This account of things often associates wickedness with the body—that dripping, dirty, lustful thing—and holiness, therefore, with getting rid of the body. Fortunately, a careful study of the biblical sources makes it clear that such a view of the body is false. Here we can say little more than that.[1]

Another misunderstanding is that, unless the "miserable sinner" account were true, we might rise to a position where we could deal with God on the basis of merit. To fend off any appearance of self-righteousness you will sometimes hear the greatest of Christians saying things like, "I'm just as wicked as anyone else." Was not the apostle Paul saying, long after his conversion, that he was the leading sinner among sinners (1 Timothy 1:15)?

But on the other hand, one can hardly imagine that Paul, at the time he wrote these words, was still the same person inwardly, full of rage and self-importance, that he was when caught up in the persecution of Christ through his people. Such a person does not write words like those in Philippians 3:7-14 or 4:4-9. And he does not say, as he did to the Corinthians, "Be imitators of me, as I am of Christ" (1 Corinthians 11:1, NRSV), nor admonish others to "flee from youthful lusts, and pursue righteousness, faith, love and peace, with those who call on the Lord from a pure heart" (2 Timothy 2:22).

❧ NEVER "THERE" YET ❧

BUT NO DOUBT THE later Paul who wrote these words was very sure that whatever spiritual formation in Christlikeness he had received might be overwhelmed. There remained in him a spark of evil that could be fanned into a flame were he not watchful or if God did not continuously direct and uphold him in every dimension of his nature.

He knew he was running a race, as you and I are. That race will not be over until we pass into God's full world. No doubt Paul had in his lifetime seen many falter and fail, many who would not be able to say at the end, as he did, "I have fought the good fight, I have finished the course, I have kept the faith" (2 Timothy 4:7).

The image of the athlete was strong and ever-present in Paul's world and in his own mind. He knew that you had to keep yourself in spiritual shape to *finish* and finish well. In 1 Corinthians 9 he discussed how he therefore conducted himself in his course of life, how he exercised and treated his body severely, making it his slave (not he its slave), "lest possibly, after I have preached to others, I myself should be disqualified" (9:27).

The valid point in "miserable sinner" Christianity is correctly expressed in these well-chosen words by St. Augustine:

If anyone supposes that with man, living, as he still does, in this mortal life, it may be possible for him to dispel and clear off every obscurity induced by corporeal and carnal fancies, and to attain to the serenest light of immutable truth, and to cleave constantly and unswervingly to this with a mind wholly estranged from the course of this present life, that man understands neither what he asks, nor who he is that is putting such a supposition. . . . If ever the soul is helped to reach beyond the cloud by which all the earth is covered (cf. Ecclus. xxiv, 6), that is to say, beyond this carnal darkness with which the whole terrestrial life is covered, it is simply as if he were touched with a swift coruscation, only to sink back into his natural infirmity, the desire surviving by which he may again be raised to the heights, but his purity being insufficient to establish him there. The more, however, anyone can do this, the greater is he; while the less he can do so the less is he.[2]

In the spiritual life one never rests on one's laurels. It is a sure recipe for falling. Attainments are like the manna given to the Israelites in the desert, good only for the day (Exodus 16:4,20). Past attainments do not place us in a position of merit that permits us to let up in the hot pursuit of God for today, for now. Paul knew that, and he knew that others missed it or forgot it to their great harm.

We deserve nothing before God, no matter how far we have advanced, and we are never out of danger. As long as we are "at home in the body" (2 Corinthians 5:6), we are still just recovering sinners. And in these respects, though *only* in these respects, do we remain "as wicked as anyone else"— Mother Teresa as Hitler.

But to distort this important truth into a claim that we can never really change, and especially in our hearts, is to substitute a glaring and harmful falsehood for a liberating and life-blessing truth. And that distortion, which sometimes is a true expression of genuine humility, can also be done by those who wish to take themselves off the hook, to enjoy remaining the same in their inner life. It is not easy to really want to be different.

❧ AND WE ARE NEVER ON OUR OWN ❧

AND THEN, FINALLY, THERE is a misunderstanding closely related to the one just discussed. This is the idea that the only alternative to "miserable sinner" Christianity is holding that human beings are somehow good apart from God and therefore capable of saving themselves, even saving themselves by merit.

The fear of many is that if you do not hold human beings to be, essentially and as such, "rotten," and forever so, you are thereby committed to the view that they are, *as such*, essentially good and therefore righteous and meritorious. This is a field of battle fought over by Pelagius and Augustine many centuries ago and repeatedly revisited through Christian history. It involves many important issues, which cannot be fully dealt with here.

We must keep clear, however, that it is the *worth* of human beings, not their righteousness, which is tied to their nature. Things of great value can still be lost and often are; and to be of great value does not mean one is not lost, but is saved and safe. "Depravity" does not, properly, refer to the inability to *act,* but to the unwillingness to act and clearly the inability to *earn.*

Everyone must be active in the process of their salvation and transformation to Christlikeness. This is an inescapable fact. But the *initiative* in the process is always God's, and we would in fact do nothing without his initiative. However, that initiative is not something we are waiting upon. The ball is, as it were, in our court. God has invaded human history and reality. Jesus Christ has died on our behalf, is risen, and is now supervising events on earth toward an end that he will certainly bring to pass, to the glory of God. The issue now concerns what *we* will do. The idea that we can do nothing is an unfortunate confusion, and those who sponsor it never practice it, thank goodness.

If we—through well-directed and unrelenting action—effectually receive the grace of God in salvation and transformation, we certainly will be incrementally changed toward inward Christlikeness. The transformation of the outer life, especially of our behavior, will follow suit. That too is "an escapable fact." "No good tree produces bad fruit" (Luke 6:43, PAR). But this means both goodness and ability in *union with* God, not apart from him—not independently, on our own.

The transformation of the inner being is as much or more a gift of grace as is our justification before God. Of course neither one is wholly passive. (To be forever lost you need only *do nothing.* Just stay your course.) But with reference to both justification and transformation, "boasting is excluded" by the law of grace through faith (Romans 3:27-31; Ephesians 2:1-10). In fact, we consume the most grace by leading a holy life, in which we must be constantly upheld by grace, not by continuing to sin and being repeatedly forgiven. The interpretation of grace as having only to do with guilt is utterly false to biblical teaching and renders spiritual life in Christ unintelligible.

Hopefully, it will now be clear that our inner (and therefore outer) being can be transformed to increasingly take on the character of Christ. That transformation is not only *possible,* but has *actually* occurred to a significant degree in the lives of many human beings; and it is *necessary* if our life as a whole is to manifest his goodness and power, and if we as individuals are to grow into the eternal calling that God places upon each life.

❧ THE GENERAL PATTERN OF PERSONAL GROWTH ❧

BUT BEFORE TURNING TO the details of transformation in the various dimensions of the human being, we also need to understand *the general pattern* that *all* effective efforts toward personal transformation—not just Christian spiritual formation—must follow. Because we are active participants in the process and what we do or do not do makes a huge difference, our efforts must be based on understanding. The degree of success in such efforts will essentially depend upon the degree to which this general pattern is understood and intentionally conformed to.

So let us begin with a couple of easy illustrations and then spell out the pattern in its generality.

❧ LEARNING TO SPEAK ARABIC ❧

CONSIDER A CASE OF those who wish to speak a language they do not presently know, say French or Arabic or Japanese. In order to carry through with this simple case of (partial) personal transformation, they must have some idea of what it would be like to speak the language in question—of what their lives would then be like—and why this would be a desirable or valuable thing for them. They also need to have some idea of what must be done to learn to speak the language and why the price in time, energy, and money that must be expended constitutes a bargain, considering what they get in return. In the ideal case, all of this would be clearly before them and they would be gripped by the desirability of it.

Now, this is the *vision* that goes into the particular project of learning the language. Unless one has it—or, better, it has them—the language will pretty surely not be learned. The general absence of such a vision explains why language learning is generally so unsuccessful in educational programs in the United States. The presence of such a vision explains why, on the other hand, the English language is learned at a phenomenal rate all around the world. Multitudes see clearly the ways in which their life might be improved by knowledge of English. If the vision is clear and strong, it will very likely pull everything else required along with it; and the language (whichever it is) will be learned, even in difficult and distracting circumstances.

Still, more than vision is required, and especially there is required an *intention*. Projects of personal transformation rarely if ever succeed by accident, drift, or imposition. Indeed, where accident, drift, and imposition dominate—as they usually do, quite frankly, in the lives of professing Christians—very little of any human value transpires. Effective action has to involve order, subordination, and progression, developing from the inside of the personality. It is, in other words, a spiritual matter, a matter of meaning and will, for we are spiritual beings. Conscious involvement with "order, subordination, and progression, developing from the 'inside' of the personality" is how a life becomes *our* life—how we "get a life," as is now said.

The will (spirit) *is* mysterious from the point of view of the physical and social world, for there it is *causes,* not choices, that dominate. But one can never get a grip on his or her own life—or that of others—from the causal point of view. It is choice that matters. Imagine a person wondering day after day if he or she is going to learn Arabic or if he or she is going to get married to a certain person—just waiting, to see whether it would "happen."

That would be laughable. But many people actually seem to live in this way with respect to major issues involving them, and with a deplorable outcome. That explains a lot of why lives go as they do. But to learn a language, and for the many even more important concerns of life, we must *intend the vision* if it is to be realized. That is, we must initiate, bring into being those factors that would bring the vision to reality.

And that, of course, brings us to the final element in the general pattern, that of *means* or instrumentalities. Carrying through with the pattern for the illustration at hand, you will sign up for language courses, listen to recordings, buy books, associate with people who speak Arabic, immerse yourself in the culture, possibly spend some intensive times in Jordan or Morocco, and practice, practice, practice.

There are means known to be effective toward transforming people into speakers of Arabic and so on. This is not mysterious. If the vision is clear and strong, and the employment of the means thoughtful and persistent, then the outcome will be ensured and, basically, adequate to the vision and intention.

❧ ALCOHOLICS ANONYMOUS ILLUSTRATES ❧

ANOTHER ILLUSTRATION OF THE general pattern of personal transformation is provided by Alcoholics Anonymous and similar "twelve step" programs. Here, of course, the significance of the transformation or change is far greater for the person involved than in the case of learning a language; and the outcome is negative—that is, refraining from doing something very harmful, something that could possibly lead to untimely death. But the pattern is basically the same.

A desirable state of being is en*visioned,* and an *intention* to realize it is actuated in decision. *Means* are applied to fulfill the intention (and the corresponding decision) by producing the desirable state of being: in this case abstinence from alcohol and a life of sobriety with all that entails. The familiar *means* of traditional AA—the famous twelve steps and the personal and social arrangements in which they are concretely embodied, including a conscious involvement of God in the individual's life—are highly effective in bringing about personal transformation.

Historically, the AA program was closely aligned with the church and

Christian traditions, and now it has much to give back to a church that has largely lost its grip on spiritual formation as a standard path of Christian life. *Any successful plan for spiritual formation, whether for the individual or group, will in fact be significantly similar to the Alcoholics Anonymous program.* There can be no doubt that the AA program originated and gained its power from Christian sources, to meet needs that Christian institutions at the time should have been meeting but were not. It works in terms of essential structures of the human self revealed by God through his people.

✌ VIM: THE GENERAL PATTERN ✌

WITH THESE TWO ILLUSTRATIONS before us (language learning and AA), the general pattern of personal transformation, which also applies to spiritual formation in the Christian tradition, should now be clear. Indeed, this is the pattern of all human accomplishment, even that which — like spiritual formation — can only occur at the initiative and through the constant direction and upholding of God, or through grace. To keep the general pattern in mind, we will use the little acronym "VIM," as in the phrase "vim and vigor."

- Vision
- Intention
- Means

"Vim" is a derivative of the Latin term "*vis,*" meaning direction, strength, force, vigor, power, energy, or virtue; and sometimes meaning sense, import, nature, or essence. Spiritual formation in Christlikeness is all of this to human existence. It is the path by which we can truly, as Paul told the Ephesians, "be empowered in the Lord and in the energy of his might" (Ephesians 6:10, PAR) and "become mighty with his energy through his Spirit entering into the inward person" (3:16, PAR).

If we are to be spiritually formed in Christ, we must have and must implement the appropriate *vision, intention,* and *means.* Not just any path we take will do. If this VIM pattern is not put in place properly and held there, Christ simply will not be formed in us.

✌ WHY WE FAIL AND DON'T GROW ✌

AND HERE, IN A nutshell, is the explanation of the widespread failure to attain Christian maturity among both leaders and followers, referred to earlier. Those who are Christians by profession — and seriously so, we must add — today do not usually have, are not led into, the VIM that would enable them to routinely progress to the point where what Jesus himself did and taught would be the natural outflow of who they really are "on the inside." Rather, what they are inwardly *is left substantially as it was,* as it is in nonChristians, and they are left constantly to battle with it. That is why today you find many professing Christians circling back to nonChristian sources to resolve the problems of their inner life.

Instead of inward transformation, some outward form of religion—often today even called "a spirituality"—is taken or imposed as the goal of practical endeavor. What is then important is to be a "good _____" (you can fill in the blank). And the respective social group—the "good _____s"—will enforce that importance, on pain of disapproval or exclusion from the group. Or the individual even enforces it upon himself or herself as what is "obviously" right. But, whatever the details, authentic inward transformation into Christlikeness is omitted. It is not envisioned, intended, or achieved.

Not so in the call of Jesus to live with him as his student or apprentice in his kingdom. By contrast, for him and for his Father, the heart is what matters, and everything else will then come along. And the process of inward renovation starts from the stark vision of life in the kingdom of God.

⚘ THE VISION OF LIFE IN THE KINGDOM ⚘

IF WE ARE CONCERNED about our own spiritual formation or that of others, this vision of the kingdom is the place we must start. Remember, it is the place where Jesus started. It was the gospel he preached. He came announcing, manifesting, and teaching the availability and nature of the kingdom of the heavens. "For I was sent for this purpose," he said (Luke 4:43). That is simply a fact, and if we are faithful to it, do justice to it in full devotion, we will find our feet firmly planted on the path of Christian spiritual formation.

The kingdom of God is the range of God's effective will, where what God wants done is done.[3] It is, like God himself, from everlasting to everlasting (Psalm 103:17; see also Psalm 93:1-2; Daniel 4:3; 7:14; and so on). The planet Earth and its immediate surroundings seem to be the only place in creation where God permits his will to be *not* done. Therefore we pray, "Thy kingdom come, Thy will be done, on earth as it is in heaven," and hope for the time when that kingdom will be completely fulfilled even here on earth (Luke 21:31; 22:18)—where in fact it is already present (Luke 17:21; John 18:36-37) and available to those who seek it with all their hearts (Matthew 6:13; 11:12; Luke 16:16). For those who do so seek it, it is true even now that "all things work together for their good" (Romans 8:28, PAR), and that nothing can cut them off from God's inseparable love and effective care (Romans 8:35-39). That is the nature of a life *in* the kingdom of the heavens now.

The vision that underlies spiritual (trans)formation into Christlikeness is, then, the vision of life now and forever in the range of God's effective will—that is, *partaking* of the divine nature (2 Peter 1:4; 1 John 3:1-2) through a birth "from above" and *participating* by our actions in what God is doing now in our lifetime on earth. Thus, "whatever we do, speaking or acting, doing all on behalf of the Lord Jesus, giving thanks through him to God the Father" (Colossians 3:17, PAR). In everything we do we are permitted to do his work. What we are aiming for in this vision is to live fully in the kingdom of God and as fully as possible *now* and *here,* not just hereafter.

This is a vision of life that cannot come to us naturally, though the human soul-depths automatically cry out for something like it; and from time to time our deepest thinkers, visionaries, and artists capture aspects of it.[4] It is a vision that has to be *given* to humanity by God himself, in a revelation suited to our condition. We cannot clearly see it on our own. And that revelation has been given through his covenant people on earth, the Jews, with the fullest flowering of the covenant people being Jesus himself.

Jesus was prepared for through centuries of rich and productive—though often painful—experience and thought among the Jews; through him the Jews have fulfilled their God-given responsibility and blessing of being a light to all the peoples of the earth (Genesis 18:18; 22:18; Isaiah 42:1-6; 60:3). Through them, indeed, all the nations of the earth *are* and continue to be blessed and will be even more blessed in the future.

↬ THE INTENTION TO BE A KINGDOM PERSON ↫

THE VISION OF LIFE in the kingdom through reliance upon Jesus makes it possible for us to *intend* to live in the kingdom as he did. We can actually *decide to do it.* Of course that means first of all to trust him, rely on him, to count on him being the Anointed One, the Christ. It is through him that the revelation and the gift of the kingdom come to us individually. If we do not count on him as "the One," we will have no adequate vision of the kingdom or of life therein and no way to enter it. He is "the door"; he is "the way." Find another whoever can.

Concretely, we intend to live in the kingdom of God *by* intending to obey the precise example and teachings of Jesus. This is the form that *trust* in him takes. It does not take the form of merely believing things about him, however true they may be. Indeed, no one can actually believe the truth about him without trusting him by intending to obey him. It is a mental impossibility. To think otherwise is to indulge a widespread illusion that now smothers spiritual formation in Christlikeness among professing Christians and prevents it from naturally spreading worldwide.

Gandhi, who had looked closely at Christianity as practiced around him in Great Britain, remarked that if only Christians would live according to their belief in the teachings of Jesus, "we all would become Christians." We know what he meant, and he was right in that. But the dismaying truth is that the Christians *were* living according to their "belief" in the teachings of Jesus. They didn't believe them!

Moreover, knowing the "right answers"—knowing which ones they are, being able to identify them—does not mean we *believe* them. To believe them, like believing anything else, means that we are set to act as if they (the right answers) are true and that we will do so in appropriate circumstances. And acting as if the right answers are true means, in turn, that we intend to obey the example and teachings of Jesus the Anointed. What else would we intend if we *believed* he is who his people through the ages have declared him to be?

Perhaps the hardest thing for sincere Christians to come to grips with is the level of real unbelief in their own life: the unformulated skepticism about Jesus that permeates all dimensions of their being and undermines what efforts they do make toward Christlikeness.

The idea that you can trust Christ and not intend to obey him is an illusion generated by the prevalence of an unbelieving "Christian culture." In fact, you can no more trust Jesus and not intend to obey him than you could trust your doctor and your auto mechanic and not intend to follow their advice. If you don't intend to follow their advice, you simply don't trust them. Period. (Of course in this case you might well have good reason.)

❧ INTENTION INVOLVES DECISION ❧

NOW, AN INTENTION IS brought to completion only by a *decision* to fulfill or carry through with the intention. We commonly find people who say they intend (or intended) to do certain things that they do (or did) not do. To be fair, external circumstances may sometimes have prevented them from carrying out the action. And habits deeply rooted in our bodies and life contexts can, for a while, thwart even a sincere intention. But if something like that is not the case, we know that they never actually *decided* to do what they *say* they intended to do, and that they therefore did not really intend to do it. They therefore lack the power and order that intention brings into life processes.

Such may have *wished* that what they supposedly intend would happen, and perhaps they even *wanted* to do it (or for it to be done); but they did not decide to do it, and their intention—which well may have *begun* to develop—aborted and never really formed.

Procrastination is a common and well-known way in which intention is aborted, but there are many other ways. And, on the other hand, the *profession* or *statement* of intentions is a primary way of negotiating one's way through life regardless of whether or not the intention professed is really there. Promises and agreements involve the profession of intentions, and such a profession is often enough to get us what we want in our social context. But how very often in human affairs is a profession empty, even in vows to God. That is why Scripture deals with swearing and vain (empty) use of God's name at such lengths. If the genuine intention is there, the deed reliably follows. But if it is not there, the deed will most likely not be there either.

Now, the robust intention, with its inseparable decision, can only be formed and sustained upon the basis of a forceful vision. The elements of VIM are mutually reinforcing. Those whose word "is their bond," or "is as good as gold," are people with a vision of integrity. They *see* themselves standing in life and before God as one who does not say one thing and think another. They "mean what they say." This is greatly valued before God, who abominates "swearing falsely" and honors those "who stand by their oath even when it harms them" (Psalm 15:4, PAR). Similarly, it is the vision of life in God's kingdom and its goodness that provides an adequate basis for the steadfast intention to obey Christ.

⁓ MEANS ⁓

THEN THE VISION AND the solid intention to obey Christ will naturally lead to seeking out and applying the means to that end. Here the means in question are the means for spiritual transformation, for the replacing of the inner character of the "lost" with the inner character of Jesus: his vision, understanding, feelings, decisions, and character. In finding such means we are not left to ourselves but have rich resources available to us in the example and teachings of Jesus, in the Scriptures generally, and in his people.

Suppose, for example, we would like to be generous to those who have already taken away some of our money or property through legal processes. Pure will, with gritted teeth, cannot be enough to enable us to do this. By what *means*, then, can we become the kind of person who would do this as Jesus himself would do it? If we have the vision and we intend (have decided) to do it, we can certainly find and implement the means, for God will help us to do so.

Here we shall only be briefly illustrative and shall leave fuller treatment to later chapters. We must start by discovering, by *identifying*, the thoughts, feelings, habits of will, social relations, and bodily inclinations that *prevent* us from being generous to these people. Our education and teachers should help us here, and perhaps they do to some extent—but nearly always insufficiently.[5]

We might with a little reflection identify resentment and anger toward the person who needs our help as a cause of not helping him. And then there is *justice*. Ah, justice! Perhaps in the form of "I do not *owe* it to him. He has no claims on me." Or perhaps we feel the legal case that went against us and in his favor was rigged or unfair.

Or again, perhaps we think we must secure ourselves by holding onto whatever surplus items we have. After all, we may say, who knows what the future holds? Or perhaps we think giving to people what is unearned by them will harm them by corrupting their character, leading them to believe one can get something for nothing. Or perhaps it is just not our habit to give to people with no prior claim on us—even if they have not injured or deprived us. Or perhaps our friends, including our religious friends, would think we are fools. And so forth.

What a thicket of lostness stands in the way of doing a simple good thing: helping someone in need, someone who just happens to have previously won a legal case against us, possibly quite justly. At this point it is the all-too-customary human thinking, feeling, and social practice that stands in the way. And, truthfully, it is very likely that little can be done *in the moment of need* to help one do the good thing that Jesus commands.

This is characteristic of all his example and teaching. When my neighbor who has triumphed over me in the past now stands before me in a need I can remedy, I will not be able "on the spot" to do the good thing if my inner being is filled with all the thoughts, feelings, and habits that characterize the ruined soul and its world. Rather, if I intend to obey Jesus Christ, I must intend and decide to become the kind of person who *would* obey. That is, I must find the means of changing my inner being until it is substantially like his, pervasively characterized by his thoughts, feelings, habits, and relationship to the Father.

❧ TRAINING "OFF THE SPOT" ❧

THE MEANS TO THAT END are not all *directly* under my control, for some are the actions of God toward me and in me. But some are directly under my control.

I can, while not "on the spot," retrain my thinking by study and meditation on Christ himself and on the teachings of Scripture about God, his world, and my life—especially the teachings of Jesus in the Gospels, further elaborated by understanding of the remainder of the Bible. I can also help my thinking and my feelings by deep reflection on the nature and bitter outcome of *the standard human way* in such situations, in contrast to the way of Jesus. I can also consciously practice explicitly "self-sacrificial" actions in other, less "demanding," situations. I can become a person for whom "looking out for number one" is not the framework of my life.

I can learn about and meditate upon the lives of well-known "saints," who have practiced continuously, in real life, Jesus' way with adversaries and those in need. I can take a close and thorough look at the bitter world of legal adversaries—at how people learn to hate one another in court—to see if I want to be a part of *that*. I can earnestly and repeatedly pray that God will directly work in my inner being to change the things there that will enable me to obey his Son. And many other things can be done as *means* to fulfilling the vision of life in God that we intend and have chosen.

What we need to emphasize here is simply that the means of spiritual formation are available. In the spiritual life it is actually true that "where there is a will there is a way." This is true here because God is involved and makes his help available to those who seek it.

On the other hand, where there is no will (firm intentions based on clear vision) there is no way. People who do not intend to be inwardly transformed, so that obedience to Christ "comes naturally," will not be—no matter what means they think of themselves as employing. God is not going to pick us up by the seat of our pants, as it were, and throw us into transformed kingdom living, into "holiness."

So the problem of spiritual transformation (the normal lack thereof) among those who identify themselves as Christians today is not that it is impossible or that effectual means to it are not available. The problem is that it is not intended. People do not see it and its value and decide to carry through with it. They do not *decide* to do the things Jesus did and said.

And this in turn is, today, largely due to the fact that they have not been given a vision of life in God's kingdom within which such a decision and intention would make sense. The entire VIM of Christ's life and life in Christ is not the intentional substance and framework of their life. Those who minister to them do not bend every effort to make it so. No wonder the example and teachings of Christ look, to many, more like fairy tales than sober reality.

We now turn to some of the things that can be done with God's assistance in *each* of the dimensions of our life and being to renovate the human heart and progressively form the inner, hidden world of the person so that "the tree is good" to the farthest reaches of root and branch.

Matters for Thought and Discussion

1. Do the common failures of Christian leaders and lay people prove that transformation into Christlikeness is impossible?

2. Is "miserable sinner" Christianity an accurate portrayal of the redeemed life in Christ? What is the valid point in the "miserable sinner" version?

3. If we are active in the process of spiritual formation, does that mean we are acting "on our own"? How do grace and effort interrelate in spiritual growth?

4. What is the general pattern of all personal growth? Discuss the "Learning to Speak Arabic" case as an illustration.

5. Consider Alcoholics Anonymous as another illustration.

6. What is the biblical vision of our life in the kingdom of God? Give some details that would fit into your life.

7. How, concretely, can we "intend to live in the kingdom of God now"?

8. How does *intention* relate to *decision*? Can "knowing the right answers" substitute for intention and decision in the spiritual life?

9. What are the main *means* that you personally use for implementing your decision to live in the kingdom of God now? Are they adequate to the intention?

10. What measures of "off the spot" training for obedience to Christ do you employ?

INTERLUDE

We have now worked our way through some difficult material that has required careful study and thought. We have distinguished and put into proper relationship profound aspects of human existence and divine operation. But it is very important that we not lose sight of the *simplicity* of spiritual formation in Christ. Otherwise its practical implementation, by individuals in their own life or by leaders for their groups, will falsely appear to be extremely difficult or even impossible.

The effect of this will be (and often is) that spiritual formation is *not seriously undertaken,* even by Christian groups, or that it is undertaken in such a way that it is bound to fail or achieve only minor degrees of success.

Individuals sometimes hear of disciplines for the spiritual life, for example, and rightly understand how important they could be for growth in Christlikeness. Perhaps they learn what an effective role the disciplines have played for "great ones" with Christ in the past or present. But they are unable to practice such disciplines to much good effect, because they do not have a sense of how such practices fit into the overall process of spiritual formation in Christ. In particular, I find, they are unable to put special practices, such as the disciplines of solitude, Scripture memorization, or fasting into a seamless unity with the rest of their life—with each of the six dimensions outlined above.

Now, the simplicity of spiritual formation lies in its intention. Its aim is to bring every element in our being, working from inside out, into harmony with the will of God and the kingdom of God. This is the simple focus. We must keep it constantly before us and not be distracted by other things, no matter how good they may appear.

Of course, we cannot realize this goal on our own. But there is no need for that. God has made provision for achieving this aim. To "grow in grace" means to utilize more and more grace to live by, until everything we do is assisted by grace. Then, whatever we do in word or deed will all be done in the name of the Lord Jesus (Colossians 3:17). The greatest saints are not those who need *less* grace, but those who consume the most grace, who indeed are most in need of grace—those who are saturated by grace in every dimension of their being. Grace to them is like breath.

In what follows I will try to say some things that will be of practical use to us in dealing with each of the six essential dimensions of human personality briefly described in chapter 2. I will try to do justice to the fact that spiritual formation is holistic. So while I shall treat each dimension separately for sake of clarity, we must all along keep a sharp awareness that they are not separate in reality and are *always* profoundly influencing one another in the flow of *real life*. (When I speak of "real life" in this book, I always mean the totality of the events we are actually involved in and the actions we actually carry out.)

I will, in the chapters to follow, briefly reemphasize the basic nature of each of the dimensions; and in each case, while pointing out some central failings peculiar to that dimension, we will do our utmost to stress the *positive* condition of it in the process and outcome of spiritual formation in Christ.

There are no formulas—no definitive how-tos—for growth in the inner character of Jesus. Such growth is a way of relentless seeking. But there are many things we can do to place ourselves at the disposal of God, and "if with all our hearts we truly seek him, we shall surely find him" (Jeremiah 29:13, PAR). Or, as the prophet Azariah said, "If you seek Him, He will let you find Him" (2 Chronicles 15:2; see also 15:4). We can count on his goodness.

Our aim will be to assist the seeker who has been found by Christ. We will indicate and encourage some small but efficacious steps through which he or she will quite certainly be met by God to accomplish the amazing work of spiritual formation in Christlikeness.

6

TRANSFORMING
THE MIND, 1

Spiritual Formation and the Thought Life

I have set the Lord continually before me;
Because He is at my right hand, I will not be shaken.
PSALM 16:8

Jesus, the very thought of Thee,
With sweetness fills my breast;
But sweeter far Thy face to see,
And in Thy presence rest.
BERNARD OF CLAIRVAUX

❧ THE FIRST MOVE BACK FROM RUIN ❧

As we first turned away from God in our thoughts, so it is in our thoughts that the first movements toward the renovation of the heart occur. Thoughts are the place where we can and must begin to change. There the light of God first begins to move upon us through the word of Christ, and there the divine Spirit begins to direct our will to more and more thoughts that can provide the basis for choosing to realign ourselves with God and his way.

The ultimate freedom we have as human beings is the power to select what we will allow or require our minds to dwell upon. We are not totally free in this respect. But we do have great freedom here, and even though "dead in trespasses and sins," we still have the ability and responsibility *to try to retain God in our knowledge*—if only in an inadequate and halting manner. And those who do so will surely make progress toward him; for if we truly do seek God as best we can, he, who always knows what is really in our hearts, will certainly make himself known to us. It is because of this fact that we always remain responsible before God, even though we are spiritually dead.

WHAT THOUGHTS ARE

WE HAVE (IN CHAPTER 2) already said something about what thoughts are, but now we must go deeper. By "thoughts" we mean *all of the ways in which we are conscious of things*. That includes our memories, perceptions, and beliefs, as well as what we would ordinarily refer to when we say "I thought of you yesterday," or "I was just thinking of our meeting tomorrow."

Now clearly, our thoughts are one of the most basic sources of our life. They determine the orientation of everything we do and evoke the feelings that frame our world and motivate our actions. Interestingly, you can't evoke thoughts by feeling a certain way, but you can evoke and to some degree control feelings by directing your thoughts. Our power over our thoughts is of great and indispensable assistance in directing and controlling our feelings, which themselves are *not* directly under the guidance of our will. We cannot just choose our feelings.

Our ability to think and represent things to ourselves also enables us to bring vast ranges of reality—and non-reality—before us. This is not always done in a way that is adequate to what we think about or in a way that is even correct. It is actually a part of the greatness of thought that it is not limited to accuracy or even reality. It can consider—bring before our mind—what is not the case but could be, or what ought to be though it is not, as well as what never should be.

Our essential nature as active and creative beings depends upon our ability to envision what is not the case as well as what is. Our ability to plan for the future must constantly run ahead of reality. And this we do in thought. A will that runs ahead depends, of course, upon our abilities to think; and *what* we think, imagine, believe, or guess sets boundaries to what we can will or choose, and therefore to what we can create.

As our senses present a landscape for our body and its actions, so our thoughts present the "lifescape" for our will and our life as a whole. Within that "thought lifescape" (including our perceptions) we make the decisions that determine what we will do and who we will become.

The realm of thought involves four main factors. These are ideas, images, information, and our ability to think, but the two most powerful ones are *ideas* and *images*.

IDEAS

IDEAS ARE VERY GENERAL models of or assumptions about reality. They are patterns of interpretation, historically developed and socially shared. They sometimes are involved with beliefs, but are much more than belief and do not depend upon it. They are ways of thinking about and interpreting things. They are so pervasive and essential to how we think about and how we approach life that we often do not even know they are there or understand when and how they are at work. Our idea system is a cultural artifact, growing up with us from earliest childhood out of the teachings, expectations, and observable behaviors of family and community.

Anthropologists observe that the world occupied by a human being comprises not only the surrounding land, water, sky, plant and animal life, human beings and works of human hands, but also a "symbolic reality," which is superimposed upon material reality. Our idea system is shareable by many— perhaps by entire social systems, such as nations or families—and it develops and changes through time and historical process, often without it being noticed that it has in fact changed.

Examples of ideas are freedom, education, happiness, "the American Dream," science, progress, death, home, the feminine or masculine, the religious, "Christian," "Muslim," church, democratic (form of government), fair, just, family, evolution, God, the secular, and so on.

If you wish to see ideas in action, look closely at artistic endeavors in their various forms (especially today, movies and music, which encapsulate most of what is called "pop culture"), and at efforts to persuade (especially today, politics and commercials). Look, for example, at the place *freedom*, a major idea now, plays in automobile ads and rock lyrics. And look at our now largely paralyzed public education system to see what ideas are dominant in students and teachers.

Now, for all their importance to human life, ideas are *never* capable of definition or precise specification; and yet people never stop trying to define them, in their vain efforts to *control* them. They are broadly inclusive, historically developing ways of interpreting things and events, which, for all their power, often do not emerge into the consciousness of the individual. Therefore, it is extremely difficult for most people to recognize which ideas are governing their life and *how* those ideas are governing their life.

This is partly because one commonly *identifies* his or her own governing ideas with reality, pure and simple. Ironically, it is often people who think of themselves as "practical" or as "men of action"—both, of course, major *ideas*—who are most in the grip of ideas: so far in that grip that they can't be bothered to think. They simply don't know what moves them. But ideas govern them and have their consequences anyway. Another illustration of "idea grip" would be how most people think of success in life in terms of promotions and possessions. One's culture is seen most clearly in what one thinks of as "natural" and as requiring no explanation or even thought.

✎ SPIRITUAL FORMATION MUST TRANSFORM IDEAS ✎

NOW, CHRISTIAN SPIRITUAL FORMATION is inescapably a matter of recognizing *in ourselves* the idea system (or systems) of evil that governs the present age and the respective culture (or various cultures) that constitute life *away from* God. The needed transformation is very largely a matter of replacing in ourselves those idea systems of evil (and their corresponding cultures) with the idea system that Jesus Christ embodied and taught and with a culture of the kingdom of God. This is truly a passage from darkness to light.

The apostle Paul, who of course understood and taught about these things, warned us that "our struggle is not against flesh and blood, but against the rulers, against the powers, against the world forces of this darkness, against the spiritual forces of wickedness in the heavenly places" (Ephesians 6:12). These higher-level powers and forces are spiritual agencies that work with—constantly try to implement and support—the idea systems of evil. These systems are their main tool for dominating humanity.

By contrast, we who have been rescued "from the power of darkness and transferred . . . into the kingdom of his beloved Son" (Colossians 1:13, NRSV) are to "let this mind be in you, which was also in Christ Jesus" (Philippians 2:5, KJV). This is an essential way of describing the substance, the underlying reality, of Christian spiritual formation. We are, in Paul's familiar language, transformed precisely by the "renewing of our mind" (Romans 12:2, PAR).

✎ THE CHANGING OF IDEAS IS EXTREMELY DIFFICULT ✎

TO CHANGE GOVERNING IDEAS, whether in the individual or the group, is one of the most difficult and painful things in human life. Genuine "conversion" is a wrenching experience. It rarely happens to the individual or group except in the form of divine intervention, revolution, or something very like a mental breakdown. It can cause deep and permanent damage to the most intimate of relationships, as Jesus forewarned (Luke 12:51-53). At a group level, the sixties illustrate this in the recent past of American and much of Western society. And in many parts of the world, Christians are persecuted and killed today because they threaten the idea system of others in their country.

In fact, we are now undergoing an even more profound change than in the sixties, though it is less noisy, with the emergence of mass "spirituality" at the end of the twentieth century.[1] This change is the equivalent of a "soul earthquake" that leaves nothing unshaken and many individuals hurt or destroyed.

From one essential perspective, of course, Jesus himself confronted and undermined an idea system and its culture, which in turn killed him. He proved himself greater than any idea system or culture, however, and lives on. He is continuing the process of a worldwide idea shift that is crucial to *his* perpetual revolution, in which we each are assigned a part.

⁓ IMAGES ⁓

CLOSELY ASSOCIATED WITH GOVERNING ideas are *images* that occupy our minds. Images are always concrete or specific, as opposed to the abstractness of ideas, and are heavily laden with feeling. They frequently present themselves with the force of perception and have a powerful emotional and sensuous linkage to governing idea systems. They mediate the power of those idea systems into the real situations of ordinary life. Every idea system is present among us as a life force through a small number of powerful images.

In recent American and European history, hair (long, short, skinhead; green, orange, and purple), brassieres (or the absence or burning thereof), flags (and their desecration), rock music, and funky or baggy clothes have provided powerful images and symbols of conflicting idea systems and the attached ways of life. Images sustaining traditional cultural authority—"The Establishment" it was called—have, by contrast, lost power.

In many Christian churches today the services have divided into "traditional" and "contemporary," primarily over imagery and the explosive feelings attached thereto. The guitar and pipe organ are no longer just musical instruments, they are powerful symbols. This is not to say that such divisions are either unimportant or sinful. But in order to act responsibly in relation to them, one does have to understand what drives such divisions.

Jesus of course understood the great significance of images and has, indeed, become one himself. Intentionally. He also carefully selected an image that brilliantly conveys himself and his message: the cross. The cross presents the lostness of man as well as the sacrifice of God and the abandonment to God that brings redemption. No doubt it is the all-time most powerful image and symbol of human history. Need we say he knew what he was doing in selecting it? He planned it all and is also the Master of images. For their own benefit, his followers need to keep the image of the cross vividly present in their mind.

⁓ STRONGHOLDS OF EVIL ⁓

BUT IDEAS AND IMAGES are also a primary stronghold of evil in the human self and in society. They determine how we "take" the things and events of ordinary life. They control the meanings we assign to what we deal with, and they can even blind us to what lies plainly before us. Again, this is seen over and over in biblical and in Christian history, and in human life generally. Their power for evil cannot be overestimated and is constantly at play in most human governments.

Ideas and images are, accordingly, the primary focus of Satan's efforts to defeat God's purposes with and for humankind. When we are subject to his chosen ideas and images, he can take a nap or a holiday. Thus when he undertook to draw Eve away from God, he did not hit her with a stick, but with an idea. It was with the idea that God could not be trusted and that she must act on her own to secure her own well-being.

This is the basic idea back of all temptation: God is presented as depriving us by his commands of what is good, so we think we must take matters into our own hands and act contrary to what he has said. This image of God leads to our pushing him out of our thoughts, as discussed in previous chapters, and putting ourselves on the throne of the universe. The condition of the ruined soul and world naturally results. The single most important thing in our mind is our idea of God and the associated images.

Thus A. W. Tozer did not exaggerate when he said,

That our idea of God corresponds as nearly as possible to the true being of God is of immense importance to us. Compared with our actual thoughts about Him, our creedal statements are of little consequence. Our real idea of God may lie buried under the rubbish of conventional religious notions and may require an intelligent and vigorous search before it is finally unearthed and exposed for what it is. Only after an ordeal of painful self-probing are we likely to discover what we actually believe about God.

A right conception of God is basic not only to systematic theology but to practical Christian living as well. It is to worship what the foundation is to the temple; where it is inadequate or out of plumb the whole structure must sooner or later collapse. I believe there is scarcely an error in doctrine or a failure in applying Christian ethics that cannot be traced finally to imperfect and ignoble thoughts about God.[2]

✎ IMAGES EMPOWER WRONG IDEAS ✎

IMAGES INCREASE THE DANGER of inadequate ideas. They have the power to obsess and to hypnotize, as well as to escape critical scrutiny. The image one has of oneself, for example, can override everything else and cause one to act in ways contrary to all reality and good sense.

Those who have been rejected or abused as children or have lived with addicted or "cold" parents, have distorted images of themselves and of "reality." These are constantly present to their minds and force them into the disastrous "lifescape" of thought where they then must live. In groups, shared images lead to fads, group-think, and mob hysteria that, once again, has no regard to fact or reasonableness.

Individuals who suffer from a poor image of themselves are caught up in self-rejection and have no defenses against group pressures. They do not see themselves as the objects of God's love, and they have no place to make a stand. Henri Nouwen noted, "Success, popularity and power can indeed present a great temptation, but their seductive quality often comes from the way they are part of a much larger temptation of self-rejection. We have come to believe in the voices that call us worthless and unlovable, then success, popularity and power are easily perceived as attractive solutions" to our desolate condition.[3] We accept it as a fact that we deserve to be pushed aside and rejected. We *see* ourselves that way. "Self-rejection," Nouwen continued, "is the greatest enemy of the spiritual life because it contradicts the sacred voice that calls us the 'Beloved.' Being the Beloved constitutes the core truth of our existence." But this profound truth will have little or no effect without powerful images of ourselves as God's beloved. Self-rejection is, ultimately, our soul's reproach to God, deriving from false images of himself and his world.

To *manipulate* images—and thereby people—is the work of the propagandist and the advertiser. Unfortunately, it is often done in the name of Christ to achieve some desired result. By contrast, to loosen the grip of fallen imagery and its underlying idea structure is a fundamental part of what mental health professionals must do to aid their patients. It is also essential to the Christian ministries of inner healing and evangelism.

DELIVERANCE FROM DESTRUCTIVE IDEAS AND IMAGES

THE PERSON AND GOSPEL of Jesus Christ—building on simple "Jesus loves me, this I know, for the Bible tells me so"—is the only complete answer to the false and destructive images and ideas that control the life of those away from God. The process of spiritual formation in Christ is one of progressively replacing those destructive images and ideas with the images and ideas that filled the mind of Jesus himself. We thereby come increasingly to see "the light of the gospel of the glory of Christ, who is the image of God" (2 Corinthians 4:4, NRSV).

As we might expect from our earlier study of the ruined self and the restored self, the contrast between the idea system of humanity and the idea system of God is very sharp, because their fundamental assumptions (about who God is and who we are) are totally different. Thus the prophet Isaiah speaks: "'My thoughts are not your thoughts, neither are your ways My ways,' declares the LORD. 'For as the heavens are higher than the earth, so are My ways higher than your ways, and My thoughts than your thoughts'" (Isaiah 55:8-9).

This is forcibly illustrated by Peter's response to Jesus' declaration that he himself would soon be tortured and killed. Peter had just acknowledged that Jesus was the promised Messiah or anointed Savior of humankind. But now he rebukes Jesus and urges that such things must never happen to him, the Messiah. "Messiah" was an idea with a content and associated images in Peter's mind totally different from what Jesus was saying. Jesus therefore called Peter "Satan," or "Adversary," and pointed out that he was thinking in human terms, not in God's terms (Matthew 16:23). The two ways are radically different. Radically different ideas and radically different images. And of course they determine radically different courses of thought and action.

Another illustration of the great difference in outlook is found in Paul's letter to the Colossians. There he contrasted the way of earth or flesh and the way of the new person. The human way is one of anger, wrath, malice, slander, abusive language, and lying (Colossians 3:8-9). Think for a moment how true this is to human life. But now, Paul says, "Lie no more, since you have stripped off the old self and its characteristic behavior and put on the new self, which sees things as they really are in God's view" (3:10, PAR). In that view the usual human distinctions (between Greek and Jew, circumcised and uncircumcised, barbarian, Scythian, slave or free person, and so on) do not matter in how we relate to people, because Christ is (or can be) in all alike (verses 10-11).

What is more unlike humans than to treat all kinds of people with equal truth and love? The ideas and images that govern unredeemed humanity make it impossible, except in highly selective circumstances and in very recent societies strongly influenced by Jesus and his followers. Paul knew we can only escape being conformed to a fallen humanity by receiving the mind of Christ himself (1 Corinthians 2:16; Philippians 2:5). Spiritual formation in Christ moves toward a total interchange of *our* ideas and images for *his*.

How is this to come about? Two other factors in our thought life can be used by God to break the power of the toxic system of ideas and images that make us "dead to God." And after he has implanted new life from above in us by Word and Spirit, we can (and must) also begin to take initiative in progressively retaking the whole of our thought life for God's kingdom. His grace will accompany us every step of the way, but it will never permit us to be merely passive in our spiritual formation in Christ.

These other two factors are *information* (or "facts") and *our ability to think*—to "connect things up," to see what must or cannot be the case if certain other things are so.

❧ INFORMATION ❧

INFORMATION IS FIRST. "HOW shall they believe in Him whom they have not heard" (Romans 10:14). Without correct information, our ability to think has nothing to work on. Indeed, without the requisite information, we may be afraid of thinking at all, or simply be incapable of thinking straight.

The hymn of Charles Wesley is true to the human situation:

> Long my imprisoned spirit lay,
> Fast bound in sin and Nature's night;

But then comes the galvanizing good news of the gospel:

> Thine eye diffused a quickening ray,
> I woke, the dungeon flamed with light:
> My chains fell off, my heart was free,
> I rose, went forth and followed Thee.

Lack of information results in everything from unpleasant burdens to stark tragedies, across the entire range of human life. Not knowing about resources at a public library or on the Internet may mean that a scholar or writer or other professional person is deprived of needed materials or at least must obtain them at considerable effort or personal expense. In the past, doctors with unwashed hands unwittingly carried deadly germs, which caused the deaths of hundreds of thousands of women from "child-bed fever."

Failure to know what God is really like and what his law requires destroys the soul, ruins society, and leaves people to eternal ruin: "My people are destroyed for lack of knowledge" (Hosea 4:6, NRSV), and "A people without understanding comes to ruin" (4:14, NRSV). This is the tragic condition of Western culture today, which has put away the information about God that God himself has made available.

Accordingly, the first task of Jesus in his earthly ministry was to *proclaim* God: to *inform* those around him of the availability of eternal life from God through himself. He made it clear that by placing their confidence in himself, "believing on him," they could immediately enter into the eternal life enjoyed by those in "the kingdom of the heavens." This is basic information for human life. It was then and is now.

Jesus had to combat much false information about the Father and bring to light the correct "Father facts" (Matthew 11:27; John 6:46). He showed the many ways in which God is love. This he did by *proclaiming* the immediate availability of the kingdom of God from the surrounding heavens, by *manifesting* its presence through use of its power to help people, and by *teaching* in various ways its exact nature (Matthew 4:23; 9:35).

On the evening before his death, his teaching ministry finished, Jesus said to his Father in prayer: "I manifested Thy name to the men whom Thou gavest Me" (John 17:6). That is, "I have made them understand what You are really like." His death was understood by his early disciples to be an ultimate revelation of the Father heart of God: "God proves his love for us," Paul wrote, "in that while we were still rebelling against him, Christ died for us" (Romans 5:8, PAR). That is, his death was a revelation of the nature of basic reality. Without knowledge of it and its meaning, we are desperately ignorant of reality, and therefore all our thinking can only result in monstrous false-hoods. The saying "Garbage in, garbage out" nowhere has greater force than in the spiritual life.

✎ SPIRITUAL FORMATION REQUIRES THINKING ✎

THE GOSPEL OF JESUS directly repudiates all false information about God and, therewith, about the meaning of human life; and it works to undermine the power of those ideas and images that structure life away from God. But for it to have this effect we must *use* our ability to think.

What is thinking? It is the activity of searching out what *must* be true, or *cannot* be true, in the light of given facts or assumptions. It extends the information we have and enables us to see the "larger picture"—to see it clearly and to see it wholly. And it undermines false or misleading ideas and images as well. It reveals their falseness to those who wish to know. It is a powerful gift of God to be used in the service of truth.

Here is Paul thinking under inspiration: "If God is for us, who is against us? He who did not spare His own Son, but delivered Him up for us all, how will He not also with Him freely give us all things?" (Romans 8:31-32).

Here is Martin Luther thinking and standing in the power of God before his examiners at Worms: "Unless I am convicted by Scripture and plain reason—I do not accept the authority of popes and councils, for they have con-tradicted each other—my conscience is captive to the Word of God. I cannot and will not recant anything, for to go against conscience is neither right nor safe. God help me. Amen." The earliest printed version of his statement added the famous words: "Here I stand, I cannot do otherwise."[4]

And so we must apply our thinking to and with the Word of God. We must thoughtfully take that Word in, dwell upon it, ponder its meaning, explore its implications—especially as it relates to our own lives. What are we to do in the light of the facts of the gospel and the revelation of God and of human destiny contained in the Bible? We must "pay greater attention to what we have heard, so that we do not drift away from it" (Hebrews 2:1, NRSV). We must thoughtfully put it into practice.

We must *seek the Lord* by devoting our powers of thinking to understanding the facts and information of the gospel. This is the primary way of focusing our mind on him, setting him before us. When we do so we will be assisted by God's grace in ways far beyond anything we can understand on our own; and the ideas and images that governed the life of Christ through his thought life will possess us.[5]

☙ THE CRUCIAL ROLE OF GOOD THINKING TODAY ❧

NOW THIS IS TREMENDOUSLY important for us today as it has been in the past. Perhaps we are in a time when it is more important than ever. *The prospering of God's cause on earth depends upon his people thinking well.*

Today we are apt to downplay or disregard the importance of good thinking to strong faith; and some, disastrously, even regard thinking as opposed to faith. They do not realize that in so doing they are not honoring God, but simply yielding to the deeply anti-intellectualist currents of Western egalitarianism, rooted, in turn, in the romantic idealization of impulse and blind feeling found in David Hume, Jean-Jacques Rousseau, and their nineteenth- and twentieth-century followers. They do not realize that they are operating on the same satanic principle that produced the "killing fields" of Cambodia, where those with any sign of education—even the wearing of glasses—were killed on the spot or condemned to starvation and murderous labor.

We too easily forget that it is great thinkers who have given direction to the people of Christ in their greatest moments: Paul, John, Augustine, Luther, Calvin, and Wesley, to name a few. At the head of the list is Jesus Christ himself, who was and is the most powerful thinker the world has ever known.[6]

Many Christians today will be surprised to learn that Isaac Watts (born 1674)—the composer of such well-known hymns as "Joy to the World," "Alas! And Did My Savior Bleed?" "When I Survey the Wondrous Cross," "Jesus Shall Reign Where'er the Sun," and "O God, Our Help in Ages Past," along with many others—also taught logic and wrote a widely used textbook, *Logic: The Right Use of Reason in the Inquiry After Truth.* Those hymns owe much of their power to the depth of thought they contain. That is one reason we need to return to them constantly.

Of logic itself Watts said,

The great design of this noble science is to rescue our reasoning powers from their unhappy slavery and darkness; and thus, with all due submission and deference, it offers an humble assistance to divine revelation. Its chief business is to relieve the natural weakness of the mind by some better efforts of nature; it is to diffuse a light over the understanding in our inquiries after truth. . . . [And] it renders its daily service to wisdom and virtue.[7]

Bluntly, to serve God well we must think straight; and crooked thinking, unintentional or not, always favors evil. And when the crooked thinking gets elevated into group orthodoxy, whether religious or secular, there is always, quite literally, "hell to pay." That is, hell will take its portion, as it has repeatedly done in the horrors of world history.

To take the "information" of the Scripture into a mind thinking straight under the direction and empowerment of the Holy Spirit, by contrast, is to place our feet solidly on the high road of spiritual formation under God. "The law of the LORD is perfect, restoring the soul; the testimony of the LORD is sure, making wise the simple. . . . The commandment of the LORD is pure, enlightening the eyes" (Psalm 19:7-8).

And "Thy word I have treasured in my heart, that I may not sin against Thee" (Psalm 119:11). "Thy word is a lamp to my feet, and a light to my path" (verse 105). "I love Thy commandments above gold, yes, above fine gold. Therefore I esteem right all Thy precepts concerning everything" (verses 127-128). "Those who love Thy law have great peace, and nothing causes them to stumble" (verse 165).

❧ THOUGHT, LOVE, AND WORSHIP ❧

TO BRING THE MIND to dwell intelligently upon God as he is presented in his Word will have the effect of causing us to love God passionately, and this love will in turn bring us to think of God steadily. Thus he will always be before our minds. As Thomas Watson beautifully wrote long ago:

The first fruit of love is *the musing of the mind upon God.* He who is in love, his thoughts are ever upon the object. He who loves God is ravished and transported with the contemplation of God. *"When I awake, I am still with thee"* (Ps. 139:18). The thoughts are as travellers in the mind. David's thoughts kept heaven-road, "I am still with Thee." God is the treasure, and where the treasure is, there is the heart. By this we may test our love to God. What are our thoughts most upon? Can we say we are ravished with delight when we think on God? Have our thoughts got wings? Are they fled aloft? Do we contemplate Christ and glory? Oh, how far are they from being lovers of God, who scarcely ever think of God! *"God is not in all his thoughts"* (Ps. 10:4). A sinner crowds God out of his thoughts. He never thinks of God, unless with horror, as the prisoner thinks of the judge.[8]

In this way we enter a life of *worship*. To think of God as he is, one cannot but lapse into worship; and worship is the single most powerful force in completing and sustaining restoration in the whole person. It puts into abeyance every evil tendency in every dimension of the self. It naturally arises from thinking rightly of God on the basis of revealed truth confirmed in experience. We say flatly, *Worship is at once the overall character of the renovated thought life and the only safe place for a human being to stand.*

An old hymn contains these lines:

In our astonished reverence we confess
Thine uncreated loveliness.

"Astonished reverence" is a good paraphrase for worship, as is "admiration to the point of wonder and delight"—more language from Tozer. That is the true outcome of renovation of the thought life. The first request in The Lord's Prayer is, "Hallowed be Thy name." It is first because it is the most important one. To the extent that God is exalted in the minds of people, and his very name is cherished with utmost respect, everything else goes right. You can verify this experimentally in yourself.

Some decades ago J. B. Phillips brought a great message to the Christian world in his book, *Your God Is Too Small*. But while the phrase "Your God is too small" is still used today, its message is usually misunderstood. The point is not "Your God is too small *to meet your needs*," but "Your God is so small that you can fail *to relentlessly worship and adore him*." In the renovated mind, God constantly stands as uniquely and supremely *worthy*. Hallowed be Thy name!

✧ THE SUPREME WORTH ✧

IN HEAVEN MYRIADS OF myriads of angels continuously say in loud unison:

"Worthy is the Lamb that was slain to receive power and riches
and wisdom and might and honor and glory and blessing." And
every created thing which is in heaven and on the earth and under
the earth and on the sea, and all things in them, I heard saying,
"To Him who sits on the throne, and to the Lamb, be blessing and

honor and glory and dominion forever and ever." (Revelation 5:12-13)

Now, this angelic vision is precisely the vision that possesses the thought life of the renovated heart; and you can see how it would grip the whole person and his or her earthly environment. This is what it is to "hallow" God's name. It is what we pray for in The Lord's Prayer. But, sad to say, even our Christian meetings and environments are for the most part far from it.

A. W. Tozer continues the passage quoted at length above as follows: "It is my opinion that the Christian conception of God current in these middle years of the twentieth century is so decadent as to be utterly beneath the dignity of the Most High God and actually to constitute for professed believers something amounting to a moral calamity."

But why a *moral* calamity? Because absolutely nothing can inform, guide, and sustain radical and radiant goodness in the human being other than this true vision of God and the worship based thereon. Only this vision can jerk the twisted condition of humanity right. Immanuel Kant said, "Nothing straight can be constructed from such warped wood as that which man is made of."[9] And humanly speaking he was right. But what is impossible with men is possible with God.

❧ STANDING BEFORE GOD ❧

WHEN GOD STANDS BEFORE us, we stand before him. Refusing to worship him is a way of trying to avoid his face and his eyes.

Two-and-a-half-year-old Larissa was enjoying water in the back yard with "Nana." Nana gently counseled her to water the purple flowers, but she had just discovered mud by pouring water on a small patch of dirt. Nana told her not to put water on the dirt because it makes mud and mud will "get *everything* dirty."

Well, mud it was anyway, and the little girl even put the mud into a small tub of water nearby, calling it then "warm chocolate."

Nana, who had been reading facing away from the action, soon discovered and cleaned up what to her was a mess, and then returned to her reading, but now seated so as to be facing Larissa. But the little girl soon resumed her "warm chocolate" routine, saying sweetly, "Don't look at me, Nana. Okay?" Nana of course agreed, and looked down at her reading. Then Larissa would make black mud and put some of it in the tub. And then some more. Three times she said, as she continued with her work, "Don't look at me, Nana. Okay?"

The tender soul of a little child shows us how necessary it is to us that we be unobserved in our wrong. The adult soul carries the same burden—

but now so great as to be crushed by it. And when the face of God will no longer be avoidable, that soul will cry out in agony "to the mountains and to the rocks, 'Fall on us and hide us from the face of Him who sits on the throne'" (Revelation 6:15-16; compare Isaiah 2:19-21). The so-called "right to privacy" of which so much is made in contemporary life is in very large measure merely a way of avoiding scrutiny in our wrongdoing.

ᴕ TRANSFORMING THE DETAILS OF LIFE ᴔ

THE EFFECT OF STANDING before God by welcoming him before us will, by contrast, be the transformation of our entire life. All else that enters our mind, and especially the thoughts that first come to mind as we encounter various kinds of events that make up our lives, will be healthy, godly, and good. The conclusions we "jump" to prompted by events around us will be those in harmony with the realities of a good-God-governed universe, not the illusions of a godless or a me-governed universe, or one where man is supreme—or no one is. My patterns of thinking will conform to the truths of scriptural revelation, and I will extend and apply those truths, under the guidance of God's Holy Spirit, to all of the details of my daily life.

Am I undertaking some task? Then I in faith do it with God, assuming and finding his power to be involved with me. That is the nature of his kingdom. Is there an emergency? I will meet it with the knowledge that God is in the midst of it with me and will be calm in a center of intense prayer. Am I praised? My thoughts (and feelings) will move immediately to the goodness of God in my life. Am I condemned or reproached? I know that God is supporting and helping me because he loves me and has a future for me. Am I disappointed and frustrated? I rest in the knowledge that God is over all and that he is working things out—that "all things work *together* for good to those who love God and are called into the fulfillment of his purposes." And so forth.

I constantly and thoughtfully engage myself with the ideas, images, and information that are provided by God through the Scriptures, his Son Jesus, and the lives and experiences of his people through the ages. In doing that, I am constantly nourished by the Holy Spirit in ways far beyond my own efforts or understanding. What I receive in response to my efforts is therefore also a gift, a grace. Spiritual (trans)formation of my thought life is achieved by the ministry of the Spirit in the midst of my necessary and well-directed efforts.

This has special importance when I am faced with the presence of evil and suffering in human life, my own or at large. I realize that I will either allow my view of evil to determine my view of God and will cut him down accordingly, or I will allow my view of God to determine my view of the evil and will elevate him accordingly, accepting that nothing is beyond his power for good.

❧ SPECIAL DANGERS IN OUR THOUGHT LIFE WITH GOD ❧

HOWEVER, SEVERAL SPECIAL DANGERS in this area should be specifically noted and guarded against.

The first is pride and overconfidence in ideas, images, or bits of "information" *simply because* they are "ours" or "mine" and I am (we are) in the habit of relying on them. This danger is not limited to our thoughts of God, but it is unfortunately common there. It takes the form of pride of doctrine, practice, and tradition.

"I did it myyyyyy way," Frank Sinatra sang, to the gratification of millions who took him to be expressing their own proper "American" attitude. But Christians often sing with misplaced satisfaction, "We did it ourrrrrr way!" Ourrrrrr way is not necessarily right or good or even "better." Of course it is not necessarily wrong or worse either. But we must be aware of the special danger of holding onto the contents of our thought life mainly because they are *ours* and therefore "obviously correct." Arrogance of doctrine or tradition is still arrogance. It is one of the things God hates (Proverbs 8:13), and not just in "others." It was first on the list of sins of Sodom, and it was what made possible the "abominations" more commonly associated with that place (Ezekiel 16:49-50).

A second danger, associated with the first, is that of simple ignorance of fact. A repeated story in Christian history is of those who have set out to prove the falsity of the way of Christ and wound up being his followers. This is, in nearly every case, simply because, in their quest, they were forced to *examine* facts and to *think carefully* about them. Therefore, as C. S. Lewis once pointed out, a "young atheist" can't be too careful about what he reads and must steadfastly protect his ignorance.

But even the followers of Jesus fall into patterns of willing ignorance about important matters, including possible objections to faith in Christ and the beliefs and practices of others who are devoted to Christ. In fact, if we are to use our minds rightly, we must live in an attitude of constant openness and learning. Before we make judgments on any serious matter, have we looked into the facts of the case and have we carefully considered all their bearings? This is especially important with reference to those we disagree with or think we disagree with.

A third great danger in the thought life of the disciple is allowing our desires to guide our thinking: especially the desire to prove we are right. This goes hand in hand with intellectual self-righteousness and is often associated with the desire to have the approval of others in "our crowd."

Often a good starting point when trying to help those who do not believe in God or accept Christ as Lord is to get them to deal honestly with the question: Would I *like* for there to be a God? Or, would I *like* it if Jesus turned out to be Lord? This may help them realize the extent to which what they *want* to be the case is controlling their ability to see what *is* the case.

And we believers should keep the question of how *we* want things to be, with respect to certain issues, in the margin of our consciousness as we conduct our thought life. We must try to remain aware of how our desires may influence how we perceive things, as well as our patterns of thought and interpretation. Many a bitter conflict among Christians could be avoided in this way. It is an essential part of "humbleness of mind," which Paul knew to be indispensable to the mind of Christ in us (Philippians 2:1-8; Colossians 3:12).

We should make it a rule never to try merely to prove that we are right.

The fourth and final great danger has to do with the images that we admit into our minds. These may be images of intellectual authority or images of financial well-being or images of the macabre and horrible or images of power (domination) and sexuality, and so on.

Our present American culture boasts of complete freedom in what one sees, says, and hears. Many professing Christians are paralyzed or even destroyed by adopting this "freedom" as a lifestyle. For they allow images into their mind that eventually overwhelm them. If we allow everything access to our mind, we are simply asking to be kept in a state of mental turmoil or bondage. For nothing enters the mind without having an effect for good or evil.

You may say, "I want to be open to think of anything, imagine anything, have all feelings, see everything. What do you think freedom of thought is all about? This is America!"

Well, then you must take the consequences. You cannot choose conditions and reject the consequences. Even a "bill of rights" cannot change that. If you choose to step off the roof, you can't then choose not to hit the ground. The mind (the person and all its dimensions) has laws just as rigorous as gravity. "The mind has cliffs," the poet Gerard Manley Hopkins said, "Cliffs of fall. Hold them cheap who never hung thereby."

If God's eyes are too pure to behold evil (Habakkuk 1:13), we had better think it might be wise for us to look away as much as is feasible—even if it is called "entertainment." We are to abhor evil and cleave to that which is good, and the foundation for doing that lies in where we choose to place our minds. The power to choose our thoughts is, as we said at the outset, our most basic freedom, our first *and* primary freedom, and we must use it well.

There are many things we need not see and are better off not seeing—

though, if you wish, you have a "right" to see them. Anyone who thinks that if I have a right to do X it is good for me to do X, simply hasn't thought deeply about the matter. Paul's wise counsel, by contrast, was, "Whatever is true, whatever is honorable, whatever is right, whatever is pure, whatever is lovely, whatever is of good repute, if there is any excellence and if anything worthy of praise, let your mind dwell on these things" (Philippians 4:8). Make no mistake; *this is a fundamental and indispensable part of our spiritual formation in Christ.*

Images, in particular, are motivational far beyond our conscious mind, and they are not under rational control. We must take care that we are nourished constantly on good and godly ones, without necessarily being able to see and say what is wrong with the others. "What is wrong" with them well may be something we cannot bring before our consciousness, but which works in the depths of our soul and body as an instrument of forces beyond ourselves.

⟳ THE WAY FORWARD ⟲

NOW, THERE ARE NO formulas in the spiritual life, because it is not a life that runs on its own. It runs in interaction with God. The key in this "thought" dimension of the person, however, as with all others, is the VIM structure. This chapter has dealt almost exclusively with the V part of the structure: *vision.* The greatest need lies there, and without it nothing moves. Unless it is properly grasped, the *intention* will be malformed or nonexistent and the *means* implemented will be chaotic and ineffectual.

The intention to be formed is to have the great God and Father of our Lord Jesus Christ a constant presence in our mind, crowding out every false idea or destructive image, all misinformation about God, and every crooked inference or belief. Thus it is the intention to use divinely powerful weapons "for the destruction of fortresses. We are destroying speculations and every lofty thing raised up against the knowledge of God, and taking every thought captive to the obedience of Christ" (2 Corinthians 10:3-5).

Given the vision, the taking of this intention is something each of us must do or not do. "Just do it." If you say, "I can't," remember, God will help you to carry out the decision and form a solid intention. But he will not do it for you. Have you decided to have God a constant presence in your mind or not?

Once you have the V and the I in place, you will begin to find appropriate, orderly, bearable, and effectual means to fulfill the decision to realize the vision. There are certain tried-and-true disciplines we can use to aid in the transformation of our thought life toward the mind of Christ.[10] Disciplines

112

are activities that *are* in our power and that enable us to do what we cannot do by direct effort. We cannot transform our ideas and images, or even the information we have or our thought processes, into Christlikeness by direct effort. But we can do things—adopt certain practices—that, indirectly, will increasingly have that effect.

The most obvious thing we can do is to draw certain key portions of Scripture into our minds and make them a part of the permanent fixtures of our thought. This is the primary discipline for the thought life. We need to know them like the back of our hand, and a good way to do that is to memorize them and then constantly turn them over in our minds as we go through the events and circumstances of our life (Joshua 1:8; Psalm 1).

The desired effect will not be realized by focusing on isolated verses, but will certainly come as we ingest *passages,* such as Romans 5:1-8 or 8:1-15, 1 Corinthians 13, or Colossians 3:1-17. When you take these into your mind, your mind will become filled with the light of God himself. And light shines into darkness and darkness loses. When the light comes into a room, we do not have to say, "Now what are we going to do about the darkness?" It's *gone!*

You say, "I can't memorize like that." I assure you, you certainly can. God made your mind for it and he will help you. He *really* wants you to do this. Of course that will be an integral part of the other changes that will permeate your life as a whole. As you choose to give your time and energy to, and plan your life around, the renovation of your mind, *it will happen!* But you must choose to do it and learn how—just like learning to program and live with your VCR. Then you will know by experience that the mind of the Spirit is life and peace, and in all the deflections of life your mind will automatically re-center on God as the needle of the compass returns to the north.

⌘ IMAGES AND SAYINGS ⌘

SIMILAR POINTS CAN BE made with references to the use of images. We need to be in the presences of images, both visual and auditory (good sayings, poetry, and songs). These can constantly direct and redirect our minds toward God, Jesus Christ, the Spirit, and the church (people of God). "Icons" have a millennia-long track record with the people of God and can be a powerful way of keeping entire stories and teachings effortlessly before the mind. We might arrange to have them tastefully present in each of our living and work spaces, so that they are always present in our visual field. We can thoughtfully use them to dispel destructive imagery and thoughts and to see ourselves as before God in all levels of our being.

Not long ago, people in the United States commonly had edifying sayings on their walls. I recall from my childhood one that said, "Only one life.

It will soon be past. Only what's done for Christ will last." This and other good sayings were constantly before the minds of all who lived in the house. They were powerfully effective because they became, through mere habit, an enduring presence and influence within the minds of those who constantly saw them. What is now constantly before the minds of those who live where we do?

Today we as a culture are schizophrenic on such matters. We want to say it doesn't make any difference what we look at or hear. This, no doubt, is because we want to be "free" to show anything and to see anything—no matter how evil and revolting. But businesses still pay millions of dollars to show us something for thirty seconds on television. They do that because they know that what we repeatedly see and hear affects what we do. Otherwise they would go out of business.

✍ FINDING OTHERS WHO ARE WALKING THE WALK ✍

OF COURSE WE NEED to do all these things that turn our thoughts to God in close association with others who know the realities of spiritual formation by such means. Spiritual formation cannot, in the nature of the case, be a "private" thing, because it is a matter of whole-life transformation. You need to *seek out* others in your community who are pursuing the renovation of the heart. Hopefully, they might even be members of your own family or in a nearby congregation of Christians. But this is not always possible. We must pray that God will lead us to others who can walk with us with Christ— whoever and wherever they may be. And then in patience stay with them.

This will naturally lead us to include, under *means,* the identification of older practitioners of The Way. We need to understand those who have learned how to live with a transformed mind and study carefully what they did—not necessarily in order to do exactly what they did, for they are not lawgivers, nor are they always right, much less perfect. But we cannot easily or wisely dispense with what they have learned and what can be learned from them.

Now we are talking about *practitioners,* not about theologians. Working backward in time, we find people such as Billy Graham, Teresa of Calcutta, Dawson Trotman, E. Stanley Jones, Frank Laubach, or at greater distance, John Wesley, William Law, Martin Luther, Ignatius of Loyola, Francis of Assisi, and many others, famous or not so famous.[11] How did they come to be able to live with "the Lord always before them"? We learn from them how to do that by making them our close companions on the way.

However, don't just look at what Dawson Trotman or John Wesley, for example, accomplished. Look at *the details of how they lived* their lives and then sensibly adapt those details to your life. Some time back my wife and I visited the haunts of St. Francis of Assisi. I noticed that the people there in charge of his remembrances were not doing the things he did. They did what we might call acts "symbolic" of Francis, but not what he did. How odd! It is not odd, however, that they fail to have his inner life and his outer effects.

There is much more to be said on the details of the *means*. But if we take in God through his Word and walk the way of those who know by experience the transformation of the mind, that transformation, with its natural and supernatural effects, will come to us and pervade every dimension of our person. *God will see to it!*

✎ Doing Justice to the Power of Thought ✎

How easily we go wrong! The simple power of thought (ideas, images, information, inferences) is so great that it gives rise to many practical plans for remedying the human situation *outside* of Christ and obedience to him. One great world religion, for example, is based entirely upon the effects on emotion, will, and body of focusing the mind in certain ways and coming to "enlightenment." Many variants of the Christian tradition follow what is, at bottom, the same path (Christian Science, Unity, Science of Mind, "Course on Miracles," and on and on). A convenient illustration of this type of teaching is to be found in Charles Roth's book *Mind: The Master Power* (published by Unity House). Nowadays some version of this viewpoint is usually present on the *New York Times* best-seller list or being widely published in so-called "new age" circles.

Within the multifloral field of psychological therapy, what is called "cognitive therapy" is based largely upon the power of "thoughts" or "words"; and classical psychotherapy (Freud) pays constant tribute to that power, as do its offshoots. "Unconscious" thoughts and images are, in such views, still thoughts or images, and may become heavily charged with powers over the body and the spirit.

Those who would understand and practice spiritual formation in the way of Jesus Christ should not deny the power of thought just because some people make a religion of it and would use it as a basis for helping and healing with *no* reference to Christ. Breakfast is a good idea, and I do not plan to give it up because Hindus practice it. For effectual spiritual formation in Christ we *must* have a realistic understanding and utilization of the powers of thought.

Indeed, it is a bad idea to deny any reality, of which the great power of thought over life is one. Rather, we should carefully inquire what "thought" is, and what can really—no hype!—be accomplished by thought and by practices based solely on its natural efficacy. And then we should thought-fully and prayerfully look into whether such practices actually are sufficient to meet the human need for spiritual formation. Especially, are they really equivalent to or better than spiritual formation in the way of Christ, when it is correctly and fully practiced?

The biblical way of personal transformation must be set in clear contrast to other ways, even if they utilize what looks like biblical language. Honesty and thoroughness is required. Many "alternative" paths of human help and healing offer themselves today *only because Jesus' formation is not widely and powerfully available* to human beings—or even known about. The transfor-mation of our thought life by taking on the mind of Christ—his ideas, images, information, and patterns of thinking—opens the way to deliverance of every dimension of the human self from the oppressive powers of darkness.

Matters for Thought and Discussion

1. What are three "thoughts" that have occupied your mind this week? Why those thoughts, and not some others? What have their effects on your life been?

2. What are the main *ideas* that rule our society today? Do you think they favor a godly life or hinder it?

3. What are the major ideas Jesus brought into human history and how do you see them affecting the contemporary world? Think broadly and of parts of our world most unaffected by Christian teaching.

4. Was the distinction between ideas and images made clear in this chapter? Where do you see images most at work in our lives today? Political cam-paigns? Advertising? Religion? Education?

5. What images of God seem most common and influential in our world? How about in your own thinking and devotional life? In that of your friends?

6. What were Peter's ideas and images concerning the Messiah? Do you think we do much better than Peter?

7. Reflect on the Gospel (New Testament) as basic *information* about reality. Is that a good way to think of it? What are the alternatives to thinking of it in that way?

8. Should followers of Jesus Christ be known as thinkers? Is thinking actually a good thing for Christians to do? How might it help us? Is it dangerous?

9. What is worship? How are thought, worship, and spiritual formation related?

10. What are some steps we can take to make sure that thought is rightly directed and used in the process of spiritual formation? How can images help that process?

7

TRANSFORMING THE MIND, 2

Spiritual Formation and Our Feelings

*For the kingdom of God is not eating and drinking, but
righteousness and peace and joy in the Holy Spirit.*
ROMANS 14:17

*Those who belong to Christ Jesus have crucified
the flesh with its passions and desires.*
GALATIANS 5:24, PAR

❧ THE POWER OF FEELING ❧

Feelings are a primary blessing *and* a primary problem for human life. We cannot live without them and we can hardly live with them. Hence they are also central for spiritual formation in the Christian tradition. In the restoration of the individual to God, feelings too must be renovated: old ones removed in many cases, or at least thoroughly modified, and new ones installed or at least heightened into a new prominence.

Our first inquiry as we greet people for the day is likely to be, "How are you feeling today?" Rarely will it be, "How are you thinking?" Feelings live on the front row of our lives like unruly children clamoring for attention. They presume on their justification in being whatever they are—unlike a thought, which by nature is open to challenge and invites the question "Why?"

The term "feeling" indicates a kind of "contact," a "touch," that is at once blind and powerful—in allure as well as in revulsion. A "touching" scene is one that evokes feelings, that "touches" us. In feelings we really know that something is "there," and solidly so. But what it is and why it is remains obscure—though hauntingly present. This aspect of "blind power" has famously led to the description of emotions as "human bondage."[1] But the quality of blind power equally extends to mere sensations or desires, which, as well as emotions, can be simply overwhelming.

The attraction of feeling to human minds is so great that we project it into angels. One of the most common themes found in literary and artistic portrayals of angels is how they desire to feel what human beings feel and, mainly, what they are capable of feeling because they have fleshly bodies. Of course, the idea is, angels would have to irreversibly give up their angel status to have what they thus desire, and as the stories go, they sometimes do give it up.

In the movie "City of Angels," Nicholas Cage's character actually does make the switch. Asked if it was worth it, he replies, "I would rather have had one breath of her hair, one kiss of her lips, one touch of her hand than an eternity without it." When you only lightly reflect on what is involved, both the blindness and power associated with such feelings become obvious. Really now, *one* breath? One kiss? For an eternity . . . of what?

The movie closes with him frolicking in the surf at sunset and the landscape full of angels (now including "her," Meg Ryan) watching him with either envy or pleasure at his pleasure. The theology (angelology) is pretty weak, but the story correctly conveys the idolatry of feeling that characterizes the human outlook.

✎ NO HEAD-ON MASTERY OF FEELING ✎

NOW, ONE THING QUICKLY becomes clear when you think about the power of feeling. No one can succeed in mastering feelings in his or her life who tries to simply take them head-on and resist or redirect them by "willpower" in the moment of choice. To adopt that strategy is to radically misunderstand how life and the human will work, or—more likely—it is to have actually decided, deep down, to lose the battle and give in. This is one of the major areas of self-deception in the human heart. The very "giving in" can be among the most exhilarating feelings known to man, though it can also be one of complete despair and defeat.

Those who continue to be mastered by their feelings—whether it is anger, fear, sexual attraction, desire for food or for "looking good," the residues of woundedness, or whatever—are typically persons who in their heart of hearts believe that their feelings must be satisfied. They have long chosen the strategy of selectively *resisting* their feelings instead of that of *not having* them—of simply changing or replacing them.

Of course this is just another way of describing the ruined person discussed in chapter 3, the one who makes himself "god" in his world. To such persons, the idea that they should not honor their feelings is an insult. "Their god is their belly," it will be recalled. They are enslaved to their feelings—hence "human bondage"—and have no place to stand in dealing with them. Jesus was referring to this situation when he said that "everyone who commits sin is the slave of sin" (John 8:34).

By contrast, the person who happily lets God be God does have a place to stand in dealing with feelings—even in extreme cases such as despair over loved ones or excruciating pain or voluptuous pleasure. They have the resources to do what they don't want to do and to not do what they want. They know and deeply accept the fact that their feelings, of whatever kind, do *not* have to be fulfilled. They spend little time grieving over non-fulfillment. And with respect to feelings that are inherently injurious and wrong, their strategy is not one of resisting them in the moment of choice but of living in such a way that they do not have such feelings at all, or at least do not have them in a degree that makes it hard to decide against them when appropriate.

Those who let God be God get off the conveyer belt of emotion and desire when it first starts to move toward the buzz saw of sin. They do not wait until it is moving so fast they cannot get off of it. Their aim is not to avoid sin, but to avoid temptation—the inclination to sin. They plan their path accordingly.

∾ My Identity Beyond My Feelings ∾

If we look at this from the viewpoint of one still at an early stage of spiritual formation, it is a major step forward just to sincerely *desire,* not to *not sin,* but to have different feelings—feelings that lead away from sin. At that early stage, one has to strongly want to *not* want what one *now* wants, and to *want* to want what one does not now want. One has to feel strong revulsion toward the wrong feeling one now has or is likely to have and at the same time strong attraction to good feeling that one does not now feel. This proves to be absolutely necessary in order to "put off the old person" (involving the wrong feeling) and "put on the new person" (involving the good feeling). So, for example, one does not merely want to not assault others verbally, or to not fall into fornication, but he or she really wants to not have the feelings that lead to it and *takes steps to avoid those feelings.*

If a strong and compelling vision of myself as one who is simply free from intense vanity or desire for wealth or for sexual indulgence can possess me, then I am in a position to desire to not have the desires I now have. And then means can be effectively sought to that end. The VIM pattern of change will work here as elsewhere.

～ THE VISION OF ONESELF AS REALLY DIFFERENT ～

BUT ACHIEVING THIS NEW vision of oneself—of *who one would be*—must not be presumed to be a mere snap of the fingers. It will require genuine openness to radical change in oneself, careful and creative instruction, and abundant supplies of divine grace. For most people all of this only comes to them after they "hit bottom" and discover the total hopelessness of being who they are. Most people cannot envision who they would be without the fears, angers, lusts, power ploys, and woundedness with which they have lived so long. They identify with their habit-worn feelings.

When Jesus said to the man by the pool of Bethesda, waiting for the angel to stir the water, "Wilt thou be made whole?" he was not just passing the time of day (John 5:6, KJV). We are not told how old he was, but this man had been in his impotent condition for thirty-eight years! If made whole, he would have to deal with a "career change" of immense proportions. To all his relatives and acquaintances he would no longer be "the one whom we take to the pool every day to wait for the angel." He would now be . . . What? Who? How would he identify himself? How would he now relate to others and they to him? He might even have to get a job. Doing what?

But, really, this man's problem was nothing compared to an individual undergoing the transformation of his feelings (emotions, sensations, desires) from those he learned in the home, school, and playground as he grew up to those that characterize the inner being of Jesus Christ. He is now not to be one who will spend hours fantasizing sensual indulgence or revenge, or who will try to dominate or injure others in attitude, word, or deed. He will not repay evil for evil—push for push, blow for blow, taunt for taunt, hatred for hatred, contempt for contempt. He will not be always on the hunt to satisfy his lust of the flesh, lust of the eyes, and the pride of life (1 John 2:16). No wonder he has no real idea of who he will be; and he must content himself with the mere identity: "apprentice of Jesus." That is the starting point from which his new identity will emerge, and it is in fact powerful enough to bear the load.

～ FEELINGS MOVE OUR LIVES—WELL, OR BADLY ～

WE MUST LOOK STILL more closely at feeling. "Feeling" encompasses a *range* of things that are "felt": specifically, sensations, desires, and emotions. We *feel* warm, hungry, an itch, or fearful. "Feelings" include dizziness and thirst, sleepiness and weariness, sexual interest and desire, pain and pleasure, loneliness and homesickness, anger and jealousy; but also comfort and satisfaction, a sense of power and accomplishment, curiosity and intellectual gratifications, compassion for others and the enjoyment of beauty, a sense of honor, and delight in God. Aesthetic experiences (of art and beauty), personal relations, and actions all involve feeling and, moreover, require that the feeling be somehow "right."

There is no complete list of human feelings, and it would be a formidable task to define what feeling is. We have not attempted that here and need not concern ourselves with it. A familiar range of feelings frames our day-to-day existence, and we know a lot about these feelings and how important they are to our lives and to how we act and relate to one another.

We know, for example, that feelings *move* us, and that *we enjoy being moved.* They give us a sense of being alive. Without feeling we have no interest in things, no inclination to action. To "lose interest in life" means we have to carry on by mere exertions of will or by waiting for things to happen. That is a condition to be dreaded, and it cannot be sustained for long. That is why so many people become dependent upon "substances" and activities that give them *feeling,* even if the dependence badly harms them and those near them. Such a condition is also the frequent background of suicide.

So feeling is essential to life. We must accept this and work with it. And you can be sure that harmful feeling, feeling associated with evil—arising from it or producing it—will eventually be taken by a human being as *better than no feeling at all.* Healthy feelings, properly ordered among themselves, are essential to a good life. So if we are to be formed in Christlikeness, we must take good care of our feelings and not just let them "happen."

The one known as the Good Samaritan, in the story by Jesus (Luke 10:30-37) was distinguished from the priest and the Levite by the fact that "when he saw him [the wounded man], he felt compassion" (verse 33). This feeling of compassion is what led him to help the man and "be a neighbor to" him (verses 36-37).

Did the priest and the Levite then have *no* feelings? Of course not. They had feelings alright: feelings of disdain, perhaps, or of fear for the harm that might come to them if they became involved, or a feeling of urgency as they remembered the business awaiting them at the end of their journey, which, being their *own* business, moved them more than did the need of this unfortunate man to be helped out of his mortally dangerous situation. They had feelings that motivated them to selfish action, and they hardened their hearts to any other feelings of sympathy and concern for the half-dead man that might have competed for their attention.

❧ DESTRUCTIVE FEELINGS ❧

MANY OF THE FEELINGS that animate us are destructive of others and ourselves. Jesus' younger brother, James, pointedly asked, "What is the source of quarrels and conflicts among you? Is not the source your pleasures that wage war in your members? You lust and do not have; so you commit murder. And you are envious and cannot obtain; so you fight and quarrel" (James 4:1-2). And elsewhere he points out that "where jealousy and selfish ambition exist, there is disorder and every evil thing" (James 3:16). This goes far to explain what happens in many homes, churches, and other social groups. But the need is to remove the cause (the underlying feelings) and not just the effect (the conflict), which, if denied or suppressed without removal of the feelings, will only break out again.

The Old Testament book of Proverbs is full of wise sayings about the good and evil of feelings in human life. As we have already seen, "The fear of the LORD is the beginning of wisdom" (9:10). Moreover,

- "Hatred stirs up strife, but love covers all transgressions." (10:12)
- "When pride comes, then comes dishonor." (11:2)
- "Anxiety in the heart of a man weighs it down." (12:25)
- "A cheerful heart has a continual feast." (15:15)
- "A joyful heart is good medicine, but a broken spirit dries up the bones." (17:22)
- "He who loves pleasure will become a poor man; he who loves wine and oil will not become rich." (21:17)
- "The reward of humility and the fear of the LORD are riches, honor and life." (22:4)
- "The heavy drinker and the glutton will come to poverty, and drowsiness will clothe a man with rags." (23:21)
- "The fear of man brings a snare, but he who trusts in the LORD will be exalted." (29:25)

And so forth.

It is part of divine and human wisdom to realize that feelings are central to our existence and to make sure they are *good* feelings. And indeed they can be strong, healthy ones. We do not have to be victimized by destructive feelings. Even the feelings that harm us are, for the most part, not bad in themselves, but are somehow not properly limited or subordinated. They are out of order. Feelings are, with a few exceptions, good servants. But they are disastrous masters.

DENIAL AND REPRESSION OF FEELING ARE NOT THE ANSWER

NOW, IF WE HAVE destructive feelings, and everyone does sometimes, we should not deny that we have them or try to repress them—though we also should not, normally, dump them on others by acting them out. In any case, let it be very clear that we are not in favor of denying feelings or repressing them. That is not the answer to our problem. The proper course of action is to *replace* destructive feelings with others that are good, or to *subordinate* them—anger and sexual desire, for example—in a way that makes them constructive and transforms their effects. The process of spiritual formation in Christ will do this by grace—effectively and intelligently received, and put into constant practice.

Several other points about feelings must be considered before we come to deal with particular feelings (emotions, sensations, desires) and what can be done for their transformation into Christlikeness.

FEELINGS AND THEIR UNDERLYING CONDITION

MOST OF THE CONDITIONS we commonly speak of as feelings are really not feelings at all; but the feeling tones or sensations that accompany those conditions are so powerful that the conditions themselves become identified with the associated sensations. This is true of love and hatred or contempt, for example, but also with hurry and peace and with self-esteem and discouragement.

Now, there are some extremely serious dangers here. When we confuse the condition with the accompanying feeling—peace, for example, with the feeling of peacefulness—we very likely will try to manage the *feelings* and disregard or deny the reality of the *conditions*. That way lie such things as "falling in love with love" and most of the well-known addictions.

The person who primarily wants the feeling of being loved or being "in love" will be incapable of sustaining loving relationships, whether with God or with other humans. And the person who wants the feeling of peacefulness will be unable to do the things that make for peace—especially, doing what is right and confronting evil. So, as far as our planning for spiritual formation is concerned, we must choose and act with regard to the *condition,* good or bad, and allow the feelings to take care of themselves, as they certainly will.

In particular, we must never directly cherish, protect, or manipulate feelings, whether in ourselves or others. The only exception to this rule is when negative feelings have themselves become so overwhelming that they threaten to take over our lives. Then we must take steps to remove the negative feeling (grief or pain, for example). Prayer or even medication for such feelings is then wise. But even so, the focus on the feeling must not be allowed to prevent our dealing, when and as we can, with the conditions from which that feeling arises.

A well-known minister, after his wife passed away, said he had to learn that there is a difference between turning loose your loved one and turning loose your grief. You will always hold your loved one in your heart, but you must let go of your grief. So far as possible, we must walk away from painful and destructive feelings. Simply that. Walk away.

✎ FEELINGS SPREAD ✎

MUCH OF THE GREAT power of feelings over life derives not just from the fact that they *touch* us, *move* us, but from the fact that they creep over into other areas of our life; they pervade, they change the overall tone of our life and our world. They spread like an unstable dye or a viral form or a yeast. They may take over all else in us, even that to which they have no relevance. Things and people around us then look different, take on a distinctive tone or meaning. And that can even determine the tendency and outcome of our life as a whole.

This explains why it is so hard to reason with some people. Their very mind has been taken over by one or more feelings and is made to defend and serve those feelings at all costs. It is a fearful condition from which some people never escape. We have noted how thoughts generate feelings. If we allow certain negative thoughts to obsess us, then their associated feelings can enslave and blind us—that is, take over our ability to think and perceive.

Here, for example, is a woman (it could just as well have been a man) who has taken in the thought that she has been treated unfairly for years in her marriage and her job. Rather than sensibly addressing the circumstances or just turning her mind away from this thought, she receives it and broods over it—for years—developing a tremendous sense of injustice and outrage, which she also welcomes and cultivates with the aid of sympathetic friends. This "root of bitterness" (Hebrews 12:15) gradually spreads over her whole personality, seeping deeply into her body and her soul. It becomes something you can see in her bodily motions and actions and hear oozing through the language she uses. It affects her capacity to see what is actually going on around her, to realize what she is actually doing, and to think thoroughly and consistently. She is in what Bob Mumford has called "the prison of resentment," though she thinks she is perhaps for the first time acting freely.

Beyond the individual level, poisonous emotions and sensations often take over entire social groups, blinding them and impelling them on terrible courses of destruction. This is nearly always what has happened in cases where repression of ethnic groups or genocide occurs. Thus, to the onlooker the participants (Nazis, and so on) seem to be deaf, blind, and insane—which, in a sense, they are. They, too, are imprisoned.

Feelings can be successfully "reasoned with," can be corrected by reality, only in those (whether oneself or others) who have the habit and are given the grace of *listening* to reason even when they are expressing violent feelings or are in the grip of them. A feeling of sufficient strength may blot out all else and will invariably do so in one who has not trained himself or herself, or been trained, to identify, to be critical of, and to have some distance from his or her own feelings. Combined with a sense of righteousness, strong feeling becomes impervious to fact and reason.

Once Oliver Cromwell, sitting in the midst of his bickering brethren, blurted out these wise words: "I beseech ye brethren, by the bowels of Christ, believe ye *may* be wrong!" One's feeling of righteousness does not mean he is right and actually should alert him to be very cautious and humble.

Those who are wise will, accordingly, never allow themselves, if they can help it, to get in a position where they feel too deeply about any human matter. They will never willingly choose to allow feeling to govern them. They will carefully keep the pathway open to the house of reason and go there regularly to listen.

THE SECRET OF ADDICTION

THIS CERTAINLY IS AN offensive proposal to modern sensibilities, with its emphasis on spontaneity and enjoying the "rush" or the "buzz" of feeling. Abandonment to feeling, allowing oneself to be "carried away" by feeling, is actually *sought* by many, and on a regular basis. That is a testimony to our epidemic deadness of soul. People want to feel, and to feel strongly, and in the very nature of life they need to do so.[2]

The opposite of peace is really not war, but deadness. The "dead soul" is one waiting to explode or fall apart, and one that will seek out trouble for reasons it cannot understand. In its desolate life away from God, there is no drama to provide constructive feeling tones that would keep life from being a burden. Such persons really have no hope. This is the key to those "lives of quiet desperation" Thoreau attributed to "most men." Feeling will then be sought for its own sake, and satisfaction in feeling alone always in turn demands *stronger* feeling. It cannot limit itself.

This simple point is what explains the powerful grip of addiction, including the various forms of sexual perversion or addiction to praise. Addiction is a feeling phenomenon. The addict is one who, in one way or another, has given in to feeling of one kind or another and has placed it in the position of ultimate value in his or her life.

Of course addicts may also hold other things to be very valuable, and their life may be (usually will be) torn and even tragic because of conflicts. But they nevertheless have inwardly conceded the final word to some feeling—emotion, sensation, or desire. It may be that they have come to fear or

125

even hate that feeling and that in their present condition their mind is blinded and they see no way out. At this point suicide sometimes occurs. But in their heart of hearts they have accepted the rule of the feeling and have conceded its right to satisfaction.

❧ MODERNITY AND DECIDING BY HOW WE FEEL ☙

ALL OF THIS HAS special relevance to our contemporary life and to spiritual formation under modern conditions. We now live within the life form called "modernity,"[3] where revered ritual and personal relations do not smoothly govern life, because human solidarity (in family, neighborhood, school, workplace, church) has been pulverized. There are few things of equal significance to this fact for serious Christians to understand today.

In the "modern" condition, feeling will come to exercise almost total mastery over the individual. This is because people in that condition will have to constantly decide what they want to do, and feeling will be all they have to go on. Here lies the secret to understanding contemporary Western life and its peculiar proneness to gross immoralities and addictions. *People are overwhelmed with decisions and can only make those decisions on the basis of feelings.*

More than a century ago, Leo Tolstoy experienced the effects of "modernity" in the circle of wealthy, upper-class Russians who made up his world. In that world, he relates, "My life came to a standstill. I could breathe, eat, drink, and sleep, and I could not help doing these things; but there was no life, for there were no wishes the fulfillment of which I could consider reasonable."

"Had a fairy come and offered to fulfill my desires," he continues, "I should not have known what to ask."[4] This is exactly the world of pointless activity portrayed in such staples of the contemporary American consciousness as television's *Cheers, Seinfeld, Friends,* and *Will and Grace.*[5]

In the course of events, however, Tolstoy became involved in the life of the Russian peasants.

I saw that the whole life of these people was passed in heavy labor, and that they were content with life. . . . And they all—endlessly different in their manners, minds, education, and position, as they were—all alike, in complete contrast to my ignorance, knew the meaning of life and death, labored quietly, endured deprivations and sufferings, and lived and died seeing therein not vanity but good.[6]

The peasants whom Tolstoy admired so much were not yet swallowed up in modernity. They had solid traditions of faith and community that provided a ritual form of life—and of death. The result was that they knew what was good to do without regard to their feelings. Good was not determined for them by how they "felt" or by what they thought was "the best deal."[7]

The same was true for the "homemaker" and the "wage-earner" of our recent past. Not to say that all was well with them or with Tolstoy's peasants. But individuals in their roles knew without thinking about it what to do with their minutes, hours, and days, and only rarely were faced with having to do what they "felt like doing." The overall order in which they lived usually gave them great strength and inner freedom derived from their sense of place and direction, even in the midst of substantial suffering and frustration.

In a situation such as today, by contrast, where people constantly have—or think they have—to decide what to do, they will almost invariably be governed by feelings. Often they cannot distinguish between their feelings and their will, and in their confusion they also quite commonly take feelings to be reasons. And they will in general lack any significant degree of self-control. This will turn their life into a mere drift through the days and years, which addictive behavior promises to allow them to endure.

Self-control is the steady capacity to direct yourself to accomplish what you have chosen or decided to do and be, even though you "don't feel like it." Self-control means that you, with steady hand, do what you *don't* want to do (or what you want *not* to) when that is needed and do *not* do what you want to do (what you "feel like" doing) when that is needed. In people without rock-solid character, feeling is a deadly enemy of self-control and will always subvert it. The mongoose of a disciplined will under God and good is the only match for the cobra of feeling.

∽ IMAGES AND "MOODS" ∾

GENERALLY SPEAKING, FEELINGS AND emotions are fostered and sustained by ideas and images, though social or bodily conditions also factor in. Hopelessness and rejection (or worthlessness and "not belonging") live on images—often of some specific scene or scenes of unkindness, brutality, or abuse—that have become a permanent fixture within the mind, radiating negativity and leaving a background of deadly ideas that take over how we think and structure our whole world.

Such images also foster and sustain moods. What we call "moods" are simply feeling qualities that *pervade* our selves and everything around us. They are, of course, extremely hard to do anything about precisely because one cannot stand outside of them. Clinical depression is an extreme form of a "bad mood," but dread, deprivation, and deficiency, as well as simple anger, fear, or pain, can *become* moods of the negative type because of the capacity of feelings to spread and pervade everything they touch.

On the positive side, there are feelings and moods associated with confidence, worthiness of good, being acceptable and "belonging," purposefulness, love, hope, joy, and peace. Being "accepted in the beloved" (Ephesians 1:6, KJV) is the humanly indispensable foundation for the reconstruction of all these positive feelings, moods, and their underlying conditions. We must be very clear on how the negative feelings rest on ideas and images. Those feelings can themselves be transformed by discipleship to Christ and the power of the gospel and the Spirit, through which the corresponding ideas and images are changed to positive ones. And we must be clear that the person given to moods faces special difficulties, though not insurmountable ones, in spiritual formation.

⊗ THE GODLY FEELINGS IN THE SPIRITUALLY TRANSFORMED PERSON ⊗

NOW, THE REALM OF feelings may appear on first approach to be an area of total chaos. But this is not so. There is also order among feelings, and it is a much simpler one than most people think. When we properly cultivate with divine assistance those few feelings that should be prominent in our lives, the remainder will fall into place.

What then are the feelings that will dominate in a life that has been inwardly transformed to be like Christ's? They are the feelings associated with love, joy, and peace. For the sake of simplicity we shall simply call them "love," "joy," and "peace," though, as we have noted, love, joy, and peace are *not* mere feelings but conditions of the whole person that are accompanied by characteristic positive feelings.

Love, joy, and peace are, we recall, the three fundamental dimensions of the fruit (note the singular) of the Spirit. They mutually interpenetrate and inform one another and naturally express themselves in the remainder of that *one* fruit: ". . . patience, kindness, goodness, faithfulness, gentleness, self-control" (Galatians 5:22-23).

Faith (confidence) and hope are also very important in properly structuring the feeling dimension of the mind and self. But they play their role in that regard in subordination to love, joy, and peace—that is, because of their relationship to them. The three primary dimensions of "the fruit" (love, joy, and peace) are in fact *not separable* from the three things "that remain" of 1 Corinthians 13:13 (faith, hope, and love) and of course are partially identical with them. All are focused on goodness and what is good, and all are strength-giving and pleasant even in the midst of pain or suffering. That is not what we seek them for, or something we try to make of them. It is, simply, their natural attire.

ꜱ HOPE AND FAITH ꜱ

HOPE IS ANTICIPATION OF good not yet here, or as yet "unseen." It is of course inseparable from joy. Sometimes the good in question is just deliverance from an evil, which *is* here. Then "we are saved by hope" (Romans 8:24, PAR) and "we rejoice in hope" (12:12, PAR), because "if we hope for what we do not see, with perseverance we wait eagerly for it" (8:25). That eager anticipation strengthens us to stay faithful to God and to stay on the path of what is right.

One of the remarkable changes brought by Jesus and his people into the ancient world concerned the elevation of hope into a primary virtue. Hope was not well regarded by the Greco-Roman world. It was thought of as a desperation measure. And while, according to the myth of Pandora's box, it may be all we have left with which to endure the agonies of life, it must be grimly held in check or it will give rise to vain expectations that only cause more misery. Christ, by contrast, brings solid hope for humanity.

Clearly, then, hope also is closely related to faith. Faith is confidence grounded in reality, not a wild, desperate "leap." It is, as Hebrews 11:1 says, *substance* and *evidence* or *proof,* not—as contemporary translations usually have it—subjective psychological states such as "being sure of" or "having a conviction of."

Rather, faith sees the reality of the unseen or invisible, and it includes a readiness to act as if the good anticipated in hope were already in hand because of the reality of God (compare 2 Corinthians 4:17-18). Jeremy Taylor drives the point home with these words: "He that believes dares trust God for the morrow, and is not more solicitous for the next year than he is for that which is past."[8] No one worries about what was going to happen last year.

Accordingly, Moses "left Egypt, not fearing the wrath of the king" (Hebrews 11:27). Egypt and its king were in the realm of "the seen." Moses was able to disregard them and to stick with his goal because he saw the One who is invisible but none the less real for that. "For he endured, as seeing Him who is unseen" (verse 27). That is "faith" as the Bible portrays it.

ꜱ FAITH AND HOPE LAY
THE FOUNDATION FOR A LIFE FULL OF LOVE ꜱ

ROMANS 5:1-5 OUTLINES AN instructive and inspiring progression from an *initial* faith in God through Christ, with an accompanying *initial* hope, to a

129

subsequent or higher-level hope that "does not disappoint." The apostle Paul wrote this way because, in the progression of our experience, the Holy Spirit pours out into our own hearts the kind of love God has. This important passage needs to be studied in depth for any adequate understanding of spiritual formation in the Christian tradition, especially as it concerns feelings.

The initial faith in Christ gives us "our introduction by faith into this grace in which we stand" (verses 1). This is the new birth into Christ's kingdom. It puts an end to the war between me and God that has gone on most of my life and surrounds me with God's gracious actions. Now, because of Christ's death for me and his continuing graces, I know that God is good, and I am thrilled with the hope that God's goodness and greatness will serve as the basis of my own existence as well as of everything else. Thus, "we exult in hope of the glory of God" (verse 2).

But this opens the path for transformation of our character. I am also thrilled about my tribulations! I know that they will prove God's power and faithfulness in love to me, and to trust him in all things becomes my settled character. Therefore "we also exult in our tribulations, knowing that tribulation brings about perseverance; and perseverance, proven character" (verses 3-4; compare James 1:2-4).

But godly character now brings about a different quality of hope (verse 4). Character is a matter of our entire personality and life, which has now been transformed by the process of perseverance under God. Hope therefore now pervades our life as a whole. And this new and pervasive hope—which is an outgrowth of our initial "hope of the glory of God," but now covers our entire life—"does not disappoint, because the love of God has been poured out within our hearts through the Holy Spirit who was given to us" (verse 5).

⤷ LOVE ⤶

THUS FAITH IN CHRIST and the initial hope it inspires lead us to *stand* in the grace (the action) of God, and standing there leads, in turn, to a life full of love. We will want to see how this love relates to joy and peace, as well as to the rest of the fruit of the Spirit. But first we need to get a clearer picture of love itself, of its four movements required to complete its work in our life, of how (when completed) it casts out fear (1 John 4:18). Then we shall see the effect of all this on the feeling dimension of our life.

And first, what exactly is love? It is *will to good* or "bene-volence." We love something or someone when we promote its good for its own sake. Love's contrary is malice, and its simple absence is indifference. Its normal accompaniment is delight, but a twisted soul may delight in evil and take no pleasure in good.

Love is not the same thing as desire, for I may desire something without even wishing it well, much less willing its good. I might desire a chocolate ice cream cone, for example. But I do not wish it well; I wish to eat it. This is the difference between lust (mere desire) and love, as between a man and a woman. Desire and love are, of course, compatible when desire is ruled by love; but most people today would, unfortunately, not even know the difference between them. Hence, in our world, love constantly falls prey to lust. That is a major part of the deep sickness of contemporary life.

By contrast, what characterizes the deepest essence of God is love — that is, will to good. His very creation of the world is an expression of will to good, and it is then to be expected that his world would be found by him to be "very good" (Genesis 1:31). His love and goodwill toward humans is, therefore, not an "add on" to a nature that is fundamentally careless or even hostile. It is another expression — one of the more important ones, of course — of what he always and in every respect is. It is not hard for God *to* love, but it is impossible, given his nature, for him *not* to love.

Our human world as we find it is not like God, though it was intended to be. We have already expanded on this in an earlier chapter, but must take note of it again here. Love is *not* natural in our world, though desire or lust certainly is. "The lust of the flesh, the lust of the eyes and the pride of life," the apostle said, is "all that is in the world" (1 John 2:16, PAR).

Pride is defined by desire, not by love. It is, above all, the presumption that my desires should be fulfilled and that it is an injustice, a crying shame, and an injury if they are not.

Lust and pride all around us inevitably result in a world of fear. For they bring us into a world of little dictators; and the most likely thing is that each person will be used and abused by others, possibly destroyed, and at least not helped and cared for. Our families, which should be a refuge from such a world, often turn out to be places where victimization is at its worst. "The dark places of the land are full of the habitations of violence" (Psalm 74:20). The tender young are initiated into an adult world hardened in evil. A baby is not even safe from its mother while in her womb. "And he who turns aside from evil makes himself a prey" (Isaiah 59:15).

Injury brings pain and loss, then fear and anger, which mingle with resentment and contempt and settle into postures of coldness and malice, with brutal feelings that drain the body of health and strength and shatter social well-being.

THE FOUR MOVEMENTS TOWARD PERFECT LOVE

IN SUCH A WORLD God intrudes, gently and in many ways, but especially in the person of Jesus Christ. It is he who stands for love, as no one else has ever done, and pays the price for it. His crucifixion is the all-time high-water mark of love on earth. "While we were still helpless, at the right time Christ died for the ungodly" (Romans 5:6). No other source, whether inside or outside of religions, even comes close to what God in Christ shows of love. This is the first "move" of love in the process of redemption. "He first loved us" (1 John 4:19). Therefore, "love is from God" (1 John 4:7, PAR). And "We know love by this, that He laid down His life for us" (1 John 3:16). All other loves are to be measured by this standard (Acts 17:31).

When we receive what is thus clearly given, the revelation of God's love in Christ, that in turn makes it possible for us to love. Love is awakened in us by him. We feel its call—and first to love Jesus himself, and then God. Thus the first great commandment, to love God with all our being, can be fulfilled because of the beauty of God given in Christ. This is the *second* movement in the return to love: "We love, because He first loved us."

But the second movement is inseparable from the *third* movement: our love of others who love God. "If we love one another, God abides in us, and His love is perfected in us" (1 John 4:12). The first great commandment makes it possible to fulfill the second: love of neighbor as oneself. And loving others under God will ensure that we are loved by others. For to the others in our community of love, *we* are the "other" whom they love because *they* love and are loved by God. The fellowship of Christ's apprentices in kingdom living is a community of love (John 13:34-35). This is the *fourth* movement in the process of redeeming love.

Here, then, is the full account of the movements of love in our lives: We are loved by God who is love, and in turn we love him, and others through him, who in turn love us through him. Thus is love made perfect or complete. And "perfect love casts out fear" (1 John 4:18). That is, those who live in the fulfillment of God's redemptive love in human life will no longer experience fear. "Fear involves torment," John notes, and torment is incompatible with living in the full cycle of love (1 John 4:18, PAR). We live in the community of goodwill from a competent God.

Now, as St. Augustine saw long ago, the opposite of love is pride. Love eliminates pride because its will for the good of the other nullifies our arrogant presumption that we should get *our* way. We are concerned for the good of others and assured that our good is taken care of without self-will. Thus pride and fear and their dreadful offspring no longer rule our life as love becomes completed in us.

❧ JOY ❧

JOY IS NATURAL IN the presence of such love. Joy is a pervasive *sense*—not just a thought—of well-being: of overall and ultimate well-being. Its primary feeling component is delight in an encompassing good well-secured. It is not the same as pleasure, though it is pleasant. It is deeper and broader than any pleasure. Pleasure and pain are always specific to some particular object or condition, such as eating something you really like (pleasure) or recalling some really foolish thing you did (pain).

But for joy, *all* is well, even in the midst of specific suffering and loss. Self-sacrificial love is therefore always joyous—no matter the pain and loss it may involve. For we are always looking at the larger scene in which love rules: Where all things (no matter what) work together for good to those who love God and are drawn into his purposeful actions on earth.

Joy is a basic element of inner transformation into Christlikeness and of the outer life that flows from it. Thus when Jesus was explaining things to his closest friends on the night before his crucifixion, he left his peace with them (John 14:27). Then, after explaining to them how he would be the vine and they the branches, constantly drawing rich life from him, he said, "These things I have spoken to you, that My joy may be in you, and that your joy may be made full" (15:11). This theme of being *full* of joy is repeated twice more in John's version of his final discourse and prayer (16:24; 17:13).

Having one's joy "full" means that there is no room for any more of it. Full joy is our first line of defense against weakness, failure, and disease of mind and body. But even when they break through into our life, "the joy of the Lord is our strength" (Nehemiah 8:10, PAR). Thus the tribulation that came upon those in Thessalonica who received the word of Christ went hand in hand "with the joy of the Holy Spirit" (1 Thessalonians 1:6). The joy of Christ that fills us is received as a gift of divine impartation. "The kingdom of God is . . . righteousness and peace and joy in the Holy Spirit" (Romans 14:17). That is, it is righteousness (love), peace, and joy of a kind that can only be produced in us by the Holy Spirit.

But here again we must not be passive. We may allow joy to dissipate through looking backward at our sins and failures, or forward at what might happen to us, or inward at our struggles with work, responsibilities, temptations, and deficiencies. But this means we have placed our hopes in the wrong thing, namely ourselves, and we do not have to do this. It is our option to look to the greatness and goodness of God and what he will do in our lives. Therefore Paul, in jail, speaks to the Philippians of his own contentment "in whatever circumstances" (4:11) and urges them to "rejoice in the Lord always; again I will say, rejoice!" (4:4). We will be empowered by the Spirit of God to do this *if* we choose it and fix our minds on the good that God is and will certainly bring to pass.

"For Thou, O LORD, hast made me glad by what Thou has done, I will sing for joy at the works of Thy hands" (Psalm 92:4).

❧ PEACE ❧

PEACE IS THE REST of will that results from assurance about "how things will turn out." It is always a form of active engagement with good, plus assurance that things will turn out well. The dead are often spoken of as "at peace," but they are not at peace unless they are actually alive and doing well.

"I am at peace about it," we say, and this means I am no longer *striving,* inwardly or outwardly, to save some outcome dear to me or to avoid one that I reject. I have released whatever is at issue and am no longer even putting "body English" or "spin" on it or inwardly gritting my teeth.

Of course everyone is at peace about *some* things, one hopes, but few have peace in general, and fewer still have peace that reaches their body and its automatic responses to such a depth that it does not live in a covert state of alarm. Most people carry heavy burdens of care, and usually about the things that are most important in life: what will happen to their loved ones, their finances, health, death, their physical appearance or what others think of them, the future of society, their standing before God and their eternal destiny. To be at peace with God and others (family, neighbors, and coworkers) is a great attainment and depends on graces far beyond ourselves as well as on our own efforts. That is also true of being at peace with oneself.

Peace with God comes only from acceptance of his gift of life in his Son (Romans 5:1-2). We are then assured of the outcome of our life and are no longer trying to justify ourselves before God or others. We have accepted that we are not righteous or even totally competent and that we cannot be so on our own. We have laid down the burden of justifying ourselves before God and are learning not to justify ourselves before men. This is the peace that grows within us.

From those around me I must simply *assume* grace and mercy, not that I will get what I deserve. I am a beggar on my way through the world. Justice is not enough for my needs, and I couldn't stand it if I got it. When others do not extend the grace and mercy I need, I have to draw on the abundance of it in God. "Who is this that is condemning me?" I remind myself, "Jesus even died for me, was raised from the dead, and is now standing up for me before God" (Romans 8:34, PAR). Assurance of this allows me to "seek peace and pursue it" (1 Peter 3:11), no matter who is involved, and to "pursue peace with all men" (Hebrews 12:14). That includes all our family members and coworkers!

Even in cases where, through no fault of my own, there must be a struggle between me and others, there does not have to be a struggle *within* me. I may have to resist others, for some good reason, but even so I do not have to *make* things come out right. I am not the one in control of outcomes. I do not have to hate those whose course of action I resist, or even get mad at them, and so I can always be at peace within myself as well as toward them.

✎ REST ON THE GREATNESS OF GOD ✎

THE SECRET TO THIS peace is, as great apprentices of Jesus have long known, *being abandoned to God*. We have to return to this for a fuller treatment in our next chapter, on the will; but the person who is heartily abandoned to God knows that all shall be well because God is in charge of his or her life. My peace is the greatness of God.

Because he, who not only loves me but *is* Love, is so great, I live beyond harm in his hands; and there is nothing that can happen to me that will not turn out to my good. *Nothing.* That is what Romans 8:28 really means. Because of this, "Thou wilt keep him in perfect peace, whose mind is stayed on thee: because he trusteth in thee," the ancient text reads (Isaiah 26:3, KJV).

It makes supreme sense, therefore, that I should accept Paul's instruction to "be anxious for nothing, but in everything by prayer and supplication with thanksgiving let your requests be made known to God. And the peace of God, which surpasses all comprehension, shall guard your hearts and your minds in Christ Jesus" (Philippians 4:6-7).

The poet Sidney Lanier put this into beautiful images:

As the marsh-hen secretly builds on the watery sod,
Behold I will build me a nest on the greatness of God:
I will fly in the greatness of God as the marsh-hen flies
In the freedom that fills all the space 'twixt the marsh and the skies:
By so many roots as the marsh-grass sends in the sod
I will heartily lay me a-hold on the greatness of God.

The greatness and love of God forms my peace, and at the same time, my love and joy. Job had many worrisome questions in the midst of his troubled life. But when he beheld God, they simply did not matter and no longer seemed to need answering. He did not raise a single one of the questions he earlier had wanted to press upon God (Job 42:2-6). He was not bullied into silence by God coming to him, but really saw the all-sufficiency of God to his life and his soul. And this brought love, joy, and peace to him at one stroke.

✎ LOVE, JOY, AND PEACE CANNOT BE SEPARATED ✎

OF COURSE IT IS impossible to separate love, joy, peace, faith (confidence), and hope from one another in practice. They lose their true nature when separated.

Try imagining love without joy and peace, joy without love and peace, or peace without love and joy, or any combination of them without faith and hope.

You will see, upon making a slight effort, that love, joy, and so on, without the others just wouldn't be themselves. Or perhaps we have all *already* seen in this world far too much of "love" without joy and peace, or "peace" without love and joy, and so on. And joy without hope is one of the most exquisitely tortured blossoms of human despair, constantly cultivated by modern secularism (Thomas Hardy, Albert Camus, and on and on).

Far too often, however, we find such a separation to be something "religion" has accomplished. And that explains why "religion" as commonly practiced does not eliminate pride and fear, but routinely makes it worse. Pride and fear are the two roots of "the deeds of the flesh" described by Paul in Galatians 5:19-21 and elsewhere, governed by sensuality and malice and trailing clouds of other poisonous feelings resulting from them. So long as the will or spirit (heart) is governed by such feelings, life is simply hopeless.

By contrast, it is the positive movement into love, joy, and peace, based on faith and hope in God, that eliminates the destructive feelings or at least eliminates them as governing factors in our life. We do not go at the change the other way around, trying first to root out the destructive feelings. That is the common mistake of worldly wisdom and of much "religion" on such matters. But we know that in being with Jesus the destructive feelings, with their actions, will drop off us as we increasingly see that "with Thee is the fountain of life," and come to realize that "in Thy light we see light" (Psalm 36:9).

Love, joy, and peace fostered in divine fellowship simply crowd out fear, anger, unsatisfied desire, woundedness, rejection. There is no longer room for them—well, perhaps there is for a while, but increasingly less so. Belonging to Christ does not immediately eliminate bad feelings, and we must not be drawn into pretense that it does. But it does *crucify* them. "Those who belong to Christ Jesus," we read, "have crucified [past tense] the flesh with its passions and desires" (Galatians 5:24).

Belonging to Christ does mean that the merely fleshly passions and desires are on the way to death and already have ceased leading a life of their own, much less, then, leading our whole life as they used to. That is how it is with all negative and destructive feelings in those who have put Christ on the throne of their life and have taken their place on his cross.

❧ SOME THINGS WE CAN DO ❧

AND SO, PRACTICALLY SPEAKING, the renovation of the heart in the dimension of feeling is a matter of opening ourselves to and carefully cultivating love, joy, and peace: first by receiving them from God and from those already living in him, and then as we grow, extending love, joy, and peace to others and everything around us in attitude, prayer, and action. Following our VIM pattern, we must intend this and decide that it shall be in all we are and do. Of course our thought life, as already described, will be focused upon God. Then through grace we can translate this intention to dwell in love, joy, and peace into the fine texture of daily existence. Our walk with Jesus and the Father will teach us and show us the details of the means required to bring it to pass.

Here is some of the work to be done. For many of us, just coming to honest terms with what our feelings really are will be a huge task. Paul says in Romans 12:9, "Let love be without hypocrisy." That is, let it be genuine or sincere. To do only this will require serious effort, deep learning, and quantities of grace.

Our ordinary life and our religious associations are so permeated with insincere expressions of love, often alongside of contempt and anger, that it is hard not to feel forced into hypocrisy in some situations. But we can learn to avoid it, and we shall immediately begin to see what a huge difference that alone makes.

But there is much more to do. Very few people are without deep negative feelings toward others who are or have been closely related to them. Wounds carried steadily through the years have weighed us down and prevented spiritual growth in love, joy, and peace. They may have seeped over into our identity. We wouldn't know who we are without them. But they can be healed or dismissed, if we are ready to give them up to God and receive the healing ministry of his Word and Spirit. This applies similarly to hopelessness over not achieving things long sought or long lost.

In general, the task, once we have given ourselves to Christ, is to recognize the reality of our feelings and agree with the Lord to abandon those that are destructive and that lead us into doing or being what we know to be wrong. This he will then help us with. We may need to write out what those feelings are in a "letter to the Lord," or perhaps confer about them with a wise Christian friend who knows how to listen to us and to God at the same time.

Perhaps individuals or our fellowship group can have a prayer ministry to us. Journaling about progress with feelings can also help. It can bring to light the ideas and images or past events on which the destructive feelings are based. Those, too, will need to be replaced or revised. Many such details may play a role as we progress toward predominance of love, joy, and peace in that dimension of our mind and our self that is our feelings.

We can be very sure that this is God's intent for us. Thus Paul prayed for his friends in Ephesus that they would be "rooted and grounded in love" and "know the love of Christ which surpasses knowledge, that you may be filled up to all the fullness of God" (Ephesians 3:17-19). And we have seen the intent of Jesus: "That My joy may be in you, and that your joy may be made full" (John 15:11). Also his, "Peace I leave with you; My peace I give to you; not as the world gives, do I give you. Let not your heart be troubled nor let it be fearful" (John 14:27). And here is Paul's benediction to the Romans: "Now may the God of hope fill you with all joy and peace in believing, that you may abound in hope by the power of the Holy Spirit" (Romans 15:13).

THE EXTREME SERIOUSNESS OF FEELINGS FOR SPIRITUAL FORMATION

UNDERSTANDING OF THE ROLE of feelings in life and in the process of spiritual formation is absolutely essential if that process is to succeed as it should. There are many ways we can go wrong with reference to feelings. They are extremely influential on all that we are and do—much more so than they should be for our own good, and mainly because we accord them greater significance than they deserve.

They, more than any other component of our nature, are the "trigger" of sinful action. If you consider all of the Ten Commandments after the first two, for example, you will see that it is feelings out of control that lead to their violation. In his own magnificent treatment of the moral life, Jesus makes a point of putting anger, contempt, and lust in their place (Matthew 5:21 and following). Until that is done, nothing else works.[9]

We have noted how we go wrong in trying to manipulate feelings themselves without regard to their underlying condition. It is often done with good intent, but it is nearly always harmful to the deeper interests of the soul. That is especially true when we try to stir up feelings as a means of getting people to do what we think is good in the course of efforts at Christian ministry.

Feelings have a crucial role in life, but they must not be taken as a *basis* for action or character change. That role falls to insight, understanding, and conviction of truth, which will always be appropriately accompanied by feeling. Feelings are not fundamental in the nature of things but become so if we assign them that role in life, and then life will not go as it should. Many sincere professing Christians suffer in their walk with God because they made a commitment prompted by a feeling of "need" and not by insight into how things are with God and their soul.

Partly because of this faulty basis of commitment, the area of feeling is, I suspect, the most likely place of defeat for those sincerely seeking to follow Christ today. Satan uses feelings to captivate us today by making them more important to our life than they really are, as well as by inducing much false guilt about what we do and do not feel. Nowhere is this more obvious than in marriage and divorce as now practiced (or mis-practiced). But at all stages of adult life, feelings are among Satan's primary instrument. They are used to devastate the soul in the processes of aging, sickness, and death among Christians and nonChristians alike. This need not be the case. Appropriate spiritual formation in Christ will prevent it. We must understand how love, joy, and peace can be our portion in every state of life and can lead us into a radiant eternity with God.

Matters for
Thought and Discussion

1. Think of the great and direct power of feeling (sensation, emotion) over human life. How do you see this at work in daily life? For good? For evil? In yourself? In others?

2. What has been your experience with controlling feeling *directly* or "head on"? Can it reliably be done? What have you seen with respect to this in lives near you? Say with anger, lust, or addiction?

3. "Who would I be if I had different feelings structuring my life (say, those of a saint)?" Is this question one that strikes you as hard to answer?

4. When you need to resist a feeling (sensation, emotion), upon what do you stand to do so? What are your available resources? Consider irritation at an interruption, or anger at another driver.

5. Did it make any sense to you that love, hatred, and so on are not just feelings but conditions of the will, body, and so on, which have feelings linked to them? Do you see any problems with trying to manage feelings directly, without changing the underlying condition?

6. What is your experience with feelings *spreading*? Over different parts of your life and activity? Over groups?

7. What are some of the problems you see with basing decisions on feelings? Can we decide *without* feelings?

8. How can feelings be "godly"? Which ones are? Aren't?

9. How are hope and faith related to love, joy, and peace?

10. How does pride affect our other "feelings," say love and peace?

11. What are the "four movements" of love in the process of coming to live "without fear"?

12. How would you distinguish peace and joy? Can you *really* have one of them without the other one? Under what conditions?

13. How can one cultivate peace, or joy, or love, or hope? What are some specific ways you have found to be helpful? How does faith fit in?

TRANSFORMING THE WILL (HEART OR SPIRIT) AND CHARACTER

If any man is willing to do His will, he shall know
of the teaching, whether it is of God,
or whether I speak from Myself.
JOHN 7:17

Would you know who is the greatest saint in the world? It is
not he who prays most or fasts most; it is not he who gives
most alms or is most eminent for temperance, chastity, or
justice; but it is he who is always thankful to God, who
wills everything that God wills, who receives everything
as an instance of God's goodness and has a heart
always ready to praise God for it.
WILLIAM LAW

By this point we are beginning to get a glimpse of what those renovated in Christlikeness look like. We know that they will have a *thought life* centered on God in his goodness and greatness, and therefore on truth. Also, their *feelings* will be dominated by the rich array of positive feelings that naturally accompany love, joy, and peace, along with their foundational conditions of faith and hope.

But such conditions of thought and feeling are not to be produced and sustained without massive changes in *other* dimensions of the human being, nor do those massive changes in the other dimensions come about without corresponding transformations of thought and feeling. Each constituent of the human being distinguished in chapter 2 is but one element in an interlocking whole. Those constituents can to some degree be distinguished and described in isolation from the others, but they cannot actually exist or develop except in tandem with the others.

⤴ HOW THE MIND DEPENDS ON THE WILL ⤵

THIS IS TRUE IN a special manner with the will (spirit, heart). We have already noted how the will is totally dependent in its functioning upon the contents of the mind (thoughts, feelings). It is not possible to choose, which is the function of the will or spirit, except in terms of thoughts and feelings. The will is hemmed in by what our thoughts and feelings actually are at the time of willing. But now we need to develop further the idea that our thoughts and feelings also have a crucial dependence on our will, on our choices.

Here, as in much of what we are covering in this book, the issues run deep, and we must be careful not to go *too* deep. But we must also not go "too shallow." What we think is, in the adult person, very much a matter of what we allow ourselves to think, and what we feel is very much a matter of what we allow ourselves to feel. Moreover, what we think is very much a matter of what we wish and *seek* to think, and what we feel is very much a matter of what we wish and seek to feel. In short, the condition of our mind is very much a matter of the direction in which our will is set.

There is a kind of "back and forth" here, which is very important to understand for our purposes of spiritual formation. Obviously, the thoughts and feelings that the will depends on in any given moment of choice cannot be changed *in* that moment. But the will or heart can change the thoughts and feelings that are to be available to it in *future* choices. It is because of this that we are responsible for our character.

Our character is that internal, overall structure of the self that is revealed by our long-run patterns of behavior and from which our actions more or less automatically arise. It is character that explains why we use credit reports and resumes and letters of reference to make decisions about people. They do not just tell what someone did, but they reveal what kind of thoughts, feelings, and tendencies of will that person habitually acts from, and therefore how he or she will act in the future.

But character can be changed. And that, of course, is what spiritual formation in Christlikeness is about.

It may be, for example, that in a certain situation I have injured someone (possibly a loved one) by speaking or acting in anger. Domestic violence is a sad fact of life and is found in many forms the world over. But in a reflective moment I also may be remorseful and ask myself if I really want to be the kind of person (have the character of one) who does such things. If I do not want that, it will be necessary to change my thoughts and feelings. Just resolving "not to do it again" will be of little use. Will alone cannot carry us to change. But will *implemented through changing my thoughts and feelings* can result in my becoming the kind of person who just doesn't do that kind of thing anymore.

Of course we must, if we would change, be in possession of whatever those thoughts and feelings are that will enable us to choose to change precisely those thoughts and feelings that brought us to abuse our loved one in the first place. And if they are to be adequate to our spiritual needs, the former thoughts and feelings ultimately must come with "repentance toward God and faith in our Lord Jesus Christ." In the last analysis the remedy to the human situation must come, as our first diagram from chapter 2 tries to show, from the impact upon the human mind and will of the good news of Jesus Christ under the influence of the Holy Spirit. The human mind and will must be transformed through interaction with thoughts and feelings deriving from the Word and the Spirit.

IDENTIFICATION OF OUR WILL WITH GOD'S WILL

NOW WE ASK, WHAT does a will or heart look like that has been transformed into Christlikeness? How is it to be characterized?

Jesus said of himself—and of course he is always the pattern—"He who sent Me is with Me; He has not left Me alone, for I always do the things that are pleasing to Him" (John 8:29).

And Paul had this to say: "I have been crucified with Christ; and it is no longer I who live, but Christ lives in me; and the life which I now live in the flesh I live by the faith of the Son of God, who loved me, and delivered Himself up for me" (Galatians 2:20).

We also recall John Calvin's words: "The only haven of safety is to have no other will, no other wisdom, than to follow the Lord wherever he leads. Let this, then, be the first step, to abandon ourselves, and devote the whole energy of our minds to the service of God."

So we have the answer to our question: *Single-minded and joyous devotion to God and his will, to what God wants for us—and to service to him and to others because of him—is what the will transformed into Christlikeness looks like.* That is the outcome of Christian spiritual formation with reference to the will, heart, or spirit. And this outcome becomes our *character* when it has become the governing response of every dimension of our being. Then we can truly be said to have "put on Christ."

But how far this is from the usual human will and character we hardly need say! Instead of being simple and transparent through a constant and coherent devotion to God, the usual human will is a place of chaotic duplicity and confusion if not darkness, because it is the playing field of pride and fear and lack of confidence in God, shrouded in layer upon layer of destructive habits.

↜ THE BASIC NATURE OF THE WILL ↝

WE RECALL THAT OUR will (heart, spirit) is that dimension of our being by which we become an underivative presence and source in the world. *What comes from it comes from nothing else but us.* This radical creativity is what makes the individual person absolutely unique and irreplaceable, and therefore an "end in itself," not just "another one of a certain kind." In other words, it is what prevents a person from being a mere thing.

Let us try to put this in other words, hoping thereby to make clearer something that really is very hard to grasp.

Will is the ability to originate or refrain from originating something: an act or a thing. It brings things into existence. Sticks and stones do not have that ability. Will is the capacity for *radical* and *underivative* origination of events and things. Therefore it is the core of who and what we are as individuals, for what arises from it is from us *alone*. It is that aspect of personality in virtue of which we have a likeness to God or are "in His image." We are created to be creators—of good.

"Our consents and non-consents," as William James said, "are the measure of our worth as men . . . the one strictly underivative and original contribution which we make to the world."[1] And our will is simply our capacity for "consents" and "non-consents." It is the core of our nonphysical being. It is, strictly speaking, *our* spirit—the human spirit, not divine—though it comes directly from God and is meant to be in his keeping through our trust in him.

It is the nature of the *spiritual* to be self-determined. Such self-determination is absolute or unrestricted in God ("I AM *THAT* I AM." Exodus 3:14, KJV, emphasis added; compare John 5:26). But it is very limited, though still very real, in man. Its primary exercise in the human, as we have already noted, is the power to select what we think on and how intently we will focus on it—from which our other decisions and actions then more or less directly flow.

Functionally, as we pointed out in chapter 2, the will is the executive center of the human self. From it the whole self or life is meant to be directed and organized, and must be if it is to be directed or organized at all. That is why we recognize the will to be the same as the biblical "heart" or *center.*

It is also clear, then, that will is not the same thing as *character,* but character does develop from it, as specific willings become habitual and, to some extent, "automatic." Character is revealed most of all in what we feel and do without thinking. But to a lesser extent it is revealed in what we repent of *after* thinking and what we then do as a result of repenting. Thought, feeling, and will give rise to character.

⤙ WILL AND HUMAN DIGNITY ⤚

WHY DOESN'T GOD JUST force us to do the things he knows to be right? It is because that would lose precisely that which he has intended in our creation: freely chosen character. The centrality of will to personhood is what makes it immediately and strongly precious and gives the person *dignity*. Dignity is a worth so great that it disallows exchanging a person for anything else.[2] The great worth of the person explains why Jesus Christ would die for the sake of individual human beings and be satisfied with the outcome (Isaiah 53:11; Hebrews 12:2).

We treasure the will or choice in ourselves and in others spontaneously, without having to learn it. Will has obvious, intrinsic, and supreme value. The small child, without *learning* to do so, values its capacity to act on its own, which it quickly identifies and stubbornly defends. The sense of things flowing from itself is unmistakable and joyous and irrepressible. And adults delight to see the child's will emerge—"Look at what she did!" and "Did you hear what he said?!" In the child and in the adult, this sense of creativity is basic to health and well-being.

Choice, the *exercise* of will and spirit, is valued and carefully guarded throughout life; and at the end of life we want to think we uniquely "have made a difference"—always for good, of course. But such an outcome is not automatically so—and certainly not so to the degree it could be and should be. For the human will in the individual is not only precious, it is a problem. From the strictly human point of view it is a devastating and unsolvable problem. Everyone has the experience of willing in a way that is contrary to other choices they have already made or ones that should be made. Human life in its usual forms is characterized by conflict within the will and between wills. But such a statement does not do justice to the facts. What we call "civilization" is a smoldering heap of violence constantly on the verge of bursting into flame. That is the true picture of the fallen human will.

⤙ THE SPLINTERED WILL ⤚

THE DRIVE TOWARD GOOD, which is naturally implanted in the human will by its Creator, is splintered, corrupted, and eventually turned against itself as a result of practical self-deification and all that accompanies it. The question, "What good can I bring about?" is replaced by "How can I get my way?" Manipulation, deception, seduction, and malice replace transparency, sincerity, and goodwill, as exaltation of self replaces submission and service to God.

Reflecting on fallen humanity "as usual," the existentialist thinkers of the last two centuries have emphasized the splintered, self-conflicted, and frustrated condition of the human will in its natural state. Freud and many other psychologists have, in their own ways, done the same. All of this has now become a part of the modern person's self-understanding and is accepted as part of standard educational programs and of the popular and other arts.

Jean-Paul Sartre and his existentialist associates accordingly turned the ridicule of *sincerity,* as necessarily a posture of self-deception, into a fine art.[3] Ambiguity of will was elevated by them and others into basic human nature, from which "freedom" was made to emerge in the form of arbitrary—perhaps totally irrational—decision and action. Doesn't that sound like *Helter Skelter* once more? As an account of the usual fallen humanity, theirs was really a very penetrating analysis—one now standard in literary, musical, and cinematic presentations of life.

Whereas in prior times a focused and coherent will was assumed to be necessary to human freedom, today the assumption is that freedom only comes with an incoherent and vagrant will. Truth, by contrast, is regarded as bondage and a rigorous identity as a prison that prevents me from endlessly creating myself and re-creating myself.

❧ THE OPPORTUNITY TO BE LOST ❧

CERTAINLY THE WILL OF a spiritual being is the one thing in his creation that God chooses *not* to override and force to take on a specific character. He allows it to go its way or ways. But that does not mean that such a being gets what it wants. Indeed, that proves to be impossible for such a will, which is following a delusion. It only means that God will not force it to do what *he* wants.

It has its choice—though it does not have its choice of the consequences of choosing what it wants. And one of the consequences of choosing what one wants without regard to God's will is enslavement to one's own self-conflicted will. On the path of self-will people eventually come to the place where they cannot choose what God wants and cannot want God. They can only want—themselves! "I wake and feel the fell of dark," the poet Gerard Manley Hopkins wrote,

> The lost are like this, and their scourge to be
> As I am mine, their sweating selves.[4]

This is the condition of the "lost," earlier described. Obviously there is something very deep here and something crucial to God's purposes in creating human beings, which we at present cannot understand.

Thus God permits there to be a world such as we live in, where the wills of human beings are often set on what is evil, wrong, or foolish and where even good and wise inclinations are frequently defeated by other components of the persons involved: the "sin in our members," social influences, mistaken ideas, overwhelming feelings, or disconnections and ruptures in the depths of the soul. The outcome may be a whole person (or even a whole society) intently focused upon accomplishing evil, or it may be a person (or society) baffled and torn by the chaos and evil it finds within itself—as is the "modern liberal" person and society of today.[5]

❧ Duplicity, Deceitfulness, and Darkness ❧

THE CONSTANT CHARACTER OF the will apart from God is *duplicity*—or, more accurately, fragmentation and multiplicity. It wills many things and they cannot be reconciled with each other. Turned away from God, thought and feeling fall into chaos, and the will, for reasons given above, cannot but follow. There is nothing outside it that can pull or push it right.

But this conflicted complexity may go unrecognized or unacknowledged. The will *seems* very simple when we first reflect upon it. We decide to go to the grocery, for example, to buy milk and bread. We decide to tell the truth (or not) in a difficult situation. The decision or choice seems as simple as a puff of wind on our cheek. But this is only because it is a nonphysical act or event, which we must strongly exert ourselves to grasp. "Who can distinguish darkness from the soul?" the poet Yeats inquired. Compared to a reading lamp or ballpoint pen, for example, its parts do not leap out at us.

When we come to reflect more deeply, however, we suddenly realize that a choice or act of will is not simple at all. The understandings, feelings, and purposes that enter into it may be highly complicated, as are the degrees of strength with which it is taken, as well as the other motivations and actions and choices to which it is related. It is a rich field for the play of good or of evil.

In a condition of alienation from God, the complexity of the human will moves irresistibly toward duplicity, not just in the harmless sense of "doubleness," but in the sense of deception. This is the result of pretending to feel and think one way while acting in another. Often the deception involved is self-deception. Our pride will constantly trap us between desire and fear. Rather than surrender our desire, we will do what we want but conceal it because of fear of the consequences of being known. And perhaps then we will also try to conceal our fear because of our pride. We will try to pretend that there is "nothing going on" at all.

Accordingly, the natural and proper complexity of the will leads those thus living as their own god in their world into ever-deeper layers of deception, and then into darkness, where they cannot even understand themselves and why they do what they do. Adults who in their childhood had to hold the lives of addicted parents and their family together may be among the clearest illustrations of this heartbreaking condition, but in some degree everyone is subject to it.

The existentialist portrayal of sincerity as *always* bogus is in fact a correct picture of the will *apart from God,* and its emphasis upon the natural complexity of the human will is correct and helpful. That natural complexity is good and God-given. It is an essential part of human greatness. But the deceitfulness and darkness of the heart *apart* from God is inevitable to those who trust only themselves and so must try to take charge of their life and their world. Then, as we have quoted previously, "the heart is devious above all else; it is perverse—who can understand it?" (Jeremiah 17:9, NRSV). And the answer to that question is, as the prophet continues in the very next verse to say: "I the LORD test the mind and search the heart, to give to all according to their ways." To God the amazing duplicity of the human heart is totally transparent.

Sad to say, we live in a world where others, including our loved ones as well as the institutions of society and government (and those running them) are with distressing regularity engaged in duplicity, deceitfulness, and darkness. It is a rare individual who does not have people around him or her who cannot be trusted to do what is right when something they desire or fear is involved. How often we have to deal with someone whom we know at the moment to be simply working out *how* he or she is going to mislead us. Perhaps very few of us could honestly say we are untouched in some way by our own duplicity. Few of us could honestly say that we do not sometimes have to struggle to overcome deceit and darkness, within ourselves as well as around us.

Our only hope is to entirely place our confidence in the God and Father of Jesus Christ, who is willing to enter the duplicity of our heart and bring it wholly to himself if we earnestly invite him. He is *"greater than our heart,* and knows all things" (1 John 3:20, emphasis added).

❧ GOD HEARS THE HEART ❧

THE HEART (WILL, SPIRIT) is precisely what God observes and addresses in human beings. He cares little or nothing for outward show. He responds to the heart because it is, above all, who we are: who we choose and have chosen to be. What God wants of us can only come from there. He respects the centrality of our will and will not override it. He seeks godly character in us and for us, to fulfill the eternal destiny he has in mind for us.

But on the other hand, he is sensitive to the slightest move of the heart toward him. This is the witness of both the Bible and of life. It doesn't matter whether you are "religious" or not ("Jew" or "Greek"), for "The same one is Lord of all, abounding in riches for all who call upon Him; for 'Whoever will call upon the name of the LORD will be saved'" (Romans 10:12-13).

Multitudes of people have come to a full knowledge of God because in a moment of complete hopelessness they prayed "The Atheist's Prayer" or something like it: "O God, if there is a God, save my soul if I have a soul." When that is the true cry of the heart, of the inmost spirit of the individual, who has no longer any hope other than God, God hears and responds without fail. It is as if he has a "heart monitor" installed in every person. And when the heart truly reaches out to God *as* God, no longer looking to itself or others, he responds with the gift of "life from above."

In fact, God is constantly *looking for* people who will worship him "in spirit and in truth." What does that mean? It means people who have free-hearted and wholehearted admiration, respect, and commitment to God as the highest being of all. They never try to conceal anything from him and always rely completely on him. God is actively seeking such people, whoever they may turn out to be—even a despised, sixth-hand woman of Samaria, so ashamed that she would dare go to the well for water only in the heat of noonday, to avoid social contacts (John 4:6). God is spirit, we recall, and nothing is hidden from him. So those who worship him must worship him in spirit and therefore in truth (4:23-24). At the level of the human spirit, nothing can be hidden. Lying always depends upon the use of our body.

❧ SHOUTING TO GOD ❧

NO GREAT SOPHISTICATION OR information about God is required to be reached by God. Edith Schaeffer tells of a man from the Lisu tribe far out in the hills back of China. There was in him a great longing for a God he did not know. One day he found on a mountain path a page torn from a Lisu catechism. He read: "Are there more gods than One?"—"No, there is only One God." "Should we worship idols?"—"No . . . " And the rest was torn away.

He went home and destroyed his altars. Immediately his daughter became very ill and his neighbors taunted him for making the demons angry. The man thought if there was one true God perhaps he could reach that God with his voice. He knew nothing about prayer, but he climbed to the top of the highest peak in the vicinity—twelve or fourteen thousand feet high—and shouted out, "Oh, God, if You really are there and You are the One I am to worship, please make my little girl well again."

It took a long time to climb back down, but upon arriving home he found the little girl completely well, with no time of recuperation needed.

She had recovered at the time he had prayed. That man became an effective evangelist across the entire area. Edith Schaeffer comments: "There will be so many stories to compare with [this man's] that I picture us taking thousands of years to find out about them all."[6] This is because of the seeking God who constantly "monitors" hearts.

And as for those whose heart is at its core completely given to him, who completely rely on and hope in him, "The eyes of the LORD move to and fro throughout the earth that He may strongly support" them (2 Chronicles 16:9). And "the eyes of the LORD are toward the righteous, and His ears are open to their cry" (Psalm 34:15). Little children, whose hearts are not fully formed are especially cared for by God. "Their angels in the heavens are always in direct contact with my Father in the heavens" (Matthew 18:10, PAR). Knowing what happens to little children in this world, how could one keep their sanity without such an assurance? Jesus assures us that children *are* cared for by God, no matter how things appear to our senses.

☙ FROM SURRENDER TO DRAMA ☙

IN THE PROGRESSION TOWARD complete identification of our will with God's there are distinctions to be noted. First there is *surrender*. When we surrender our will to God we consent to his supremacy in all things. Perhaps we do so grudgingly. We recognize his supremacy intellectually, and we concede to it in practice—though we still may not like it, and parts of us may still resist it.

We may not be able to do his will, but we are willing to will it. In this condition there is still much grumbling and complaining about our life and about God. Andrew Murray comments that "we find the Christian life so difficult because we seek for God's blessing while we live in our own will. We should be glad to live the Christian life according to our own liking."[7]

Still, this is an important move forward. The center of the self, the heart or spirit, is now willing for God to be God—even if with little hope or enthusiasm. Perhaps it is only willing to be made willing. But it is for lack of this minimal identification with God's will that multitudes of people are unable to *understand* the truth of Jesus (John 7:17). Such persons are *not* willing to do his will, and hence God does not open their understanding, and they cannot do so. They are left to struggle in the darkness, which in fact they desire. And they will certainly reproach God for not giving them more light, though they are unwilling to act on the light they have.

But if grace and wisdom prevail in the life of the one who only surrenders to God's will, he or she will move on to abandonment. Then the individual is *fully* surrendered. There is no longer any part of himself or herself that holds back from God's will. Typically, at this point, surrender now covers all the circumstances of life, not just the truth about God and his explicit will (commandments) for human beings, given through the Bible.

While some things that happen to us may clearly not be what God would wish or has brought about, yet he does allow all — the tragic loss of a loved one, for example, or of health or opportunity, or a grievous wrong done to us by the sins of others. Otherwise such things would not happen. We therefore no longer fret over "the bad things that happen to good people," though we may undergo much hardship and suffering. While he does not cause these things to happen, we now accept them as within his plan for good to those who love him and are living in his purposes (Romans 8:28). *Irredeemable* harm does not befall those who willingly live in the hand of God. What an astonishing reality!

Accordingly, older Christian writers often speak of how we are privileged to "kiss the rod" of affliction which strikes us, even while trembling with weakness and pain. What a crucial lesson this is for spiritual transformation! We cease to live on edge, wondering, "Will God do what I want?" Pain will not turn to bitterness or disappointment to paralysis. Such a one has learned, in the words of Tennyson, to

> . . . so forecast the years,
> And find in loss a gain to match,
> And reach a hand through time to catch
> The far-off interest of tears.

But there is still more. Beyond abandonment is *contentment* with the will of God: not only with his being who he is and ordaining what he has ordained in general, but with the lot that has fallen to us. At this point in the progression toward complete identification with the will of God, gratitude and joy are the steady tone of our life. We are now *assured* that God has done, and will always do, well by us — no matter what! Dreary, foot-dragging surrender to God looks like a far distant country. Also, at this point, duplicity looks like utter foolishness in which no sane person would be involved. Grumbling and complaining are gone (Philippians 2:14-15) — not painstakingly resisted or eliminated, but simply unthought of. "Rejoice evermore" is natural and appropriate.

From Abandonment to Contentment — and Participation

But we are not done yet! Beyond contentment lies intelligent, energetic *participation* in accomplishing God's will in our world. We are no longer spectators, but are caught up in a vivid and eternal drama in which we play an essential part. We embrace our imposed circumstances, no matter how tragic they seem, and act for the good in a power beyond ourselves. "We are reigning—exercising dominion—in life by One, Christ Jesus" (Romans 5:17, PAR), looking toward an eternity of reigning with God through ages of ages (Revelation 22:5). We take action to accomplish the will of God in his power. *Our* tiny "willpower" is not the source of our strength. We hardly notice any exercise of it, though it is fully dedicated to carrying out God's purposes in every respect. But we are carried along by the power of the divine drama within which we live actively engaged. So far from struggling to resist sin, we are devoted to realization of righteousness all around us. This is the real meaning of "Yet not I, but Christ liveth in me." The strongest human will is always the one that is surrendered to God's will and acts *with* it.

This progression toward full identification of our will with God's will is one that, perhaps for most people, may not be fully realized in this life. But that does not really matter. It is a progression that is *there* for us to enter into *now,* through the power at work within us as disciples of Jesus Christ. It may be that at present we cannot even imagine what it would be like for us to have a will significantly identified with God's will as just described. But we must never forget that he "is able to do exceeding abundantly beyond all that we ask or think, in terms of the power that is working within us" (Ephesians 3:20, PAR; compare Isaiah 64:4). Our part is to begin as best we can.

❧ "To Will One Thing" ☙

NOW, WHEN WE SET out on the path of the surrendered will we find we must come to grips with our fallen character. This character will have taken over our habitual or "automatic" ways of thinking and feeling, shaped our social world past and present, permeated our body and its responses, and even sunk down into the unconscious depths of our soul. As the diagram on page 40 indicates, what we actually do arises out of all these factors. In their fallen character these factors will usually not be in accordance with the genuine intentions of our reborn spirit or will. The fallen character in fact poises every element of our being against God.

The condition we find ourselves in can best be described as one of *entanglement.* By contrast, the condition we must move to is that of single-minded focus upon doing the will of God in everything, distracted by nothing.

C. T. Studd once upset some of his missionary comrades in the Congo by what he called his "DCD Campaign." "DCD" stood for "Don't Care a Damn" for anything but Christ. He made up a skull and crossbones insignia and imposed "DCD" upon it, to wear on jackets and caps and to stick on buildings and equipment. "His intention was that he and his missionary team should care for *nothing* before Christ (not even their family and friends). Nothing should be allowed to detract from that or conflict with it. All lesser desires had to be done to death (hence the macabre badge!)."[8] Some people, of course, were more concerned about language they thought was wrong than about hearts not set wholly on Christ.

In our fallen world very few people live with a focused will, even a will focused on an evil. We have heard from W. B. Yeats that "the best lack all conviction, while the worst are full of passionate intensity." But, in fact—and we can be thankful for this—even "the worst" rarely have much intensity about them. There are always the "Hitlers" of this world, however. Evil people who are genuinely focused can gain the great power they do over others because of the fact that good people and evil people alike are, for the most part, simply drifting through life.

The "CEO" of the self has abandoned its post to other dimensions of the self and is dragged hither and thither by them. In our culture today the direction of the self is usually left to feelings; and the will, if it is recognized at all, is either identified with feelings or else regarded as helpless in the face of feelings. The cognitive side of the mind is hijacked to rationalize it all by producing or borrowing suitable "insights," usually lying ready to hand in surrounding culture.

David Hume's eighteenth-century claim that "reason is and ought only to be the slave of the passions" was prophetic of a world to come—our present world—to the existence of which he significantly contributed: a world of perpetual drift in which manipulation and entanglement of the will is simply unavoidable.

"Purity of heart," Kierkegaard once said, "is to will one thing." Before we can come to rest in such single-mindedness as the habitual orientation of all dimensions of our being, to allow it and to sustain it, a serious battle is required. But the call of grace and wisdom is nonetheless to "lay aside every encumbrance, and the sin which so easily entangles us, and . . . run with endurance the race that is set before us, fixing our eyes on Jesus" (Hebrews 12:1-2) and on his own example of single-minded pursuit of God's will, even to the point of death.

"No soldier in active service entangles himself in the affairs of everyday life," Paul reminded Timothy, "so that he may please the one who enlisted him as a soldier" (2 Timothy 2:4). Dear Martha was "worried and bothered about so many things," as Jesus pointed out, while only a few things are necessary, really only one, "Mary has chosen the good part, which shall not be taken away from her" (Luke 10:41-42). And Paul's own testimony was that he really did only one thing, which was to "press on toward the goal for the prize of the upward call of God in Christ Jesus" (Philippians 3:13-14).

ᔰ THE POWER OF UNTAMED DESIRE ᔰ

NOW, THE PRIMARY SOURCE of our entanglement is our desires—really, not just our desires themselves, but our enslavement to them and confusion about them. Temptation to sin always originates in desire (James 1:14-15). We have set our hearts on too many different things, some of which are wrong or evil, and all of which are in conflict with some others. We have already discussed this matter with reference to James 4:1-3. Here, perhaps, we need to add that habitual following of a desire leads to strengthening the power of that desire over us. In the realm of the will there is something like the power of inertia in the physical realm. It is easier to do what you have done than what you have not, and especially than what goes *contrary* to what you have done. You tend to keep on doing what you have done; and the more so, the more you have done it. That is spiritual inertia.

We may come to identify our will with our desire, and a powerful desire may throw us into something like a hypnotic state in order to achieve its satisfaction—often in horrible deeds. In addition, when the will is enslaved to a desire, it will in turn enslave the mind. To justify itself in satisfying the desire, the will enlists the intellect to provide rationalizations, frequently so bizarre that they amount to selective insanity. Then of course the individual in question does and says things that make no sense to anyone. They are hypnotized by their evil desires.

That is where the entanglements of the will with desire can lead and do lead. The "news" and the media keep cases of this constantly before us, and we need to understand what we are looking at. Otherwise we too will stand at a loss with those who say, "How could people do such things?" We need to realize that the less sensational entanglements of ordinary lives—perhaps Christian lives—are precisely what keep well-intentioned people from following Christ into the depths and heights of spiritual transformation.[9]

ᔰ GETTING FREE FROM ENTANGLEMENT ᔰ

OUR PRIMARY, PRACTICAL AIM in stepping free from the "entanglements" must be to overcome duplicity. And to overcome it we must become conscious of it, confront it, and take appropriate steps to forsake it. The point of reference in all of this is *the explicit teachings of the Bible concerning the will of God.* He that "has my commandments and keeps them, he it is that loves me," Jesus said (John 14:21). The person who intends to will what God wills—to identify his or her will with God's—begins with what God has *said* he wills. And we do not need to know *all* he has said, though under New Testament teaching that is not as difficult as it sounds (Romans 13:8-10). We can begin with what we know he has said. Let us firmly decide to do that. This will quickly lead us into the depths of spiritual transformation, including adequate knowledge of all of his will for us.

Who does not know, for example, that it is God's will we should be without guile and malice? Then let us decide never to mislead people and never to do or say things merely to cause pain or harm. Let us decide that today, right now, we will not do such things. You might think that this is a very small part of identifying with God's will. But in fact lying and malice are *foundational* sins. They make possible and actual many other sins. If you removed them, the structure of evil in the individual and in society would be very largely eliminated. From family fights and breakups to warfare, the human landscape would be transformed beyond recognition.

Of course when we begin to implement our decision, we discover that it is no simple task. We discover what a grip duplicity and malice have on us in every dimension of our being. Our thoughts and feelings and our usual routines of action, and perhaps even forces beyond our conscious grasp or understanding, have an influence over our choices that is much more powerful and complicated than we ever imagined while we simply went along with them.

We can never sufficiently emphasize the fact that spiritual formation cannot be a matter of just changing the will itself. That is central, of course, but it cannot be accomplished except by transformation of the other dimensions of the self. We discover that mere intention or effort of will is not enough to bring about the change in us that we have hoped for and to free us from duplicity and malice. Still, we must hold to that intention and sincerely make the effort, and then we will find that help is available.

◦ THE ROLE OF SPIRITUAL DISCIPLINES HERE ◦

A MAJOR SERVICE OF spiritual disciplines—such as solitude (being alone with God for long periods of time), fasting (learning freedom from food and how God directly nourishes us), worship (adoration of God, as discussed in chapter 6), and service (doing good for others with no thought of ourselves)—is to cause the duplicity and malice that is buried in our will and character to surface and be dealt with. Those disciplines make room for the Word and the Spirit to work in us, and they permit destructive feelings—feelings that are usually veiled by standard practices and circumstances and by long accepted rationalizations—to be perceived and dealt with for what they are: our will and not God's will. Those feelings are normally clothed in layer upon layer of habitual self-deception and rationalization. Typically, they will have enslaved the will, and it in turn will have coerced the mind to conceal or rationalize what is really going on. Your mind will really "talk to you" when you begin to deny fulfillment to your desires, and you will find how subtle and shameless it is. I know this from experience.

For example, our "righteous judgments" on others may, as we practice solitude or service, be recognized as ways of putting them down and us up. Our extreme busyness may be revealed as inability to trust God or unwillingness to give others a chance to contribute. Our readiness to give our opinions may turn out to be contempt for the thoughts and words of others or simply a willingness to shut them up.

Truly becoming one who wills above all to act with the kingdom of God and to have his kind of goodness (Matthew 6:33) will not happen overnight. But upon a path of clear intention and decision, with appropriate spiritual disciplines and accompanying grace to illumine and correct us when we fail, it is not as far away as many would suppose. The duplicities, entanglements, and evil intents that infect our will *can* be clarified and eliminated as we keep our eyes on Jesus, who initiated and perfects our faith, and "who for the joy set before Him endured the cross, despising the shame, and has sat down at the right hand of the throne of God" (Hebrews 12:2).

⨳ SWEET WILL OF GOD ⨳

DO WE THEN LOSE ourselves? To succeed in identifying our will with God's will is not, as is often mistakenly said, to have no will of our own. Far from it. To have no will is impossible. It would be to not even be a person. Rather, it is for the first time to have a will that is fully functional, not at war with itself, and capable of directing all of the parts of the self in harmony with one another under the direction of God. Now we do not hesitate to do what is right; and to do wrong we would have to work against ourselves.

In chapter 2 we said that a person with a well-kept heart is "a person who is *prepared* and *capable* of responding to the situations of life in ways that are 'good and right'." When through spiritual transformation we have in some measure come to know the well-kept heart in real life, we experience it as a gift of grace, no matter how hard we may have had to struggle in the process of growing into it. And it is a gift in which we find, precisely, ourselves, as Jesus taught: "He who has lost his life for My sake shall find it" (Matthew 10:39).

For the first time we not only have a fully functioning will, but we also have a clear identity in the eternal kingdom of God and can day by day translate our time into an eternity embedded in our own life and in the lives of those near us. The will of God is not foreign to our will. It is sweetness, life, and strength to us. Our heart sings,

Sweet will of God,
Oh, hold me closer,
'Til I am wholly lost in Thee.

Matters for
Thought and Discussion

1. How can we be responsible for our character if *in the moment of choice* we are always dependent upon the thoughts and feelings we have at the moment? How can we purposively set about to change our own character (with God's assistance of course)?

2. What, in your own words, does it mean to have "put on Christ," to have put off the old person and put on the new (Colossians 3:9-10)?

3. What in our makeup constitutes our *will*?

4. How does "getting my way" result in a "splintered" will that is ambiguous and incapable of sincerity?

5. What is the condition of the will in a "lost" person?

6. How do duplicity, deception, and darkness descend upon those who would be their own god?

7. What kind of person is God actively seeking?

8. How does *drama*—a dramatic life—arise out of surrender to God's will?

9. "Kiss the rod of affliction"—is that for you and me?

10. What do you think of C. T. Studd's "DCD Campaign"? Could you have one in your church?

11. Have you seen first-hand the effects of the "entanglements" of desire on life?

12. Do you know anyone who cannot tell the difference between desire and will, and hence does not know how to oppose his of her own desires?

13. Does it make sense to you that spiritual disciplines could retrain the will and reform character?

14. What would it be like for you to be "wholly lost in the will of God"?

TRANSFORMING
THE BODY

*Are you unaware that your body is a shrine to the Holy Spirit
from God, Who is within you? And that you are not your own
property? A price has been paid for you. So make your body
a showplace of God's greatness.*
1 CORINTHIANS 6:19-20, PAR

*No longer present the parts of your body to sin as weapons of
wickedness, but present yourselves to God like people who,
coming out of death, have eternal life; and present your
bodily parts to him as weapons of righteousness.*
ROMANS 6:13, PAR

Spiritual transformation into Christlikeness, I have said, is the process of
forming the inner world of the human self in such a way that it takes on
the character of the inner being of Jesus himself. The result is that the "outer"
life of the individual increasingly becomes a natural expression of the inner
reality of Jesus and of his teachings. Doing what he said and did increasingly
becomes a part of who we are.

But for this to happen *our body* must increasingly be poised to do what
is good and refrain from what is evil. *The inclinations to wrongdoing that literally inhabit its parts must be eliminated.* The body must come to serve us as a
primary ally in Christlikeness.

For good or for evil, *the body lies right at the center of the spiritual life*—a
strange combination of words to most people. One can immediately see all
around us that the human body is a (perhaps in some cases even *the*) primary
barrier to conformity to Christ. But this certainly was not God's intent for the
body. It is not in the nature of the body as such. (The body is not inherently
evil.) Nor is it even *caused* by the body. But still it is a fact that the body usually hinders people in doing what they know to be good and right. Being

formed in evil it, in turn, fosters evil and constantly runs ahead of our good intentions—but in the opposite direction.

Still our body is a good thing. God made it for good. That is why the way of Jesus Christ is so relentlessly incarnational. The body *should* be cherished and properly cared for, not as our master, however, but as a servant of God. For most people, on the other hand, their body *governs* their life. And *that* is the problem. Even professing Christians, by and large, devote to their spiritual growth and well-being a tiny fraction of the time they devote to their body, and it is an even tinier fraction if we include what they worry about.

What is going on here? Can our body truly become our ally in Christlikeness? It can and it must, but its essential role in spirituality is the one thing most likely to be overlooked in understanding and practicing growth in grace.

✎ OUR BODY WRONGLY POSITIONED IN LIFE ✐

IN THE CHAPTER "RADICAL Evil in the Ruined Soul" I explained how human ruin comes from placing oneself at the center of one's universe, in place of God. We further saw how this naturally, if not inevitably, leads to worship of the body and to the life of sensuality that results. The body becomes our primary source of gratification and the chief, if not the only, instrument for getting what we want. That is a perversion of the role of the body in life as God intended it; and it results in "death," in alienation from God and the loss of all we will have invested our lives in (Galatians 6:8).

Therefore Paul tells us that those who live in terms of the "flesh"—the merely natural powers of the human being, based in the human body—have their minds set on (or are totally preoccupied with) the flesh (or what they can manage on their own). He continues on to say that to have the mind "set on" the flesh in this way is "death" (Romans 8:5-6). Such a mind is naturally hostile toward God because God threatens *its* god. And it is unable to live in accordance with what God says, because it is working against God (Romans 8:7).

To understand this situation and how it must be transformed, we must look more deeply into the role of physical reality, especially of our own body, in the human life. What is the body, and what is its main function in relation to us?

✎ THE BASIC NATURE OF OUR BODY
AND OF PHYSICAL OBJECTS ✐

FROM ONE ESSENTIAL PERSPECTIVE, our body, and physical objects in general, are *potential energy*. To possess and access that energy is the constant human goal and problem. Only by succeeding here can we extend our "kingdom." If there is gasoline in my tank, I can liberate the energy in it and make it do work by driving my car. I can liberate the energy in a piece of wood by burning it in a fireplace to warm myself, or in a stove to cook my food, or (in other days) in a steam engine to move myself across the countryside over a stretch of railroad track. I can liberate some of the energy in a hamburger by eating it. We can now liberate the energy in atoms by "splitting" them. (I am told there is enough energy in a raisin to supply power to New York City for an entire day.)

But now notice how central my *own* body is in all of this. I can only liberate and use the energy in other physical objects by using my own body. It too is potential energy. But there is a great difference. My body is the only body whose energy is *directly accessible* for my own use and satisfaction. I access it by choice. Even the child that sucks its thumb has mastered this basic fact. It gets little energy, perhaps, but obviously a lot of satisfaction from this direct use of its body.

ᴥ My Body Becomes Me ᴥ

THEREFORE MY BODY IS the original and primary place of *my dominion* and my responsibility. It is only through it that I have a *world* in which to live. That is why it, and not other physical objects in my world, is part of who I am and is essential to my identity. My life experiences come to me through or in conjunction with my body. Thus my parents and my date and place of birth are bodily realities that are foundational to who I am.

It is only with and through my body that I receive a place in time and space and human history. Through it I am given a family, a gender, a language and national culture, and a set of talents along with opportunities to use them.

But there is more. Upon this already very complicated basis I begin to extend *my kingdom* and I take on voluntary aspects of my identity. First I must take dominion over my body itself (eye movement, voice, motions of limbs and bowels, and so on), but very quickly over other bodies—Mama and Papa, toys, playmates and animals, and on and on. I generate a realm in which I am driven by desire and channeled by ideas, sensations, and emotions that play over my body. I come to have a history, a track record that tells the truth about me in depth and from which I can never escape.

ᴥ My Body, My Character, and My Body Language ᴥ

NOW, IN DEVELOPING MY dominion I soon run into realities that do not yield to my will. Often these are the kingdoms of other individuals, organized around their desires and contrary to my own. So I begin to experience destructive emotions, especially fear, anger, envy, jealousy, and resentment. (Here is Cain.) These may, in time, develop into settled attitudes of hostility, contempt, or indifference.

Such attitudes make me ready to harm others or to see them suffer, and these attitudes quickly settle into my body. There they become more or less overt tendencies to act without thinking in ways that harm others or even myself. These attitudes are quite apparent to others, even if they are unwilling or unable to say it; and they come to form what has been called, in a useful concept, "body armor." (Notice how we hold and use our body and its parts as a soldier might use armor.) If left unchecked, our parts will rule the rest of our lives and will constantly inject poison into our social world and personal relations.

Of course the development of the body in the domain of the self is not all negative. It is in fact largely positive. We learn many things that are productive of good for ourselves as well as for those around us. Most of these positive learnings, along with their accompanying ideas, sensations, and emotions, become positioned in our body, which then enables us to do by far most of what we do without any special thought or conscious direction. Only so can we handle the complexities of day-to-day existence. Only our body and what it learns permits this.

Most of what is called "character" (good *or* bad) in normal human life consists in what our bodies are or are not "at the ready" to do in the specific situations where we find ourselves. Those "readinesses" enter our consciousness primarily, if at all, through how we feel about things, how we are directly "moved" by things and events around us.

Finally, those readinesses and feelings that run our life, whether we are aware of them or not, *reside in fairly specific parts* of our body, and they reveal themselves to others through our body language—in how we "carry" our bodily parts. They not only govern our immediate responses in action, but also are read with great accuracy by observant people around us and then determine how they react to us. We wear our souls "on our sleeve," even when we ourselves are oblivious to them, and that governs the quality of our relations to others.

ﾠ INCARNATION AND OUR PRESENT BODY ﾠ

ALL OF THIS MAKES clear *why* the way of Christ is so relentlessly incarnationist, so *bodily*. Incarnation is not just an essential fact about Jesus: that "Christ is come in the flesh." Rather, he came in the flesh, a real human body, in order that he might bring redemption and deliverance to our bodies. Our body is, we have now seen, an essential part of who we are, and no redemption that omits it is full redemption. Those who deny that Christ has come in real flesh are antichrist, John said (1 John 4:3).

Such a strong position is taken in the New Testament because redemption is in the first place for "the life which I now live in the flesh" (Galatians 2:20). This present life is to be caught up *now* in the eternal life of God. But of course "the life I now live in the flesh" is inseparable from the mortal body I now have. So it too must become holy, must "come over" to Christ's side. Otherwise my life itself could not "come over," and so it would be impossible that "as He is, so also are we in this world" (1 John 4:17).

The redemption of the body will be *completed* later, but even now, "if the Spirit of Him who raised Jesus from the dead dwells in you, He who raised Christ Jesus from the dead will also give life to your mortal bodies because of His Spirit who indwells you" (Romans 8:11). We are to know now "the power of His resurrection" (Philippians 3:10). Our body is not just a physical system, but is inhabited by the real presence of Christ.[1]

❧ THE PROFUNDITY OF PAUL ❧

ONCE WE ARE CLEAR about the centrality of the body to our identity and the normal course of life, the profundity of Paul's teachings about the body will strongly impress us.[2] Without understanding this, however, his words become incomprehensible. I'm afraid that's what they are to most people today. They cannot understand how Paul could literally mean what he said about the role of the body in the life of one who belongs to Christ.

For example, in Colossians chapter 3 he tells the "holy ones (saints) and faithful brothers" (Colossians 1:2, PAR) to whom he is writing, to "kill off" ("mortify") their "members (*mela*) which are upon the earth" (Colossians 3:5, PAR). And as such "members" he lists "fornication, uncleanness, passion, evil desires, and covetousness, which" he says, "is idolatry."

What does this mean, "members which are upon the earth"? It means those parts of a life lived *entirely in terms of the natural powers of the embodied self*. You need no help from supernatural sources to engage in fornication, the many sexual pollutions—"short of intercourse," we now say—indulgences in passions and desires for what is evil, or greed to possess what belongs to others. Just follow the inclinations now built into your bodily existence and they will all happen. Just let the demands of your "members" guide your life. These are the "parts" of our life that are "upon the earth," in the sense that they do not come "from heaven" or God. Because of them, human beings become "children of disobedience." Their basic nature becomes disobedience or rebellion. They are inherently at war with God and therefore subject to God's wrath (Colossians 3:6-7).

ல "NICE" FLESH ஐ

BUT OFTEN THE PARTS or members that "are upon the earth" are also very nice. This is generally true among religious people, and it is a deadly trap. When Paul explained to the Philippians what "flesh" he could have had confidence in he lists: "Circumcised the eighth day, of the nation of Israel, of the tribe of Benjamin, a Hebrew of Hebrews; as to the Law, a Pharisee; as to zeal, a persecutor of the church; as to the righteousness which is in the Law, found blameless" (Philippians 3:5-6). You can easily translate this into modern-day terms by listing the things religious people are apt to present as "good qualifications."

However, Paul actually regarded all this "nice flesh" as loss, and even as feces, compared to the real treasure of the resurrection life of Christ moving in him (verses 3-11).

That is why he said to the Colossians: "Therefore kill off your parts (members) that are of the earth." The "therefore" refers back to the fact he had just cited in this passage, that Christ's people have received a different life, one not "of earth" but of Christ himself, raised up beyond natural death. "You have died," he said, "and your real life is now concealed along *with* Christ *in* God" (Colossians 3:1-3, PAR).

This, as is well known, is a theme developed at many other points in Paul's writings, but at greatest lengths in Romans chapters 5 through 8. There Paul had been describing how sin (and therefore death) has *reigned* over (governed) human life. But now as he comes toward the end of chapter 5, a new kind of "reign" emerges. Death had reigned because of sin, which came into the human world by one man (Adam). Yes, but "much more those who receive the abundance of grace and of the gift of righteousness will reign [govern] in life through the One, Jesus Christ" (Romans 5:17). Sin indeed has flourished. But grace (life from above) has and will flourish all the more, "that, as sin reigned in death, even so grace might reign through righteousness into eternal life through Jesus Christ our Lord" (Romans 5:21).

Now we must emphasize that the grace in question is not merely a judicial action, though it involves that too. It is above all a presence and power *in life,* which provides an alternative to the merely natural forces (flesh) accessible to the individual in and through the body without any specific divine intervention from above.

So now Paul lays out the alternative open to the one *already* born from above and therefore experiencing a life that is not of the flesh. Such a one is given the option of *walking* in the new, different life that is already "doing things" in them. "Just as Christ was raised from the dead by the glory of the Father," Paul said, "so we too might *walk* in newness of life" (Romans 6:4,

NRSV, emphasis added). *Walk* in it, as a steadily moving force, not just feel it in spurts and starts!

But because we are now in the grip of grace it is *up to us*—though never on our own—to "not let sin have dominion in our death-bound (mortal) body to obey Sin's desires" (verse 12, PAR). And *this we do by refusing to surrender our body parts to sin as weapons of wickedness.* Instead, having been invaded by a life beyond death, and hence by one that is not *of* the body or flesh, we "present our body parts (members) to him as weapons of righteousness" (verse 13, PAR).

Because we *are* in the grip of grace, sin does not exercise control over us except insofar as we allow it. And, with divine assistance provided, we can break whatever strict control remains to it in every aspect of our life (verse 14). So, just as once—while "dead in . . . trespasses and sins" (Ephesians 2:1)—we surrendered our body parts to be servants of impurity, and to lawlessness leading to more lawlessness, so now we are to "present our body parts to be servants of righteousness leading to sanctification" (Romans 6:19, PAR).

Now, these words of Paul refer precisely to the process and outcome of *spiritual formation,* of which we have spoken. "Now that you have been released from slavery to sin and enslaved to God by your dependence on him for your new kind of life, the benefit you get is sanctification, and the outcome is eternal life" (verse 22, PAR), "the life that really is life" (1 Timothy 6:19, NRSV). The parts of our death-bound body are not mere physical things, but now carry *in* them a life that is not *of them.* He who raised Jesus from the dead now dwells in us and "will give life to your mortal bodies also through his Spirit that dwells in you" (Romans 8:11, NRSV).

❧ THE CENTRALITY OF SPIRITUAL FORMATION OF THE BODY ☙

MY HOPE IS THAT this rather lengthy discussion of the place of the body in our life and of how the apostle Paul understood its transformation will make very clear *why* spiritual formation requires the transformation of the body. The proper retraining and nurturing of the body is absolutely essential to Christlikeness. The body is not just a physical thing. As it matures, it increasingly takes on the quality of "inner" life. (The body of a small child, by contrast, has almost no inner quality to it, which is why the child can really hide nothing.) That is, the body increasingly becomes a major part of the hidden source *from which* our life immediately flows.

The outcome of spiritual formation is, indeed, the transformation of the inner reality of the self in such a way that the deeds and words of Jesus become a natural expression of who we are. But it is the nature of the human being that the "inner reality of the self" settles into our body, from which that inner reality then operates in *practice*. Formed in sin, our character and its body is set against God and God's ways, and as we look about us, we find it running pretty much on its own—at least for a while.

When our heart (will, spirit) comes to new life in God, the old "programs" are still running contrary to our new heart, and for the most part they are running *in* our body and its parts or members. "Sin dwells within me . . . that is, in my flesh " (Romans 7:12-18, PAR). "Sinful passions" are still "at work in our bodily parts" (Romans 7:5, PAR), even though they no longer can, in the long run, "bring forth death." That is because my identity before God has been shifted over to another life that is also now in me as God's gift. While the spirit is willing but the flesh is weak (Matthew 26:41), I may find myself doing the thing I hate (Romans 7:15). But it really is no longer I who is doing it, but the sin still functioning as a living force in the members of my body (verse 23).

However, this is only a transitional state for those who can say with David, "My soul follows hard after you" (Psalm 63:8, PAR). The law or force of the Spirit of life that is in Christ Jesus is now also a real presence in my body and it opens the way to liberation from the force of sin in my bodily parts (Romans 7:23). By not walking in terms of the flesh but in terms of the Spirit, we are increasingly able to do the things that Jesus did and taught (Romans 8:4). We move toward the place where both the spirit is willing and the flesh is strong for God because the Spirit has now occupied *it*. We have presented the members of our body "as slaves to righteousness, resulting in sanctification" (Romans 6:19).

❧ WE MUST TAKE THIS ALL VERY LITERALLY ❧

THE GREATEST DANGER TO our prospects for spiritual transformation at this point is that we will fail to take all this talk about our bodily parts very literally. It may help us to consider ordinary situations of temptation. We said earlier that temptation is a matter of being inclined to do what is wrong. But where do those inclinations primarily reside? The answer is, they primarily exist in the parts of our body.

Those inclinations are actually present in those parts and can even *be felt* there by those who are attentive to their body and who are informed, thoughtful, and willing to admit what they find upon careful reflection. Others, too, can recognize the tendencies present in our bodily parts— hands, feet, shoulders, eyebrows, loins, tongue, overall posture—and they can *play upon* those tendencies, to trap us, ensnare us, use us, destroy us. Those who purposefully prey upon others constantly do this. They become experts at it.

These various tendencies actually present in our bodily parts can *move* our body into action independently of our overall intentions to the contrary—often quite genuine—and of our conscious thoughts. Thus we act or speak "before we think." The part of our character that lives in our body carries us away.

The tongue, for example. James said that "the tongue is a small part [member, *mela*] of the body" (James 3:5). However, "the tongue is a fire, the cosmos of iniquity. The tongue is set among our members as something which defiles the entire body, setting fire to the natural course of things and itself set on fire by hell" (James 3:6, PAR).

James had no doubt observed the incredible power of the tongue to stir up the inclinations of the whole body and of all of its parts—our own body as well as that of others. Have you observed this? It is perhaps the last bodily part to submit to goodness and rightness. No one can tame it, James said, and indeed that is right. Physical violence nearly always is introduced by verbal violence.

It is only as we habitually subject the tongue to the grace of God as an instrument reserved for him, to do his will, that grace comes literally to inhabit and govern it. And when that happens the effects spread throughout all the body. "If anyone does not stumble in word," James said, "that is a perfect man, able even to guide his entire body aright" (James 3:2, PAR). "The tongue of the righteous is as choice silver" (Proverbs 10:20), and "A healing tongue is a tree of life" (15:4, PAR).

Other members of the body, though not as central to life as the tongue, have their own readiness to act wrongly, with the associated feeling states—"Haughty eyes," the wise man said, "a lying tongue, hands to shed innocent blood, . . . feet that run quickly to do evil" (Proverbs 6:17-18, PAR). The shoulders, the stomach and the genitals, the fists and the face are constantly moving us away from God, if they have not *already* been permeated by the real presence of Christ.

A person caught up in rage or lust or resentment—or religious self-righteousness, for that matter—is basically one whose body has taken over and, at least for the moment, is totally running his or her actions or even life. Sometimes we say, "I just lost my temper." "Temper" refers to the capacity to handle all kinds of situations and maintain one's balance. It is in fact close to *character*, as when we say of someone that they are "acting out of character" or "are not themselves" today.

But what does one lose one's temper or character *to*? Things will be happening around us, of course, and *they* may get blamed, as a baby spanks the floor where it falls on it. But what we lose our temper or our "control" to, what begins to govern our actions at that point, is precisely *our body and the inclinations to wrong that, as Paul and James both knew, actually inhabit its parts as living forces.* You can verify this by carefully observing the bodily behavior of the next person you see in a rage.

✎ CHRIST DELIVERS FROM BODY HATRED ✎

A BURNING SENSE OF these powers of evil actually inhabiting our body and specific parts thereof is one of the reasons *body hatred,* throughout the ages and across cultures, has been such a dreadful fact. Sincere people really do find evil in their body and wrongly blame the body for it.

This misguided and terribly harmful attitude toward the body correctly sees the power of sin that really is in the actual body and its parts. But it mistakenly assumes that the evil *is* the body and its parts, and does not know how to think about the readiness to sin, the sinful meanings and intentions, that have come to possess those parts through their habituation in a world of sin.

In this respect Paul's teaching, explained above, that we are to "present our bodily parts as servants to righteousness for sanctification" (Romans 6:19, PAR) stands in shocking opposition to the assumptions of classical thought of his day, as well as to those of most human thinking up to now. The same is true for his teaching that the body of the redeemed is a shrine of the Holy Spirit, and that therefore "the body is meant not for fornication but for the Lord, and the Lord for the body" (1 Corinthians 6:13, PAR). "Do you not know," he continues on to say, "that your bodies are members [*mela*] of Christ?" (1 Corinthians 6:15).

Well, they did not know, we can be sure, and could hardly think or imagine such a thing. We today do little better. Theirs was the same understanding of the body that led Paul's hearers in Athens to scoff at the idea of a resurrection of the body (Acts 17:32). "Who wants *that* thing back?" you can almost hear them say. It was inconceivable to them that the physical body and its parts should be honored and treasured as the habitation of God in redeemed human personality. And the same is true for most people today — and indeed for most professing Christians.

For usual human beings in the usual circumstances, their body runs their life. Contrary to the words of Jesus in Matthew 6:25, life is, for them, *not* more than food, nor the body more than clothing. As a matter of simple fact, their time and energy is almost wholly, if not entirely, devoted to how their body looks, smells, and feels, and to how it can be secured and used to meet ego needs such as admiration, sexual gratification, and power over others.

It is this bodily orientation of the self that runs the human cosmos, as the elderly apostle John pointed out: "For all that is in the world, the lust of the flesh and the lust of the eyes and the boastful pride of life, is not from the Father, but is from the world" (1 John 2:16). This is "the mind of the flesh" discussed earlier from Paul, which is in opposition to "the mind of the spirit" (Romans 8:4-11). And John saw exactly the same outcomes for these two human options that Paul and all of the biblical writers knew: "The world is passing away, and also its lusts; but the one who does the will of God abides forever" (1 John 2:17; compare Isaiah 40:6-8; James 1:10; 1 Peter 1:24-25).

❧ THE BODY BETRAYED ❧

NOW, THE HUMAN BODY is betrayed in its own nature when it is thus made central to human life. It is created for spiritual life in the kingdom of God and to be honored—indeed, glorified—in that context.[3] But when taken out of that context and made the central focus of human experience and endeavor, it is betrayed—robbed of the spiritual resources meant to sustain its life and proper functioning—and in turn it then betrays those who center their life on it.

The sense of this betrayal is what lies at the heart of youth worship in Western societies. It also is the source of the fear, shame, disgust, and even the anger directed at fat, old age (or just aging), and death and dying that dominate our culture. An outlook focused entirely on the body finds the body's failure and cessation to be, of course, the ultimate insult from which there is no recovery. You have to understand this if you want to understand Western life and culture.

The same mis-location of the body explains many other intractable problems now facing much of our world: the sexualization of practically everything, abortion, eating disorders, and racial and other discriminations. All of these are rooted in taking the body—our own or that of others—to *be* the person and thereby depriving ourselves of the spiritual perspective on the person, which alone can enable us to cherish the body and its central role in our life.

Body hatred also comes from disappointment about our future with it, even from outright fear of the body—of what *it* is going to *do to* us. Not accepting God as God puts *us* in his place, I have noted, and leaves us with nothing to trust and worship but our body and its natural powers. The frenzy over physical attractiveness that we see all around us today and the despair over its loss—eventually, in aging and death, for everyone—are the main characteristics of the contemporary climate of life. But that only illustrates, once more, that to be carnally minded—that is, obsessed with the merely natural—is death indeed. We should now be able to see the truth of this in everything we view or read in today's world. But, by contrast, to be spiritually minded—that is, to be focused on our nature as spiritual beings and on our place in God's eternal life and kingdom—"is life and peace" (Romans 8:6). Then the body is beautified and beatified in its proper place.

✑ MY BODY IS *NOT* MY PROPERTY ✑

NOWHERE DOES THE MODERN frenzy of self-assertion and the "me" god come more clearly into view than in the claim now often made that "my body is my own." This is taken to mean that I alone have the right to say what is done in and with it. Now, there is an important truth here—especially in a world where there are so many ways of getting at you through your body. But it is a truth misstated and misunderstood. Our only safety lies in a proper solidarity with others, not in isolation and pretending to go it alone.

Because we are essentially social beings and what is done with our body strongly affects others around us, I do *not* have exclusive say over what happens in and with my body. It is not mine to do with as I will. To think it is is only the irrational response of a being terrified and hostile about its vulnerability through its body.

But "no man is an island," nor any woman either. I did not produce my body. I could not care for it for many years. It is not self-sufficient now. (Ask yourself where your food and water come from.) There will probably come a time when I cannot care for it again. I did not determine its basic properties, and there is very little about my body of any great importance that is due to me.

As a mature and competent individual, I am *responsible for* the care of my body, and it is the center of all the other responsibilities I have. But that does not imply that I and I alone have the right to say what is to be done with it, or in short, that *I own* my body.

And this is all the more true for an apprentice of Jesus, whose body and whole being has literally been bought back from evil by God through the death of his Son. It is therefore God's to do with as he pleases, and he pleases that our body should be "a showplace of God's greatness" (1 Corinthians 6:20, PAR). Christians are the last people on earth who could say, "My body is my own, and I shall do with it what I please."

✑ THE ONLY REASONABLE USE OF OUR BODY ✑

ACCORDINGLY, OUR "REASONABLE service," the only thing that makes any sense for a human being who trusts Christ, is to "present our bodies as a living and holy sacrifice, very pleasing to God" (Romans 12:1-2, PAR). This total yielding of every part of our body to God, until the very tissues and muscles that make it up are inclined toward God and godliness and are vitalized in action by the powers of heaven, breaks all conformity with worldly life in this age and transforms us into conformity with the age to come, by completing the renewal of our minds—our powers of thought and imaginations and judgment, deeply rooted in our bodies.

"Don't even think it," we sometimes say. And the mark of the renewed mind is what it will "not even think." And this freedom from even the *thought* of evil—"thinketh no evil" (1 Corinthians 13:5, KJV)—requires that the automatic responses toward evil are no longer running the body and its parts. The bodily tendencies of the "living sacrifice" no longer incline us or start us toward evil *without thinking,* and then drag our thoughts and feelings after them—and very likely our will (heart, spirit) also.

❧ THE DISTRAUGHT BODY ❧

FOR MANY OF US today, our body is in a constant state of agitation and discomfort. That is the contemporary condition and explains our astonishing degree of dependence on prescription and other drugs. In some cases, of course, this may be due to strictly physical conditions. But more often it is not so, but is due to tendencies of the self that have settled into our body's parts and put it at war with itself. Wounds, fears, unsatisfied desires, shames, losses, and unhealthy ambitions and images of the self sink beneath the horizon of our awareness. We may even deny them. But they continue to disrupt our body and can even take over our life through the body's "automatic" responses.

Frank Laubach—partly because, to be "noble," he had voted for the other candidate—was denied a position as president of a college in the Philippines, where he had been serving as a missionary. He lost by one vote. He was frustrated and bitter, and for two years was almost continuously ill. A biographer writes,

> He suffered from flu, appendicitis, paratyphoid, a strained leg muscle, an ulcerated eye, and shingles! In a state of bitter self-pity, he hobbled around, worked inefficiently, and wore a patch over one eye much of the time. His failure to accept the defeat was costing him his health. The fact that his desire to exercise Christian principles resulted in hurting himself increased the inner tension and conflict. These were years of despondency and aimlessness. He was fighting the battle of his soul.[4]

In fact, what we see in such a case is *soul disruption* manifesting itself in disorders of the body, which in turn threaten to take over life as a whole and could even lead to physical death. Thank God, Laubach in time found the spiritual key to turning all this around and bringing his body into the health of a person radiant with the presence of Christ.[5]

❧ TAKING STEPS ❧

WE NOW HAVE THOROUGHLY examined the nature of the human body and its place in life. What are some things that can be done to place our body and its parts fully at the disposal of the redeeming power that God intends to live in them? We acknowledge once again that changes are required in other dimensions of our person than our body and that these other dimensions and changes can never be adequately understood or dealt with in total isolation from each other. We must never forget this. But as in each of the other cases we have discussed, so here too there are avenues of intervention for the sake of spiritual (trans)formation that bear precisely on the body.

Before looking at some particular steps, however, I would like to mention two books that, though not widely known or available, are of great practical help with the matters here discussed. The first is a little book by Frances Ridley Havergal, *Kept for the Master's Use*. Many know of and perhaps have sung her song, "Take My Life, and Let It Be,"[6] but the fundamental spiritual attitude briefly and beautifully indicated in the words of the song is spelled out with remarkable intelligence and biblical force in her book.[7]

The second book is by Margaret Magdalen, *A Spiritual Check-up: Avoiding Mediocrity in the Christian Life*.[8] This lovely treatment envisions each bodily part, from the feet up, as it enters the waters of baptism, and what that should mean for the transformation of all our life in godliness. It is extremely helpful in thinking about our body and our spiritual life.

So, now, in approaching the spiritual formation of our body, what should we do? There are a number of things:

1. We must actually *release our body to God*. That is what Paul means when he tells us "to present our body to God as a living sacrifice" (Romans 12:1, PAR). It needs to be a definite action, renewed as appropriate, perhaps on a yearly basis. You will not drift into this position before God, and you will not, without decisive action, stay there.

Perhaps you could do it like this. Decide to give your body to God on the basis of understanding how important it is and that scriptural teaching requires it. Know, therefore, that it is a good and indispensable thing to do. Then take a day in silent and solitary retreat. Quiet your soul and your body, and let them get clear of the fog of your daily burdens and preoccupations. Meditatively pray some central Scriptures before the Lord, especially those dealing directly with the body, already cited and emphasized in this chapter.

I recommend that you then lie on the floor, face down or face up, and explicitly and formally surrender your body to God. Then take time to go over the main parts of your body and do the same for each one. What you want to do is to ask God to *take charge* of your body and each part, to fill it with his life and use it for his purposes. Accentuate the positive; don't just think of not sinning with your body. You will find this following naturally from active consecration of it to God's power and his purpose. Remember, a sacrifice is something to be *taken up* in God.

Give plenty of time to this ritual of sacrifice. Do not rush. When you realize it is done, give God thanks, arise, and spend some time in praise. An ecstatic reading (chant and walk or dance) of Psalms 145–150 would be an excellent exercise in this context. Put your *body* into it. Later, share what you have done with a spiritual friend or pastor, and ask him or her to bless it. Review your ritual of sacrifice in thought and prayer from time to time over the following weeks, and *plan* to renew the same ritual surrender year by year.

2. *No longer idolize your body.* What does that mean? It means that you no longer make it an object of "ultimate concern." You have, after all, now given it up to God and he can do with it as he wishes. You have taken your hands off of "outcomes" with respect to it, and you care for it only as it serves God's purposes in your life and the lives of others. You don't worry about what will happen to it—sickness, repulsiveness, aging, death—for you have placed God in charge of all that, and any issues that arise in this area you freely take up with him in prayer. You take good care of your body, but only within the framework of values clearly laid down by God and exemplified in Jesus Christ. You don't live in fear of your body and what it might "do to you."

3. Closely allied with the above is that you *do not misuse your body.* This means primarily two things: First, you do not use it as a source of sensual gratification, and you do not use it to dominate or manipulate others. Addictions of various kinds are cases where sensual gratification is accepted as a necessity. These are, whatever else must be said about them, misuses of the body. Bodily pleasure is not in itself a bad thing. But when it is exalted to a necessity and we become dependent upon it, then we are slaves of our body and its feelings. Only misery lies ahead.

The second thing this means is that we do not use our bodies to dominate or control others. This means different things to different people. For example, we do not present our bodies in ways that elicit sexual thoughts, feelings, and actions from others. We do not try to be "sexy." We can be naturally attractive without that. This would of course be a fatal blow to the fashion industry and to other large segments of the economy, but we have to leave them to look after themselves.

Another example on this point has to do with intimidation by means of our body. There are many aspects of this, up to and including brute force. The most common forms of it are social: for example, "power dressing," sarcasm, and "knowing" looks and remarks. Having given up our body to God, we do not then use it or its parts in these ways.

A final example, for now, is overwork. In our current world this is a primary misuse of the body. It is now said that work is the new "drug of choice." Often this is associated with excessive competition and trying to beat others out in some area of our common life. Sometimes this is just a matter of wearing our body out in order to succeed—often in circumstances that we regard (perhaps rightly) as imposed upon us by others. It is still a misuse of the body and a failure to work things out with God. God *never* gives us too much to do. He long ago gave us these words: "It is vain for you to rise up early, to sit up late, to eat the bread of sorrows: for so he giveth his beloved sleep" (Psalm 127:2, KJV).

4. The positive counterpart of the remarks just made is that *the body is to be properly honored and cared for.* The first step in this direction follows from what has already been said. That is, the body is to be regarded as holy, because it is owned and inhabited by God.

Of course that means it will be withheld from engagement in what is wrong. "The body is not for immorality, but for the Lord; and the Lord is for the body" (1 Corinthians 6:13). That being so, "Do you not know that your bodies are members [*mela*—that is, in organic, living communion] of Christ? Shall I then take the members of Christ and make them members [that is, put them into organic, living communion] of a harlot?" (verse 15). The answer is obvious, as obvious as whether or not one should kick a sleeping baby. Of course not! "May it never be!" is Paul's response. But it is equally true of theft, murder, or lying, once you think of it. Any part of the body of Christ is too holy for that.

But because it is holy (separated to God) we will also properly care for it: nourish, exercise, and rest it. The practical center of proper care for the body is Sabbath. Now, Sabbath is a quite profound and intricate subject, and we cannot deal adequately with it here. But no treatment of spiritual formation and the body can be complete without at least touching upon the meaning of Sabbath.

The Christian philosopher and scientist Blaise Pascal commented, "I have discovered that all the unhappiness of men arises from one single fact, that they cannot stay quietly in their own chamber."[9] This remark, though somewhat of an exaggeration, contains a deep insight. The capacity to simply be, to rest, would remove one from most of the striving that leads to misery. This is a capacity that comes to fullness only when it reaches our body. Peace is a condition of the body, and until it has enveloped our body it has not enveloped us. Peace comes to our body when it is at home in the rightness and power of God.

ᕗ AND THAT IS SABBATH ᕐ

SABBATH FULFILLED IN HUMAN life is really celebration of God. Sabbath is inseparable from worship, and, indeed, genuine worship is Sabbath. As the fourth commandment, Sabbath is the fulfillment in practice of the first three. When we come to the place where we can joyously "do no work" it will be because God is so exalted in our minds and bodies that we can trust him with our life and our world and can take our hands off of them.

Now, for most of us Sabbath is first to be achieved in the practice of solitude and silence. These must be carefully sought, cultivated, and dwelt in. When they become established in our soul and our body, they can be practiced in company with others. But the body *must* be weaned away from its tendencies to always take control, to run the world, to achieve and produce, to attain gratification. These are its habitual tendencies learned in a fallen world. Progress in the *opposite* direction can only be made in solitude and silence, for they "take our hands off our world" as nothing else does. And that is the meaning of Sabbath.

Rest is one primary mark of the condition of Sabbath in the body, as unrest is a primary mark of its absence. So if we really intend to submit our bodies as living sacrifices to God, our first step well might be to start *getting enough sleep*. Sleep is a good first use of solitude and silence. It is also a good indicator of how thoroughly we trust in God.

The psalmist, who knew danger and uncertainty well, also slept well: "I lay down and slept; I awoke, for the LORD sustains me" (3:5-6), he said, and "In peace I will both lie down and sleep, for Thou alone, O LORD, dost make me to dwell in safety" (4:8).

Of course we do not mean that we can just sleep our way to sainthood. Sometimes people sleep because they are depressed, or are sad, or have a physical condition, or are just evading reality. Nor do we mean that really godly people—call them saints—do not work hard and are never exhausted. But the saints who have separated their bodies to God have resources not at the disposal of the ordinary person running on fumes and promises, where so many of us find ourselves today. We have to learn how to get where those resources are and to take our bodies into the rest of God.

If we are not rested, on the other hand, the body moves to the center of our focus and makes its presence *more strongly* felt, and the tendencies of its parts call out more strongly for gratification. The sensual desires and ego demands will have greater power over us through our desperate body and its parts. In addition, our awareness of what it is doing—it is very subtle—and what is happening around us will be less sharp and decisive. Confusion is the enemy of spiritual orientation. Rest, properly taken, gives clarity to the mind. Weariness, by contrast, can make us seek gratification and energy from food or drugs, or from various illicit relationships, or from egoistic postures that are, in Paul's words, "upon the earth." They pull us away from reliance upon God and from living in his power.

Much more could be said of the role of spiritual disciplines on behalf of the spiritual formation of the body. A full discussion of disciplines focused on the body would have to deal with how exercise and diet can contribute to easing the influence of the "sin that is in our members." As finite, bodily creatures we cannot ignore such things. In particular, specific disciplines go far in retraining particular parts of our body away from the specific tendencies to sin that are localized in them. They enable us to *stop* the practice and remove the tendency in question by entering special contrary practices and circumstances, and thereby breaking the force of habit that has us in bondage. But for now we must leave further treatment of these details aside.

❧ THE BODY SPIRITUALLY ADORNED ❧

WHAT WE MUST BE sure about, in concluding this chapter, is that God has made every provision for the body we actually have to serve us and him well for his purposes in putting us here on earth. There may be severe problems with our bodies, at least from the human point of view. We do not mean to deny or disregard that. But, as Peter said to women apprentices of his day (and of course it applies equally well to men), the real power of life lies in who we are as redeemed people and how our behavior is caught up in that.

So we should "not let [our] adornment be merely external—braiding the hair, and wearing gold jewelry, or putting on dresses; but let it be the hidden person of the heart, with the imperishable quality of a gentle and quiet spirit, which is precious in the sight of God" (1 Peter 3:3-4). This is no legalistic ban on jewelry and so on—though such things can be wrongly used, and perhaps nearly always are. But it is a clear indication of where genuine beauty, health, and strength of the body come from and of what incredible grace lies in the spiritual transformation of the body.

Matters for
Thought and Discussion

1. Do you agree that "the body lies right at the center of the spiritual life"? Why or why not?
2. How is the body "wrongly positioned" in life on our own?
3. In what respects are my life and identity inseparable from my body?

4. Is it possible that much of our character consists in what our body is "ready" to do without "being told"?

5. What does Paul mean by "mortify . . . your members which are upon the earth" (Colossians 3:5, KJV)? Can we do that?

6. Discuss James' view of the power of the tongue to run "on its own" and influence our whole body (James 3:1-12). How does that happen?

7. Do you agree or disagree that when we "lose our temper" we lose it to our activated body, which then takes off on its own?

8. What is the source of body hatred, and how does Christ deliver us from it?

9. Is my body my property to do with as I wish? Why or why not?

10. What are some of the ways we can bring our body to peace and strength in God?

11. What does Sabbath mean to your body?

12. Can the body have a spiritual beauty? In what way?

10

TRANSFORMING OUR SOCIAL DIMENSION

*The communities of God, to which Christ has become teacher
and guide, are, in comparison with communities of the
pagan people among whom they live as strangers,
like heavenly lights in the world.*
ORIGEN[1]

*We know that we have passed out of death into life, because
we love the brethren. He who does not love abides in death.*
1 JOHN 3:14

Now we must find out what our relationships to others must be like if we are to be spiritually formed in Christlikeness.

❧ CIRCLES OF SUFFICIENCY ❧

THE NATURAL CONDITION OF life for human beings is one of reciprocal rootedness in others. As firmness of footing is a condition of walking and secure movement, so assurance of others being *for* us is the condition of stable, healthy living. There are many ways this can be present in individual cases, *but it must be there*. If it is not, we are but walking wounded, our life more or less a shambles until we die.

When the required type of "for-ness" is adequately present, human "circles of sufficiency" emerge. The most fundamental form is that of a mother and child. Then perhaps mother and child and father. ("Just Molly and me, and baby makes three.") Then there are young lovers, reciprocally absorbed, as well as mature mates. Of course numerous forms of human association can take on some degree of this "sufficiency," and always with a distinctive character arising out of the precise nature of the relationships involved.

179

These circles of sufficiency, natural and essential to the human condition and so profoundly beautiful to behold, are always illusory at the merely human level, and even the illusion itself is terrifyingly fragile. To assure an anxious child we may say, "Everything is okay now." But it never is. In this world it is never true that *everything* is okay, and perhaps it is least true in those very situations where we feel the need to say it.

Every human circle presupposes for its *"really* being okay" a larger context or circle that supports it. The mother and child, for example, presuppose the larger family that cares for and sustains them, making it possible for them to be absorbed in one another as they need to be, ignoring all else. These larger circles also depend upon yet larger circles, which, while ever less intimate, are still crucial to making the inner circles possible. That is just how human life is. The togetherness of the mother and child may be drastically affected by economic conditions on the other side of the earth.

Ultimately, every human circle is doomed to dissolution if it is not caught up in the life of the only genuinely self-sufficient circle of sufficiency, that of the Father, Son, and Holy Spirit. For that circle is the only one that is truly and totally self-sufficient. And all the broken circles must ultimately find their healing there, if anywhere.

Only when rooted in that divine Trinitarian circle can the broken individuals from the broken circles recover from the wounds received in their circles of origin and find wholeness on their long journey from the womb to the eternal City of God. Of course it was never God's intention that the natural human circles of sufficiency, of reciprocal rootedness, would be illusory, fragile, and eventually broken; and if they were lived within his kingdom, they would not be.

❧ THE REALITY OF REJECTION ❧

MOST PEOPLE KNOW A great deal about being rejected, being left out, or just not received, not welcome, not acceptable. As the parent/child relationship is perhaps the most perfect illustration of a circle of sufficiency in human life, so it is also the place where the deepest and most lasting wounds can be given. If a child is totally received in its early years by its parents and siblings, it will very likely have a rootedness about it that enables it to withstand most forms of rejection that may come upon a human being in a lifetime. It will carry its solid relationships to and from its family members throughout life, being sustained by them even long after those loved ones are dead. It will receive a steady stream of rest and strength from them.

By contrast, a small child *not* adequately received can actually die from it; or if it survives, it is very likely to be incapable of giving and receiving love in decent human relationships for the rest of its life. It will be perpetually "left out," if only in its imagination. And in this matter, imagination can have the force of reality. Thus the final words of the Old Testament speak of one who must come and "restore the hearts of the fathers to their children, and the hearts of the children to their fathers" to avoid a curse coming to rest upon the land (Malachi 4:6).

Of course severe wounds to our rootedness in others may also occur in later life. Failures of various kinds, real or imagined, can bring rejection or detachment from parents and other significant figures. Unfaithfulness in a mate, divorce, failure in career advancement, collapse of a profession, disloyalty of children, or just never making it "in," wherever "in" may be[2]—all of these break up our human circles of sufficiency. They may leave us unconnected to others at levels of our soul where lack of nourishment from deep connections with others means spiritual starvation and loss of wholeness in our every dimension.

Framing all the many human rejections and broken circles is real or imagined rejection by God because of sin, and a sense of worthlessness from moral failures, often too deep for conscious awareness or words.

❧ THE TWO BASIC FORMS OF EVIL IN RELATIONS TO OTHERS ❧

SO WHEN WE COME to deal with spiritual formation of our social dimension, we have to start from *woundedness*. It is hard to imagine anyone in this world who has not been deeply injured in his or her relationships to others. The exact nature of the poison of sin in our social dimension is fairly easy to describe, though extremely hard to deal with. It has two forms. They are so closely related that they really are two forms of the same thing: of lovelessness, lack of proper regard and care for others. These two forms are *assault* or attack and *withdrawal* or "distancing." They are so much a part of ordinary human existence that most people think they are just "reality," and never imagine that we could live without them.

If spiritual formation in Christ is to succeed, the power of these two forms of evil in our own life—within our self—absolutely *must* be broken. So far as it is possible, they must be eliminated as indwelling realities, as postures we take toward others. They also must be successfully disarmed as they come toward us. And they must be eliminated in our social environment— especially in the fellowships of Christ's followers—so far as that is possible. Perhaps we must be reconciled to the fact that they cannot be entirely eliminated from our world, or even from our fellowships of Christian believers, until a new epoch dawns, but we can eliminate them from our own being. We *can* live without them.

❧ UNDERSTANDING ASSAULT AND WITHDRAWAL ❧

WE ASSAULT OTHERS WHEN we act against what is good for them, even with their consent. It is not only when we harm them or cause them pain against their conscious will. Hence, seduction is assault, as is participation in or even compliance with the social structures that institutionalize wrongdoing and evil. The more explicit and well-known forms of assault are dealt with in the last six of the Ten Commandments — murder, adultery, theft, and so on. These are deepened in their meaning by the teachings of Jesus, especially in his Sermons on the Mount and on the Plain (Matthew 5–7; Luke 6) and the teachings of Paul in such passages as Colossians chapters 3–5 and 1 Corinthians 13.

We withdraw from someone when we regard their well-being and goodness as matters of indifference to us, or perhaps go so far as to despise them. We "don't care."

Both assault and withdrawal primarily involve our relations to those close to us, those affected by what we do and who we are in the natural course of our living. Clearly that means members of our family or household, those who live intimately with us — our "nigh boors" — those with whom we work or play, and those with whom we share common goods, our community. In the modern world it is hard to draw a boundary to the latter because of significant worldwide connections for everyone, though in practice some distinctions *must* be made because of our finitude. We cannot effectively extend care or receive it from very many people.

Now we always "distance" ourselves from those we assault, and withdrawal — including threats or suggestions thereof — is nearly always a way of assaulting those we withdraw from. So we should think of the distinction between assault and withdrawal as only a matter of emphasis, useful for the understanding of how lovelessness works.

❧ SPIRITUAL FORMATION IS NECESSARILY SOCIAL ❧

SPIRITUAL FORMATION, GOOD OR bad, is always profoundly social. You cannot keep it to yourself. Anyone who thinks of it as a merely private matter has misunderstood it. Anyone who says, "It's just between me and God," or "What I do is my own business," has misunderstood God as well as "me." Strictly speaking there is *nothing* "just between me and God." For all that *is* between me and God affects who I am; and that, in turn, modifies my relationship to everyone around me. My relationship to others also modifies me and deeply affects my relationship to God. Hence those relationships must be transformed if I am to be transformed.

Therefore Jesus gave a sure mark of the outcome of spiritual formation under his guidance: we become people who love one another (John 13:35). And he does not leave "love," that "many splendored thing," unspecified. Instead he gives "a *new* commandment, that you love one another. *Just as* I have loved you, you also should love one another" (verse 34, NRSV, emphasis added). The age-old command to love is transformed, made a new command, by identification of the love in question with that of Jesus for us (see 1 John 2:7-8).

Love of "the brethren" in this supernatural way allows us to know that "we have passed out of death into life" (1 John 3:14). We simply can't love in *that* way unless we have a different kind of life in us. And the "love" here in question is identified as that which is in Christ *because* it is one that makes us ready to "lay down our lives for the brethren" (1 John 3:16).

Failure to love others as Jesus loves us, on the other hand, chokes off the flow of the eternal kind of life that our whole human system cries out for. The old apostle minces no words: "He who does not love abides in death" (1 John 3:14). Notice that he did not say, "he who hates," but simply, "he who does not love." The mere absence of love is deadly. It is withdrawal.

Notice also that he did not say, "he who is not *loved*," though that also is true. That too is death, but our purpose cannot be to get others to love us. Love comes *to* us from God. *That* must be our unshakable circle of sufficiency. Our purpose must then be to become one who loves others with Christ's *agape*. That purpose, when developed, will transform the social dimension of the human self and all of our relationships to others. Love is not a feeling, or a special way of feeling,[3] but the divine way of relating to others and oneself that moves through every dimension of our being and restructures our world for good.

❧ LOVE DEEPLY ROOTED IN HUMAN NATURE ❧

THESE TEACHINGS OF JESUS are deeply rooted in our basic nature. Love expresses itself in the beautiful circles of sufficiency with which we opened this chapter. We reemphasize: The life of the human being is one of relating to others. We are born of relations and into relation, though many are cursed to live and die alone.

One of the heart-rending stories from Mother Teresa of Calcutta is about an untouchable who had lived beyond human care, upon the streets or wherever he could find a place simply to be. Dying, he was brought by Mother Teresa into her shelter and cleaned and cared for. His words were, "I have had to live my life like an animal, but now I can die like a human being." Simply because he had been "taken in" by others who *gave to* him! To merely welcome another, to provide for him or her, to make a place, is one of the most life-giving and life-receiving things a human being can do. They are the basic, universal acts of love. Our lives were meant to be full of such acts, drawing on the abundance of God, and they achieve their greatest fulfillment precisely when, like Jesus, we "lay down our lives for the brethren."[4]

This "relating" quality reaches into every dimension of human existence. It characterizes the basic nature of all thought and feeling, which is always a thought *of* or feeling *of* something other than itself. It pervades the deepest reaches of our body, soul, and world, where our very identity—who we really are—is always intermingled (if sometimes negatively, by reaction) with others who have given us life, sustained us, or walked with us—or perhaps have deeply injured us. The call of "the other" on our lives is a constant for everyone. It is the basic reality of a moral existence, which we retreat from only into a living death of isolation. If we make it our purpose to save our life by withdrawal, we lose it. So Jesus said. But this is not only a revealed truth, it is also a testable fact of life. If you would live, then give—and receive. (Recall chapter 4.)

❧ GOD *IS* LOVE ❧

THIS IS POSSIBLE AND can be actual for each of us because of what God, the source and governor of all, is. "God is Love." Yes. But we must not miss the essential point. The profound good news is *not* just that he loves *us*, as is often said. A pretty mean person can love someone for special reasons (Matthew 5:46-48). But he *is* Love and sustains his love *for us* from his basic reality as Love, which dictates his Trinitarian nature.

God is in himself a sweet society of love, with a first, second, and third person to complete a social matrix where not only is there love and being loved, but also *shared* love for another, the third person. Community is formed not by mere love and requited love, which by itself is exclusive, but by *shared* love for another, which is inclusive. And within the Trinity there is, I believe, not even a thought of "First, Second, and Third." There is no subordination within the Trinity, not because of some profound metaphysical fact, but because the members of the Trinity *will not have it.*

The nature of personality is inherently communal, and only the Trinity does justice to what personality is. Aristotle, pagan but profound, says of human personality:

> The individual, when isolated, is not self-sufficing, and therefore he is
> like a part in relation to the whole. But whoever is unable to live in
> society, or who has no need of it because he is sufficient for himself,
> must be either a beast or a god.[5]

But this fundamental fact about human personality is rooted in the nature of its Creator, and the writers of the Bible were well aware of it long before Aristotle. We are told on the earliest pages of the Bible that "it is not good that the man should be alone," and so God decided to make "a helper to be a match for him" (Genesis 2:18, PAR). Centuries later Paul pointed out that "not one of us lives unto himself and not one dies unto himself" (Romans 14:7, PAR). He knew something that Aristotle could not know, however: "whether we live or die we are the Lord's" (verse 8, PAR) and for this purpose "Christ died and lived again, that He might be Lord both of the dead and of the living" (14:9). Human beings are really *together* only in God, and all other ways of "being with" fall short of the needs of basic human nature.

The secret of all life-giving relation to others, and of all that is social, lies in the fact that *the primary other for a human being, whether he wants it or not, is always God.* John Donne wrote the following beautiful extension of Paul's words:

> All mankind is of one author, and is one volume; when one man
> dies, one chapter is not torn out of the book, but translated into a
> better language, and every chapter must be so translated. God
> employs several translators: some pieces are translated by age, some
> by sickness, some by war, some by justice. But God's hand is in every
> translation, and his hand shall bind up all our scattered leaves again
> for that library where every book shall be open to one another.[6]

❧ ONE NATION UNDER GOD? ❧

NOW, HERE IN AMERICA we pledge our allegiance to a flag that represents "one nation under God, indivisible, with liberty and justice for all." But who has any idea of what this would mean for real life on the street and how it applies to them? And the biblical vision of human unity under God is even more so one that few people today can even imagine, much less regard as realistically possible for themselves or others. Only the message and people of Jesus Christ can give it substance.

Perhaps someone with no real knowledge of Christ could imagine that kind of "communal solidarity" for a *few* people, carefully selected—people of "the right kind." But certainly not for people generally, and especially not for those *imposed* upon us by "accidents" of birth, and thereby of history and society. Sin structures embedded deeply in our souls and bodies have almost totally disabled us for those relationships to others that our hearts desire and that were meant by God to be—relationships that our public discourse in America idealizes without understanding what they are.

Larry Crabb beautifully writes,

When two people *connect,* when their beings intersect as closely as two bodies during intercourse, something is poured out of one and into the other that has power to heal the soul of its deepest wounds and restore it to health. The one who receives experiences the joy of being healed. The one who gives knows the even greater joy of being used to heal. Something good is in the heart of each of God's children that is more powerful than everything bad. It's there, waiting to be released, to work its magic.

Then he adds, "But it rarely happens."[7]

SPIRITUAL FORMATION IN CHRIST WOULD MAKE IT SO

THAT IS SADLY SO. The power of life in Christ is seldom realized, but spiritual formation in him, carried to fulfillment, would mean that what Crabb describes would *routinely* happen between Christ's people. That is the meaning of the church as the body of Christ, the members nourishing one another with the transcendent power that raised up Christ from the dead and is now flowing through each member to the others. That is what produces "the Church as we see her spread out through all time and space and rooted in eternity, terrible as an army with banners."[8]

The visible church, which anyone can look at if he or she wills, is—with all her imperfections—the outward manifestation in history and society of the invisible church, which God alone sees. Of this invisible reality Dietrich Bonhoeffer said,

> The spiritual unity of the Church is a primal synthesis willed by God. It is not a relationship that has to be established, but one that is already posited (*iustitia passiva*), and remains invisible. It is not made possible by concord, similarity or affinity between souls, nor should it be confused with unity of mood. Instead it is real just where seemingly the most intractable outward oppositions prevail, where each man leads his quite individual life, and it is perhaps absent where it seems to prevail most. It can shine more brightly in the conflict between wills than in concord.[9]

Into *this* church, the invisible body of her risen Lord, we come when we place our confidence in Jesus. He takes us in and forms a circle of sufficiency that is real and ultimate. It is first in relation to him that we begin to know what Crabb above described about *connecting;* and we can then begin to see how the flow of loving presence from him extends

186

through others to us and from us to others.

This must happen within the imperfect communities and congregations available to us now. But the new life can and must eventually transform the entire social dimension of our self toward the heavenly future in which we shall know as we are now known by God — "where every book shall lie open to one another."

∾ THOROUGHLY UNDERSTANDING THE WRONGNESS ∾

HERE AS IN ALL the other dimensions of our life, the progression of redemption in our relations to others depends upon what we do as well as what God does for us and in us. And in order to do our part in the process of spiritual formation of social relations we must deeply *identify and understand what is wrong in our relations* with others (whether that wrong is coming from us or toward us) and how it can be changed. Thus we have spoken of *assault* and *withdrawal*.

Assault comes first in the development of a child, and it arises primarily from conflicts of desire. The child wants something that another has. It does what it can to take that thing away from the other. But the other resists, and the children involved become angry with each other. They therefore try to harm each other. This is the story of Cain.

Or perhaps they experience envy and are displeased with one another because of that. Perhaps there is a status that one enjoys and the other does not. Feelings of resentment and contempt may arise and play back and forth between them. As we grow older, theft, lying, murder, adultery, and settled attitudes of covetousness fall into place. These are all forms of assault on others.

Central to them all is the will to make another suffer and suffer loss. As we have already noted, the last six of the Ten Commandments therefore deal with *assault,* with the primary ways in which we are likely to injure, by the aggressive action, those in social relation with us. With the exception of the sixth commandment, they are all explicitly negative — "Thou shalt not . . ." The sixth commandment, "Honor your father and mother," deals with a relation so intimate in its nature that the command with reference to it must be positive, for to omit the positive here would amount to an injury to both parties involved. That also is why this is "the first commandment with a promise," as Paul said (Ephesians 6:2). Violation of it disrupts the human soul and makes dysfunctional people as nothing else does.

Now we can see immediately that spiritual formation in Christ will mean becoming persons who *would* not, and therefore do not, assault those to whom they stand in relation, those whom they are *with*. Of course the overall teaching of the Bible about assault is much more profound and subtle than just these six commandments, which can be regarded as the rock bottom essentials for right relations to others. But there are many ways of assaulting people, and these merge into our other category of wrong in relationships, that of withdrawal.

Here we see again, for example, the power of the tongue. A verbal assault (which can be done in very refined as well as brutal ways—we speak of a "cutting remark") is specifically designed to hurt its object and to inflict loss of standing or respect in their own eyes and before others. You will find many people who never in their lifetime recover from a particular verbal assault, or a pattern thereof, or from other nonverbal forms of harassment or degrading treatment they have received. Most often this happens to people while very young or otherwise weak and unprotected.

But withdrawal within a relationship, like assault, also wounds those involved. And the tongue, as is well known, can assault by withdrawal, by not speaking. So, to reemphasize an essential point, we do not want to draw too sharp a line between assault and withdrawal, for withdrawal is often by intention a form of assault or attack. Some forms of it are not, however, and may instead be motivated by weakness, fear, uncertainty, or even aesthetic considerations ("pretty," "ugly," and so on), rather than any direct will to harm. Often our own weaknesses and limitations make us withdraw without intending injury or even recognizing its possibility. Yet injure it does. To those *without* full consciousness of God's enfolding love and power, no combination of good motives and explanations can prevent or heal the wounds of withdrawal. Without God, we can at most become hardened against them and "carry on."

So far from assault and withdrawal, the social area of our life is meant by God to be a play of constant mutual blessing. Pain and dysfunctionality result from the lack of this. Of course there are degrees of "withness" or involvement that human beings have with one another, and these make a difference in the precise character of the "mutual blessing" appropriate in the given case. But *every* contact with a human being should be one of goodwill and respect, with a *readiness* to acknowledge, make way for, or assist the other in suitable ways.

✿ OUR CURRENT COLDNESS IS NOT *NORMAL* ✿

TODAY WE ARE NOT so far removed in time from a social world in which such a constantly generous response was the presumed ideal. I recall from my childhood that my father, as he drove along in his car, always raised his hand to the driver of an oncoming vehicle, and he or she nearly always reciprocated. (Just recently while driving in rural Georgia, a man acknowledged me in this way. I was mildly shocked.) Of course there were not that many oncoming vehicles then. My father also never passed *anyone* on the sidewalk without acknowledging him or her, unless he was in a crowd; and he would always tip his hat to a woman (who, as such, was assumed to be a *lady*).

These, it might be thought, are small things, and you would probably wreck your car if you tried to acknowledge all the drivers you meet today. If you spoke to people on the sidewalk they would think you were crazy or dangerous. No doubt the profound moral insight of our times would also point out the "hypocrisy" involved in such responses.

Admittedly, we now live in a different world. But is it a better world for that? Could the epidemic of addictions and dysfunctions from which the masses suffer possibly be related to the fact that we are constantly in the presence of people who are withdrawn from us, who don't want to acknowledge we are *there* and frankly would feel more at ease if we weren't — people who in many cases explicitly reject us and feel it only right to do so? Isn't the desperate need for approval that drives people so relentlessly today — causing them to go to foolish and self-destructive lengths to be "attractive" or at least to get attention — nothing but the echo of a lost world of constant mutual welcome and blessing in family, neighborhood, school, and work? "Being attractive" and getting attention is the absolute bottom of the barrel of being "with others" — the fifteen minutes of fame (for which Andy Warhol is famous) that is now down to fifteen seconds or less.

I do not mean to suggest that anyone can overcome our desperate social situation by an individual act of will. Far from it. Whatever might be done, *that* isn't it. This is the world we now have. To do *anything* of substance about it will require a grace and wisdom that is at no individual's disposal, and a *long-range plan* of personal and social development is required. No doubt God has one in mind.

But to make a start where we are, we must recognize that this our world is not normal, but is only *usual* at present. We must try to see it for what it is and then begin to think of specific ways grace and truth can begin to change it. And above all, we who follow Jesus must understand that a couple of hours per week of carefully calibrated distance in a church setting will be of little help, and may only enforce the patterns of withdrawal that permeate our fallen world. What *could* we do in our fellowships that would really help make a difference?

❧ THE CENTRALITY OF FAMILIES ❧

BUT IT IS ESPECIALLY in our families and similarly close associations that we must identify the elements of assault and withdrawal that defeat love and right relation to others. By insight and practice we must break away from them and reverse them, first by learning a calm but firm non-cooperation with those poisonous elements, and then by initiatives of goodwill and blessing in the midst of them. What we do in our meetings as Christians should be focused on enabling us to do this effectively wherever we are. Those meetings should and could be centers from which powerfully redemptive community spreads.

Where to start? In various parts of the United States, publicly owned vehicles (police, street maintenance, schools) wear a bumper sticker that says, "There's No Excuse for Domestic Violence." It's a wonderful idea. But we need to go deeper, of course. We need to become the kind of people for whom domestic violence is unthinkable and never an option. We must be transformed in such a way that our minds and bodies—our very souls—simply do not have the makeup for it. This is the work of Christian spiritual formation.

We must begin in the family. Now the slogan must be, "There's No Excuse for Assault or Withdrawal in the Home." Do you think that would take care of domestic violence? Of course it would. But the reverse is not true: merely avoiding domestic violence can still leave the home a hell of cutting remarks, contempt, coldness, and withdrawal or noninvolvement. Such a hell is often found in the homes of Christians and even of Christian leaders. Frequently they seem to honestly think that such a condition is normal, and they have no knowledge of any other way. Their very theology may strengthen this tragically false outlook.

❧ MARRIAGE ☙

TODAY THERE IS ABOUT a fifty-percent divorce rate in America, and the rate is not much lower for professing Christians. But the problem is not divorce—though divorce generates a set of problems all its own. The problem is that people don't know how to be married. They don't actually get *married* in many cases, though they go through a legal and possibly a religious ceremony. They are, sad to say, incapable of *marriage*—the kind of constant, mutual blessing that can make two people in conjugal relation literally one whole person (Ephesians 5:22-33). It is not their fault. In their world, how could they know? Who would teach them? This is the soul-searing fact at the heart of our modern sadness.

To be married is to *give oneself to* another person in the most intimate and inclusive of human relationships, to support him or her for good in every way possible—physically, emotionally, and spiritually, of course, but in every conceivable dimension of his or her being. Nothing ever given to humanity more adequately portrays what *marriage* is than the "traditional service," the "Form of Solemnization of Matrimony," in the old *Book of Common Prayer* of the Church of England.

Just consider some of its wording. Anyone who wishes to really understand the situation with divorce and family breakup today should begin with careful study of the giving of oneself and the receiving of another that is manifested in the vows of this traditional service: "I . . . take thee . . . to have and to hold from this day forward, for better for worse, for richer for poorer, in sickness and in health, to love and to cherish, till death do us part. . . ." Insight into the meaning of the vows will clearly bring out *why* the ideal intent of marriage is one man, one woman for life. The "mutual submission to each other in awe of the Lord," which is the vision of marriage in Christ, eliminates both assault and withdrawal from this most basic of human relationships. Thereby it provides the matrix or womb from which (in God's plan) whole human beings can emerge to form whole human communities, under God.

This "womb" is then, of course, the overall home life of the child, not just a particular part of the female body. Birth should only be a move from one part to a larger part of the same home. This home is as much or more the man's responsibility as the woman's, for it is the man's role to make it possible for the woman to do what she alone can do for the child—and for him. And for her part, then, she is to help in making it possible for him to do what he alone can do for her and the child—and this in the midst of constant sacrificial submission on the part of each to the overall good of the other. In case there are no children involved, they still "lay down their life" for each other. That is what *marriage* involves.

The "Market" Approach to Marriage

IN THE CONDITIONS OF modern life, especially since the two World Wars, it has, for various reasons, been increasingly unclear how such a union of souls could be carried out in practice. *Individual desire has come to be the standard and rule of everything.* How are we to serve one another in intimate relations if individual desire is the standard for everything and if what we desire can be acquired from many competing providers?

The ways in which man and wife, or parents and children, would "naturally" serve one another—and traditionally have done so—are increasingly viewed as available (usually less expensively and perhaps with "better quality") from various sources.[10] This is true all the way from food, clothing, entertainment, and attractiveness, to romance, sexual gratification, and surrogate "motherhood" and "fatherhood." The perilous condition of laborers competing with others to sell their labor is now the condition of everyone in current society. Individual desire is accepted as a principle governing everything.

What, then, does devotion to another mean when one or both parties are constantly shopping for "a better deal" or constantly appraising one another in the light of convenient alternatives? Withdrawal, rejection, and assault will naturally become a constant factor in the most intimate of human relations. This is what Satan has always used to defeat God's plans for human community on earth, from Adam blaming Eve for his own sin, to Cain killing Abel, to the latest cases of "ethnic cleansing," and the millions of children living on their own in the streets and sewers of urban centers around the globe or starving in rural poverty. The very same principle of withdrawal and assault operates at the highest levels of cultural, social, and political interaction, with constant glorification in the popular arts and media.

◈ THE DEVASTATION OF CHILDREN ◈

THE SPIRITUAL MALFORMATION OF children is the inevitable result. Their little souls, bodies, and minds cannot but absorb the reality of assault and withdrawal in a climate where their parents or other adults are constantly engaged in them. And of course they are soon in the line of fire themselves. They soon are being attacked and frozen out. In such a context you can almost see the children shrivel.

Their only hope of survival is to become *hardened*. This amounts to a constant posture of withdrawal, even from oneself. It is a defensive posture, which, incidentally, makes attack (on others *and* on oneself) easy and inevitable. Hardened, lonely little souls, ready for addiction, aggression, isolation, self-destructive behavior, and for some, even extreme violence, go out to mingle their madness with one another in nightmarish school grounds and "communities." They turn to their bodies for self-gratification and to control others, or for isolation and self-destruction.

The wonder is not that they sometimes destroy one another, but that the adults who produced them and live with them can, with apparent sincerity, ask "Why?" Do they really not know? Can they really not see the poison in the social realm? It is another profound case of the blind leading the blind and both falling into a pit (Matthew 15:14).

Marching onward in life, these little people become big people and move on with their malfunctioning souls into workplace, profession, citizenship, and leadership. From them proceeds the next generation of wounded souls. Many of these now "big people," perhaps "the best and brightest," try hard to rectify the situation. They sponsor sickeningly shallow solutions to the human problem, such as "education" or "diversity" or "tolerance."

Not that these are not good things in themselves. They are. But they do not come close to the root of the human problem. They are superficial. The deep root is not ignorance (at least not ignorance of the things you learn getting an "education"), not prejudice, and not intolerance. A very small percentage of human evil comes from them, everything considered; and almost none of that does which affects our most intimate relations and turns us into the kind of people we are. Ignorance, prejudice, and intolerance, far from being the primary sources of evil, draw upon the still deeper-lying soul structures of assault and withdrawal, without which they would have little effect.

"Difference" only serves as *one occasion* of assault and withdrawal. Unless the sources deeper than it are effectively dealt with, education, diversity, and "tolerance" will only yield another version of secular self-righteousness and legalism. They will further crush the already famished human frame, being just the opposite of what Crabb calls "connecting." Instead of healing relationships, they will only establish a somewhat more socially stable context within which people shrivel and die.

MINISTER TO MARRIAGE

SO, TO HEAL THE open sore of social existence, there is no doubt we must start with the marriage relationship—or, more inclusively, with *how men and women are together in our world.* If that relationship is wrong in its many dimensions, all who come through it will be seriously damaged. And they will be further damaged by a surrounding world of similarly damaged people, who are trying to manage their ways of being together on the assumption that assault and withdrawal are just "the facts of life." Consequently, spiritual formation, and all our efforts as Christians to minister to people, must focus on this humanly most central relationship.

Frankly, however, we sometimes see families arriving at church frozen in coldness or seething in anger about many things, even about what it took to get them there on time. And then we may have people conducting the services who can hardly endure one another because of disagreements and painful incidents that have occurred between them—even in the process of determining how the service should be done. Do we need a bumper sticker that says, "There is no excuse for hostility and coldness among Christians"?

Yes, that might help. Obviously it is relevant. But we can only begin to recover the correct social dimension of our lives under Christ by unshakable recognition that there is no human answer to human problems, not even a "religious" answer—which is why the various humanistic "spiritualities" of our day are dead ends. Of course they may offer some help to the distressed human condition. But they are powerless to dissolve the pervasive structures of assault and withdrawal that characterize our individual and corporate existence. Or, if they are not, then let them do it. They in turn can rightly say to the church, "You do it." And that too is fair enough.

The visible churches, congregations of apprentices to Jesus, must return to the transcendent power of Christ for which they stand. They must *drain the assault and withdrawal, the attack and coldness, from the individual men and women who form families under their ministry of Jesus and his kingdom.* We must affirm, and make clear by teaching and example, both *that* and *how* it takes "three to get married," as Fulton Sheen taught years ago. (The "Third" of course is God.) That is the true meaning of the union "with benefit of clergy" that the people of Christ offer. From this basis in the home, established through the church of Jesus Christ, the power of God on earth can break up the deadly hold of assault and withdrawal over the entire social dimension of the human self.

⮞ Main Elements in Spiritual Formation of Our Social Dimension ⮜

WHAT WILL THIS LOOK like in ordinary human relations? This is what must be explained and abundantly exemplified in the context of the redemptive local gathering. It all must start there, though it will be *immediately* applied to conjugal relationships and the families arising out of them. Above all it must be seen in the family relationships of those who lead and teach. Here are four major elements in the new world of redeemed relationships.

⮞ Receiving God's Vision of Our Wholeness in Him ⮜

THE *FIRST* MAIN ELEMENT in the transformed social dimension is for individuals to come to see themselves *whole,* as God himself sees them. Such a vision sets them beyond the wounds and limitations they have received in their past relationships to others. It is this vision of oneself from God's point of view that makes it possible to regard oneself as blessed, no matter what has happened. "We are dead," Paul tells us, and "our life is hid with Christ in God. When Christ, who is our life, shall appear, then we will appear with him, glorious" (Colossians 3:3-4, PAR). We have stepped into a new life where the primary relationship is with Christ and we are assured of a glorious existence forever.

God has a plan for each of us in the work he is doing during our lifetime, and no one can prevent this from being fulfilled if we place our hope entirely in him. The part we play in his plans now will extend to the role he has set before us for eternity. Our life in him is whole and it is blessed, *no matter what has or has not been done to us, no matter how shamefully our human circles of sufficiency have been violated.*

It is God's sufficiency to us that secures everything else. Paul again said, "Our sufficiency is of God" (2 Corinthians 3:5; 9:8, PAR). It is the God-given vision of us as whole in him that draws all the poisons from our relationships to others and enables us to go forward with sincere forgiveness and blessing toward them. Only in this way can we stand free from the wounds of the past and from those who have assaulted or forsaken us.

✎ DEFENSIVENESS GONE ✐

THE SECOND ELEMENT IN the spiritually transformed social dimension is abandonment of all defensiveness. This of course could occur only in a social context where Christ dwells—that is, among his special people. But it is natural it would occur in the absence of attack and withdrawal, wherever that may be, or where we have an impregnable defense against it.

This abandonment of defensiveness includes a willingness to be known in our most intimate relationships for who we really are. It would include abandonment of all practices of self-justification, evasiveness, and deceit, as well as manipulation. That is not to say we should impose all the facts about ourselves upon those close to us, much less on others at large. Of course we shouldn't. But it does mean that we do not hide and we do not follow strategies for "looking good."

Jesus' teachings about not performing for public approval, about letting our "yes" be a "yes" and nothing more, and about not being a hypocrite—having a face that differs from our reality—all find application here (Matthew 5–6).

✎ GENUINE LOVE PREDOMINATES IN OUR GATHERINGS ✐

AND THEN ALL PRETENSE would vanish from our lives. That would be the *third* element in the spiritually transformed social dimension of the self. Love between Christians then would, as Paul says to the Romans, "be genuine." And that is the central factor in the beautiful picture of what the local gatherings of disciples into "churches" should be like, given by Paul in Romans 12:1-21. Christ's apprentices would be carrying out their particular work in the group life with a grace and power that is not from themselves, but from God (verses 3-8), and each one would be exhibiting the following qualities (verses 9-21):

1. Letting love be completely real
2. Abhorring what is evil
3. Clinging to what is good
4. Being devoted to one another in family-like love (*philostorgoi*)
5. Outdoing one another in giving honor
6. Serving the Lord with ardent spirit and all diligence
7. Rejoicing in hope
8. Being patient in troubles

9. Being devoted constantly to prayer
10. Contributing to the needs of the saints
11. Pursuing (running after) hospitality
12. Blessing persecutors and not cursing them
13. Being joyful with those who are rejoicing and being sorrowful with those in sorrow
14. Living in harmony with each other
15. Not being haughty, but fitting right in with the "lowly" in human terms
16. Not seeing yourself as wise
17. Never repaying evil for evil
18. Having due regard for what everyone takes to be right
19. Being at peace with everyone, so far as it depends on you
20. Never taking revenge, but leaving that to whatever God may decide
21. Providing for needy enemies
22. Not being overwhelmed by evil, but overwhelming evil with good

This is the most adequate biblical description of what the details of a spiritually transformed social dimension look like. We should pause to contemplate it. Just think for a moment what it would be like to be part of a group of disciples in which this list was the conscious, shared *intention,* and where it was actually lived out, even if with some imperfection. You can see, I think, how it would totally transform the marriage relation and the home and family. Its effect on the community would be incalculable, as it in fact has been wherever realized throughout the history of Christ's people on earth.

The abandonment of all defensiveness and its many strategies would clearly be achieved in such a group. There would no longer be any need for them. In their place would be receptiveness and blessing for all, even enemies. Certainly, to achieve this in our social dimension we must have heard and accepted the gospel of grace, of Jesus' defenseless death on the cross on our behalf, and of his acceptance of us into his life beyond death and beyond the worst that could be done to him or to us. We must stand safe and solid in his kingdom.

The *fourth* element is an opening up of our broader social dimension to redemption. Not having the burden of defending and securing ourselves, and acting now from the resources of our new "life from above," we can devote our lives to the service of others. This is the positive moment in redemption of the social side of the self. It is not just a matter of *not* attacking or withdrawing. That redemption will naturally and rightly be chiefly focused in blessing upon those closest to us, beginning with our family members and moving out from there, proportional to our degree of life involvement with others.

The social world is set before us as an infinite task, which can only be carried out in the power of God. We accept that. Just as we cannot be the husband or wife or parent God intends except in the power of God, so for our life as a whole. We do not even know how to pray as we ought, Paul tells us (Romans 8:26). What then, shall we not pray? By no means, for "the Spirit Himself intercedes for us with groanings too deep for words" (verse 26). And the Spirit of God will enter into all of our social connections if we invite him, wait on him, and proceed as best we can. We have the promise of Jesus to those who live by his "living water." That water "shall become in him a well of water springing up to eternal life" (John 4:14), and "'from his innermost being shall flow rivers of living water'" (John 7:38; compare Isaiah 58:11).

Spiritual formation in Christ obviously requires that we increasingly be happily reconciled to living in and by *the direct upholding of the hand of God*. This is clearly what the entire biblical view of life calls for, and especially what Jesus himself lived and presented as the truth. Only from within this gospel outlook on life can we begin to approach the godly reformation of the self in its social world. But from within that outlook we can cease from assault and withdrawal and can extend ourselves in blessing to all whose lives we touch.

Matters for Thought and Discussion

1. What "circles of sufficiency" have you enjoyed in your lifetime? Describe in detail some occasions when you experienced "completeness" in them. Or occasions when they were "broken."

2. How does rejection affect us? Why does it affect us as it does? Can you recall an occasion, perhaps as a child or youth, when you rejected someone and how they responded?

3. Do assault and withdrawal cover the field of the evils people do to others? Think about the role these play in ordinary life. Is it possible to disagree with or correct others without assault or withdrawal?

4. Consider violations of each of the last six of the Ten Commandments as forms of assault. Do you see how they are? What they *do to* people?

5. How would love as Jesus loved eliminate assault and withdrawal within familiar personal relationships?

6. How does the Trinitarian nature of God cast light on what human relations could and should be?

7. "One nation under God." How could that possibly be realized?

8. How do assault and withdrawal find their way into the lives of children?

9. Must we accept coldness between people as *normal* now?

10. Do you agree that redemption of the marriage relation is central to any hope for transforming our broader social situation today? Or is that just "too much" to put on man–woman relationships?

11. How can we come to "see ourselves whole in God's life," and how would that help heal our social dimension?

12. Could Paul's picture of the redemptive fellowship of Christ's people (Romans 12:1-21) be put into place in your group?

TRANSFORMING THE SOUL

Only give heed to yourself and keep your soul diligently, lest you forget the things which your eyes have seen.
DEUTERONOMY 4:9

Take My yoke upon you, and learn from Me, for I am gentle and humble in heart; and you shall find rest for your souls.
MATTHEW 11:29 (SEE ALSO JEREMIAH 6:16)

What is running your life at any given moment is your soul. Not external circumstances, or your thoughts, or your intentions, or even your feelings, but your soul. The soul is that aspect of your whole being that *correlates, integrates,* and *enlivens* everything going on in the various dimensions of the self. It is the life-center of the human being. It regulates whatever is occurring in each of those dimensions and how they interact with each other and respond to surrounding events in the overall governance of your life. The soul is "deep" in the sense of being basic or foundational and also in the sense that it lies almost totally beyond conscious awareness.[1]

In the person with the "well-kept heart," the soul will be itself properly ordered under God and in harmony with reality. The outcome will be, as we have said, "a person who is *prepared* for and *capable* of responding to the situations of life in ways that are good and right." For such a person, the human spirit will be in correct relationship to God. With his assisting grace, it will bring the soul into subjection to God and the mind (thoughts, feelings) into subjection to the soul. The social context and the body will then come into subjection to thoughts and feelings that are in agreement with truth and with God's intent and purposes for us. Any given event in our life would then proceed as it should, because our soul is functioning properly under God.

☙ PSALM 1 MAN ☙

THAT IS HOW IT is with the man in Psalm 1. He is first characterized in terms of what he does *not* do, which is perhaps the most immediately obvious thing about him. He does not determine his course of action by what those without God are saying—even their latest brilliant ideas. That is, he does not live as if God does not exist nor make plans from within strictly human understanding. He plans on God (verse 1).

Because of that he also does not position himself or stand in life where and as those do who live by doing wrong. If you live within only human "wisdom" you will find it constantly "necessary" to do what is wrong. And in that case you will become an "authority" on what is right and wrong—because, after all, you will have to *manage* right and wrong. You will have to have ready explanations of why, though you do wrong things, you are still a good person, and why those who do not do as you do are fools. You will become an expert scorner, able to put everyone in their place with appropriate doses of contempt, which is an essential element of scorn (verse 1).

In contrast to all this, the Psalm 1 man delights in the law that God has given. Note, he *delights* in it (verse 2). He loves it, is thrilled by it, can't keep his mind off of it. He thinks it is beautiful, strong, wise, an incredible gift of God's mercy and grace. He therefore dwells upon it day and night, turning it over and over in his mind and speaking it to himself. He does not do this to please God, but because the law pleases him. It is where his whole being is oriented.

The result is a flourishing life. The image used here is that of a tree planted by water canals. No matter what the weather or the surface condition of the ground, its roots go down into the water sources and bring up life. As a result, it bears fruit when it is supposed to, and its foliage is always bright with life. It prospers in what it does. And likewise the man who is rooted in God through his law: "in whatever he does, he prospers" (Psalm 1:3; compare Joshua 1:8). We must come back to the absolutely vital relationship between the law and the soul later.

☙ THIS IS NOT THE ORDINARY CASE ☙

FOR MOST OF US, however, this ideal arrangement of life under God will be only partially realized, at best. For many, it remains an impossible dream, for their soul is running amuck and their life is in chaos. They are "dead in trespasses and sins," living off of incoherent dreams and illusions. Enslaved to their desires or their bodily habits or blinded by false ideas, distorted images, and misinformation, their soul cannot find its way into a life of consistent truth and harmonious pursuit of what is good. It is locked in a self-destructive struggle with itself and with all around it. Normally, unfulfilled desires and poisonous relationships are the most prominent features of such lives. I confess that as a sometimes counselor of those in trouble, I am often stunned with the reasons people give for not doing the only things that could possibly be of help to themselves.

The individual soul's specific formation—the character it has taken on through its life course—is seen in the details of how thoughts, feelings, social relations, bodily behaviors, and choices unfold, and especially how they interact with each other. In most actual cases, the individuals are not at harmony with themselves, much less with truth and with God. Their habitual condition is one of conflict, and one of acting other than how they themselves intend or regard as wise.

Their intentions of good are, precisely, not effectively related to the other components of their person—the thoughts and feelings, the bodily habits, the social dynamics, the relationship to God's kingdom—in a way that would bring the good to pass. The failure of good intentions is the outcome of the underlying disconnects or "wrong connects" between thoughts, feelings, and actions, permitted or enforced by their disordered soul. The dimensions of the self are not coherently drawn together by the soul to form a whole life devoted to God and to what is acknowledged as good. Such a person cannot "get it all together" or "get his (or her) act together," as we say now. That language is not metaphorical, but expresses the reality of his or her life.

Extreme cases of this are found in people for whom everything in personal and social life is painful or unmanageable. They cannot find a place in human affairs. This can take many forms, but their inner condition makes it impossible for them to deal with life. Often this comes from early experiences. Severe deprivation or suffering in the early years will invariably distort the soul and leave it receptive to malfunction and evil in many forms, or simply *stunted*. The protective walls of the soul seem to have been broken down by pain and evil, leaving the person at the mercy of everything that happens.

There is a developmental order in the soul, such that if it does not receive what it needs to receive within appropriate periods of time as it grows, its further progression toward wholeness is permanently hindered. It will never be what it might have been. Sometimes horrible events of later life, such as being tortured or cruelly betrayed, have similar effects, from which the soul may never recover.

However, one must not overgeneralize on such matters. And one must not underestimate the powers of recovery of the soul under grace. Robert Wise observes, "Reconnected to the Spirit of God, lost souls discover they have power and capacity beyond anything they could have dreamed. The restoration of soul is more than a recovery of connectedness. Significant strength, ability to achieve, guidance, and awareness are imparted."[2]

Truly we are "fearfully and wonderfully made" (Psalm 139:14). The human soul is a vast spiritual (nonphysical) landscape, with resources and relationships that exceed human comprehension; and it also exists within an infinite environment of which, at our best, we have little knowledge. We only know that God is over it all and that the soul, if it can only acknowledge its wounded condition, manifests amazing capacities for recovery when it finds its home in God and receives his grace.[3]

☙ MODERN DIFFICULTIES WITH THE SOUL ❧

NOW, OF ALL THE dimensions of the human being that must be dealt with in understanding spiritual formation, the soul is by far the most controversial and inaccessible in today's world. For various reasons, it was rejected by the field of "psychology" — by very name the "theory of the soul" — as that field tried to develop itself into a "scientific" understanding of humans. The alleged failure to "find" an enduring, nonphysical center that organizes life into a whole has become a part of what is regarded as the outcome of modern thought, as everyone with a high-school education now knows.

The issues here certainly run deep, and we do not mean to dismiss them lightly. However, they are not the kind of matters that can be dealt with in a book such as this. Instead, we shall indicate some relevant literature for those who wish to go deeper into questions about the soul,[4] and then point to the obvious necessity in life of treating ourselves and others as having a deeper unity and continuity than can be understood from within science as "science" is now generally understood, under the philosophical influence of empiricism and naturalism.

☙ SOUL UNAVOIDABLE ❧

THIS "OBVIOUS NECESSITY" HAS in recent decades expressed itself in a great wave of popular publications and media presentations on the soul. "Soul" has become almost as attention-getting as "sex," and is widely used as a selling point. People pride themselves on having and knowing and expressing "soul." The superficial conditions of ordinary life in most Western contexts have brought this forth. It is a natural reaction to a deeply felt need, for indeed the soul—or, more generally, the spiritual side of life—simply cannot be indefinitely suppressed. Fundamental aspects of life such as art, sleep, sex, ritual, family ("roots"), parenting, community, health, and meaningful work all are in fact soul functions, and they fail and fall apart to the degree that soul diminishes. It is possible that the reason modern intellectuals have failed to find soul is that soul really is no longer present in their individual lives. Perhaps something like a soulless life really is possible and not just something to be portrayed in fashionable literary works.

That would explain why meaning is such a problem for human beings today. "Meaning" in action is fundamentally a matter of "carry over" or transcendence. Meaningful experience *flows*. It does not leave you stuck on something you can't get past—whether a word you don't understand or a pointless social situation. Meaning is one of the greatest needs of human life, one of our deepest hungers—perhaps it is, in the final analysis, the most basic need in the realm of the human experience.[5] Almost anything can be born if life as a whole is meaningful. But in the absence of meaning, boredom and mere effort or willpower are all that is left. "Dead" religion or a dead job or relationship is one that has to be carried on in "meaningless" human routine.

In boredom and carrying on by mere willpower, almost nothing can be endured, and people who are well off by all other physical and social standards find such a life unbearable. They are "dead souls." By contrast, though in meaningful experience we are very active, the presence of meaning, with its power of "carryover," relieves the pain of effort and makes even great strain exhilarating. It is as if a power beyond us meets our action and *carries* us. That is always, in some measure, the presence of soul.

✺ PERFORMANCE, FANATICISM, AND THE BROKEN SOUL ✺

WHERE LIFE MEANING IS lacking, performance is at a premium. "Performance"—in art or sports, for example—creates the illusion of meaning for a magical moment, *if* the performance is successful. Performance presupposes an *artificial context* in which some portion of life, action, or experience is present as a whole, meaningful, unique, flowing—transcendent to ordinary existence. This may be in some area of art, or in sports, or in politics. Unfortunately, it may also be in religion, or in the intimate relations of life. But in these latter areas, performance is not really valued unless it deals effectively with life and reality as a whole and does not presuppose an artificial context. Otherwise the performance is a sham. Here performance really must mean *competence* and must eliminate illusion. Mere "acting" will not do.

It will further help us to understand the reality of soul in life if we see how *fanaticism* comes in. Fanaticism—in art, politics, sports, or religion, to name some of the main kinds—is the result of inherently meaningless lives becoming obsessed with performance and then trying to take all of their existence into it. Being a fan of . . . is treated as something deep and important. Because those who do this do not have a whole soul directing their lives toward good, rooted in God, they allow a "flow" they find outside themselves to take over their thoughts, feelings, behavior, and social relations. That flow intoxicates them. They absolutize the flow and no longer subject it to ordinary tests of truth, reality, and tried-and-true human values.

Thus the winning of a championship by a city team can lead to looting, burning, and death. Romantic/sexual relationship can play the same obsessing role, as can "success," leading to workaholic absorption. All of these are reflections of a nonfunctional or broken or recessive soul with inadequate resources to deal with the whole human life. The nonfunctioning soul falls easy prey to the mob and to pressures from others. It is the source of the "other-directed person" and "the lonely crowd" that are so prominent today.[6]

So it really doesn't matter what our *theories* are, or how "modern" we may be. Soul will always reassert itself as a reality, if only by the shambles left behind when it departs. What Hitler preyed upon was soul, as have all the great twentieth-century destroyers—or rather, upon the loss of soul and the revenge that loss takes upon the masses. Similarly for those who produce the wasteland of contemporary pop culture, from *Jerry Springer* to *Seinfeld*.

Those who deny the soul, perhaps for what they regard as the most overwhelming of scientific and philosophical reasonings, still have *to live a life,* and they need to find the resources for it. If they cannot deal with that need in terms of a healthy soul, they still have to deal with it in *some* terms. What shall those terms be? They have to find them in one way or another, and not all ways are equal. The soul will strike back.

⤬ OUR STRATEGY HERE ⤬

BECAUSE I CANNOT DEAL with the soul here in a thorough and systematic manner that would address main issues (I refer again to the literature noted), my strategy will be twofold: First, I will elaborate a picture or image of the soul, and second, I will look at certain things said about the soul in the Bible. Now the image:

Our soul is like an inner stream of water, which gives strength, direction, and harmony to every other element of our life. When that stream is as it should be, we are constantly refreshed and exuberant in all we do, because our soul itself is then profusely rooted in the vastness of God and his kingdom, including nature; and all else within us is enlivened and directed by that stream. Therefore we are in harmony with God, reality, and the rest of human nature and nature at large. As is usual in biblical themes, a little child that has been allowed to develop naturally and has been nurtured in all the aspects of its being gives us the best presentation of what a life flooded with a healthy soul looks like.

Now, beyond the image or picture of an inner stream is this reality: *Life* is self-initiating, self-directing, self-sustaining activity and power. In this full sense, of course, *only God has life*. That is the biblical view. Moreover, in his "hand is the soul of every living thing," Job tells us (Job 12:10, PAR). "The Father has life in Himself," Jesus taught, and "gave to the Son also to have life in Himself" (John 5:26). "He alone possesses undying life" (1 Timothy 6:16, PAR), according to Paul, and is the one "who gives and preserves life to all things" (verse 13).

The individual living thing receives its *relatively* "self-initiating, self-directing, self-sustaining power" from the hand of God. This derivative life flows through the living being in the form of its own soul. As for the human, its peculiar form of soul is related to the unique spirit relationship it has to God (Genesis 2:7). It is its peculiar form of soul that enlivens everything else in the creature, and its overall condition reflects the state of its soul. In the human being, spiritual life in the kingdom of God is central to its soul and its life.

This, we seriously suggest, is not an image but a reality, and one that the image of a stream of water can portray with some force. When we speak of the human soul, then, we are speaking of the *deepest level of life and power* in the human being.

✸ GOD HAS A SOUL ✸

THAT THIS IS THE meaning of the soul in the Christian understanding can, I think, be seen from what the Bible says about *God's* soul. Many people are surprised to learn that God, too, has a soul, and even translators of the Bible often do not seem to know what to do about it. Referring to the gross wickedness into which Judea had fallen, the prophet Jeremiah gives the Lord's word: "Be thou instructed, O Jerusalem, lest my soul depart from thee; and lest I make thee desolate, a land not inhabited" (Jeremiah 6:8, KJV). But more recent versions translate this as " . . . or I shall turn from you in disgust" (NRSV) or "Lest I be alienated from you." Similarly in Jeremiah 9:9: "Shall not my soul be avenged on such a nation as this?" (KJV); "Shall I not bring retribution on a nation such as this?" (NRSV); and "On a nation such as this shall I not avenge Myself?"

In these and other cases the word *"nephesh"* (or soul) occurs in the Hebrew texts with reference to God. That is done in order to indicate the utter depth of the response of God to the wickedness of his people. That depth is not successfully communicated by the alternative language offered. The true meaning is hollowed out and lost. Similar observations must be made about Isaiah 1:14 (where KJV and NRSV, but not NASB, use "soul"). In speaking of the *soul* of God, reference is always made to the deepest, most fundamental level of his being. And similarly in New Testament texts such as, "BEHOLD, MY SERVANT WHOM I HAVE CHOSEN; MY BELOVED IN WHOM MY SOUL IS WELL-PLEASED" (Matthew 12:18; see Leviticus 26:11; Psalm 11:5; and numerous other passages referring to God's soul).

The heart of the matter is that to refer to someone's soul is to say something about the ultimate depths of his or her being and something that cannot be communicated by using terms like "person" or "self" or various available pronouns. (See Matthew 11:29, cited at the head of this chapter; and Luke 21:19.)

✎ APPLIED TO THE HUMAN SOUL: BIBLICAL CASES ✐

NOW, IF YOU TAKE this idea of the deepest and most fundamental level of a life and apply it to biblical references to the *human* soul, you will see that it makes great sense of what the Scripture is saying in the given case. Human life has many aspects that are superficial, not the real essence of life. They are not *soul*. Let us consider a few texts.

Lot, fleeing the destruction of Sodom, doesn't want to have to live out in the mountains, and he pleads with God to let him go into a tiny town nearby: "Please let me escape there! Is it not a little thing, that my soul may live?" (Genesis 19:20, PAR). His exterior life has been wiped out, and he is pleading for his soul, his essence, to be able to survive. He doesn't think it will survive in the mountains, even though that is where he seems to have wound up anyway (verse 30).

Or consider Isaac wishing to give his blessing to his eldest son, Esau. And to enable it to come from his most profound depths he asks Esau to prepare a favorite meal of wild game that he has caught: "Prepare a savory dish for me such as I love, and bring it to me that I may eat, so that my soul may bless you before I die" (Genesis 27:4). And when the blessing has come from those depths, he cannot retract it or produce another.

Or consider Jesus' teaching that it does not profit one to gain the whole world and lose his or her own soul (Matthew 16:26). One might well ask, before taking up the question of profit, how is that possible? What does it mean to lose your soul? Can you actually do that? Does it describe anyone you know?

Well, what it means is that your whole life is no longer under the direction of your inner stream of life, which has been taken over by exteriors. The rich farmer who said, "Soul, you have many goods laid up for many years to come; take your ease, eat, drink and be merry" (Luke 12:19), is simply a case in point. He had abandoned his soul in favor of externalities. He had laid up treasure for himself, and was not "rich toward God" (verse 21). He is an illustration of those who do not recognize that they are meant to be "aliens and strangers" upon the earth, and who, as a result, turn their life over to "desires of the flesh that wage war against the soul" (1 Peter 2:11, NRSV).

A step beyond the misguided farmer is the person who delights in doing evil. He is a wicked, not just a misguided or foolish person. "The soul of the wicked desires evil," the proverb tells us, and will even harm those closest to him (Proverbs 21:10). In his deepest depths he is committed to wrongdoing.

On the positive side we see Mary calling upon her soul to "magnify the Lord" (Luke 1:46, KJV). That is, the deepest part of her being. James spoke of how the engrafted word "is able to save your souls" (1:21). Paul and his coworkers strengthened "the souls of the disciples" as he returned through the cities of Asia Minor (Acts 14:22), and he spoke to the Thessalonians of how they not only gave them the gospel of God, but also imparted "our own souls" (1 Thessalonians 2:8). Peter speaks of disciples purifying their souls in obedience (1 Peter 1:22).

The book of Psalms is, of course, the great "soul book" in the Bible, simply because it, more than any other, deals with life in its depths and with our fundamental relationship to the One who is the keeper of our soul (Psalm 121:7). "My soul thirsts for Thee, my flesh yearns for Thee, in a dry and weary land where there is no water" (Psalm 63:1). Of course the "water" spoken of here is not H_2O, but the water of life, which Jesus promised. "My soul longed and even yearned for the courts of the LORD" (84:2). "As the deer pants for the water brooks, so my soul pants for Thee, O God. My soul thirsts for God, for the living God" (42:1-2). The water image earlier noted naturally stands out in these passages because of the similarity of water to the nourishing flow of God's life from which the soul draws its strength and direction. "There is a river, the streams whereof shall make glad the city of God" (46:4, KJV). But then it turns out that the river is God himself: "God is in the midst of her; she shall not be moved: God shall help her, and that right early" (verse 5, KJV).

These and many other passages make clear that the soul is the most basic level of life in the individual, and one that is by nature rooted in God. We must take care to do whatever we can to keep it in his hands, recognizing all the while that we can only do this with his help.

✆ ACKNOWLEDGING OUR SOUL ✆

AND THE VERY FIRST thing that we must do is to be mindful of our soul, to acknowledge it. In spiritual formation and transformation it is necessary to take the soul seriously and deal with it regularly and intelligently. We must be sure to do this for ourselves, individually, and also in our Christian fellowships.

I suspect it will seem strange to some that we emphasize this. Isn't the soul something "religious," after all? And doesn't religion deal with the soul all the time? Such questions have a historical point to them, for the soul has very much been at the center of traditional Christianity. But in the contemporary context you will hear very little about the soul in Christian groups of whatever kind in the Western world, and you will see very few people seriously concerned about the state of their own soul. There is very little said from the pulpit about the soul as an essential part of our lives and almost no serious teaching about it at any level of our various Christian educational undertakings.

Some conservative and evangelical churches still sometimes talk about *saving* the soul, but even this much less than used to be the case; and once the soul is "safe" it is usually treated as needing no further attention. Ignoring the soul is one reason why Christian churches have become fertile sources of recruits for cults and other religious and political groups. It is not reasonable to think the soul would be properly cared for when it isn't even seriously acknowledged. So this has to change.

The acknowledgment of the soul, which is necessary to carry through with spiritual formation, is made more difficult by the elusiveness of the soul and the loss of Christian traditions and terminologies for comprehending it. Here too our religious contexts have suffered from harmful influence by the secular intellect, which frankly abhors the soul. We all more or less dimly feel and discern our own soul's condition and that of others. But we rarely can articulate or express those conditions and bring them to a level of comprehension required for helpful reflection and discussion. We have very much lost "soul" language and are embarrassed by it—though it still breaks through in the Bible and older Christian writings and in odd places here and there in contemporary life and art.

Now, this is not a desirable situation, to say the least, and certainly it is not compatible with the serious undertaking of spiritual formation. Our preachers and teachers must emphatically and repeatedly acknowledge the soul as the living center of Christian life that it is, and they must reassume their responsibility for the care of souls, long assigned to them in Christian tradition.[7] We as individuals must "own" our souls and take responsibility before God for them, turning to our pastors and teachers for the necessary help.

On the other hand we must recognize the recent upsurge of "soul talk" in publishing (see the many titles) and in business books and seminars. "Soul" has become profitable. That would be well if it were joined with a proper presentation of the soul in relation to God. But unfortunately, this rarely is the case. We must never forget that the indispensable first step in caring for the soul is to place it under God.

☙ THE CRIES OF THE SOUL ☙

ONCE WE CLEARLY ACKNOWLEDGE the soul, we can learn to hear its cries. Jesus heard its cries from the wearied humanity he saw around him. He saw the soul's desperate need in those who struggled with the overwhelming tasks of their life. Such weariness and endless labor was, to him, a sure sign of a soul not properly rooted in God—a soul, in effect, on its own. He saw the multitudes around him, and it tore his heart, for they were "distressed and downcast" like "sheep without a shepherd" (Matthew 9:36). And he invited such people to come and become his students ("learn of me") by yoking themselves to him—that is, letting him show them how he would pull their load. He is not "above" this, as earthly "great ones" are, for he is meek and lowly of heart (Matthew 11:28-30).

His own greatness of soul made meekness and lowliness the natural way for him to be (Philippians 2:3-11). Being in his yoke is not a matter of taking on additional labor to crush us all the more, but a matter of learning how to use his strength *and* ours together to bear our load *and* his. We will find his yoke an easy one and his burden a light one *because,* in learning from him, we have found rest to our soul. What we have learned is, primarily, to rest our soul in God. Rest *to* our soul is rest *in* God. My soul is at peace only when it is with God, as a child with its mother.

☙ ABANDONING OUTCOMES ☙

WHAT WE MOST LEARN in his yoke, beyond acting *with* him, is to abandon *outcomes* to God, accepting that we do not have in ourselves—in our own "heart, soul, mind, and strength"—the wherewithal to make *this* come out right, whatever "this" is. Even if we "suffer according to the will of God," we simply "entrust our souls to a faithful Creator in doing what is right" (1 Peter 4:19). Now, this is a major part of that meekness and lowliness of heart that we also learn in his yoke. And what rest comes with it!

Humility is the framework within which all virtue lives. Angela of Foligno observed, "Our Lord did not say: Learn of Me to despise the world and live in poverty . . . but only this: Learn of Me for I am gentle and lowly of heart." And "One of the signs by which a man may know that he is in a state of grace is this—that he is never puffed up."[8] Accordingly, we are to "clothe [ourselves] with humility," Peter said (1 Peter 5:5), which certainly means loss of self-sufficiency. "God gives grace to the humble," he continues.

"Humble yourselves, therefore, under the mighty hand of God, that He may exalt you at the proper time, casting all your anxiety upon Him, because He cares for you" (verses 5-7). Humility is a great secret of rest of soul because it does not presume to secure outcomes.

Here is a simple fact: We live in a world where, *by God's appointment,* "the race is not to the swift, and the battle is not to the warriors, and neither is bread to the wise, nor wealth to the discerning, nor favor to men of ability; for time and chance overtake them all" (Ecclesiastes 9:11). The Lord "does not delight in the strength of the horse; He does not take pleasure in the legs of a man" (Psalm 147:10). He has a plan for our life that goes far beyond anything we can work out and secure by means of strong horses and good legs.

We simply have to rest in his life as he gives it to us. Knowledge, from Christ, that he is good and great enables us to cast outcomes on him. We find this knowledge in the yoke of Christ. Resting in God, we can be free from all anxiety, which means deep soul rest. Whatever our circumstance, taught by Christ we are enabled to "rest [be still] in the LORD and wait patiently [or longingly] for Him" (Psalm 37:7). We don't fret or get angry because others seem to be doing better than we are, even though they are less deserving than we.

✎ NO SOUL REST WITH SIN ✎

ON THE OTHER HAND, sin or disobedience to what we know to be right *distances* us from God and forces us to live on our own. That means it makes soul rest impossible and is very destructive to the soul. "He who is partner with a thief hates his own soul," the proverb says (29:24, PAR).

Those are surely right who have recognized in *pride* the root of all disobedience. We think we are "big enough" to take our life into our own hands and disobey, instead of "humbling ourselves under the mighty hand of God." And this will certainly be driven by the thought that if we do not take things into our own hands, we will not get what we want—another blow to our pride. Our attitude should be, to the contrary, that there is no particular reason why I should get what I want, because I am not in charge of the universe.

The understanding of all this no doubt lies back of the warning already quoted from Peter: "abstain from fleshly lusts, which wage war against the soul" (1 Peter 2:11). How do fleshly lusts war against the soul? Very simply, by enticing us to uproot our dependent life, pulling it away from God, which will deprive our soul of what it needs to function correctly in the enlivening and regulation of our whole being. To allow lust (or strong desires) to govern our life is to exalt our will over God's.

That is why Paul calls covetousness "idolatry" (Ephesians 5:5; Colossians 3:5). *We* are the idol, in that case, prepared to sacrifice the well-being and possessions of others to ourself. He also speaks of those whose God is their belly—that is, their desire center (Romans 16:18; Philippians 3:19). James also assigns the origin of sin to our strong desires or lusts (1:14), and now, perhaps, we see clearly how that works.

So sin, through desire and pride, alienates the life in us (the soul) from the life that is in God and leaves us in the turmoil of a soul struggling with life on its own. Those who go so far as to *abandon* themselves to evil—consciously choosing evil as their goal (the "wicked" of Proverbs 21:10)—will be totally abandoned by God. Arrogant wrongdoing is the deepest possible wound people can inflict on their soul. Efforts at spiritual formation in Christlikeness obviously must reverse this process of distancing the soul from God and bring it back to union with him. What can help us to do that? The law of God.

≈ "THE LAW OF THE LORD IS PERFECT, CONVERTING THE SOUL" ≈

THE WRITTEN LAW THAT God gave to the Israelites is one of the greatest gifts of grace that God has ever conveyed to the human race. It is a part of the blessings that God promised would come to all the families or nations of the earth through Abraham and his seed. Of course there is much more to the law than just rules or commandments. It provides a picture of reality: of how things are with God and his creation. The Prophets and the Gospels share with "the Law" this vital function of enabling human beings to know God, what God is doing, and what we are to do—wherein our true well-being lies.

Thus Moses challenges his people: "For what great nation is there that has a god so near to it as is the LORD our God whenever we call on Him? Or what great nation is there that has statutes and judgments as righteous as this whole law which I am setting before you today?" (Deuteronomy 4:7-8).

The law of the Lord gratefully received, studied, and internalized to the point of obedience is "perfect," as Psalm 19:7 says. There is nothing lacking in it for its intended purpose. It therefore converts or restores the soul of those who seek it and receive it. It is a spiritual power in its own right, as is the Word of God generally. It is a living and powerful being capable of distinguishing soul from spirit in man and dealing with them appropriately and redemptively (Hebrews 4:12).

There is nothing in all of the glory of the law according to the Old Testament that suggests for a moment that what the law does in the human heart is a human accomplishment. Rather, all benefit is ascribed to the law itself and to its giver. (Study Psalm 119 carefully.) Viewed as something we can or must achieve by somehow using the law on our own, the benefit of the law would be, simply, a loss. For in attempting to *use* it, we would have thrown ourselves back into the position of self-idolatry, utilizing the written law as *our* tool for managing ourselves and God.

This mistake is what led to the horrible degradation of "the Law" at the time of Jesus and Paul, turning it from a pathway of grace to an instrument of cultural self-righteousness and human oppression. "Woe to you lawyers!" Jesus said, "For you have taken away the key of knowledge; you did not enter in yourselves, and those who were entering in you hindered" (Luke 11:52).

"HE RESTORETH MY SOUL"

NOW, IT IS ALWAYS true from the beginning to the end of the Bible, as well as of human history, that human deliverance comes from a personal relationship with God established in God's gracious love and power. *But the law is an essential part of that relationship.* The inadequacy of human effort taken by itself is simply assumed. Still, the law was given as an essential meeting place between God and human beings in covenant relationship with him, where the sincere heart would be received, instructed, and enabled by God to walk in his ways. God is the only restorer of souls. When those walking in personal relationship with him take his law into their heart, that law, as a living principle, quickens and restores connection and order to the flagging soul. But that never happens in the absence of the personal presence and gracious action of God with the person involved.

Thus some of the greatest assurances of God's personal presence are found in the Old Testament. In the book of Isaiah, for example:

> "Do not fear, for I am with you; do not anxiously look about you,
> for I am your God. I will strengthen you, surely I will help you,
> surely I will uphold you with my righteous right hand. . . . I will
> open rivers on the bare heights, and springs in the midst of the val-
> leys; I will make the wilderness a pool of water, and the dry land
> fountains of water . . . that they may see and recognize, and con-
> sider and gain insight as well, that the hand of the Lord has done
> this, and the Holy One of Israel has created it." (Isaiah 41:10,18,20)

Spirit, covenant, and law always go hand in hand within the path of spiritual formation, for it is the path of one who walks with God.

LAW HATE: ANTINOMIAN CHRISTIANITY?

AND ON THIS POINT we are in the greatest of dangers today. There are many who in effect, if not in intent, do just what Jesus said not to do. They annul the law and teach others to do the same (Matthew 5:19). That ends all prospects of spiritual formation.

We in the Western world live today in an antinomian culture. This culture in part derives from our religious and secular history, but it in turn reinforces antinomianism among professing Christians. "Antinomian" means "against the law." It was a term coined by Martin Luther to designate some in his day (Johann Agricola and his followers) who held that God's law was not a factor in conversion to Christ.

However, the antinomian tendency is much older than Luther and possibly as old as some reactions to Paul's gospel. It is based upon the mistaken conclusion—strongly rejected by Paul—that because we are not *justified* by keeping the law, but through our personal relationship of confidence in Jesus, in his death and his life, we have no essential use for the law and can simply disregard it.

Does not faith in the saving merits of Christ abolish any obligation to keep the moral law, including the Ten Commandments and the teachings of Christ in the Gospels? We are free to hate the law, our "oppressor," or despise it, or regard it as at best a good thing that failed. These are common attitudes among professing Christians today—more often than not, one must admit, based on simple ignorance of Scriptures rather than on a carefully worked out understanding.

Details vary from group to group down through history, but the essential point of antinomianism is that sinning or not sinning—obeying or not obeying the law—has nothing to do with being "saved" or not. Some groups have advocated extreme license, others not. God's law is irrelevant to one's standing before God in either case.

During the Commonwealth period in England (1649-1660), antinomianism was present among high Calvinists who maintained that an elect person, being predestined to salvation, need not keep the moral law and doesn't even need to repent. No one should be urged to repent, therefore.

Others have said "that good works hinder salvation, and that a child of God cannot sin; that the moral law is altogether abrogated as a rule of life; that no Christian believes or works any good, but that Christ only believes and works good."[9]

⟿ THE EFFECT ON SPIRITUAL FORMATION ⟿

NOW, YOU HAVE ONLY to think for a moment to see what a disaster this will be for spiritual formation and the development of character. It amounts to rejecting it entirely except in so far as it may be done *to* you by God, passively. And you have only to glance briefly at the behavior of professing Christians currently to realize the practical outcome of holding the law and obedience to the law to be irrelevant to the life of faith in Christ.[10]

The basic practice of Western Christianity today is, I fear, strongly antinomian. Here is a true story from the current Christian scene. Test our theology on it: A man—a long-time, faithful church member—comes to his pastor and says, "I'm going to divorce my wife and marry someone else." The pastor, aghast, says, "You can't do that! You're a devoted Christian, and so is your wife. Divorce in these circumstances is clearly wrong." "Yes," the man replies, "I know that, but I'm going to do it anyway. I just can't stand her any longer. I know it's wrong, but after it's all over I'll ask God for forgiveness and he will forgive me. He must, because I believe that Christ died for me. That's what you teach."

You can extend this to imaginary cases: murdering someone who "deserves it," a once-in-a-lifetime, career-making, crooked deal, and so forth. *How,* precisely, does our version of salvation rule out a judicious use of sin? And what does growth in Christlikeness mean if one can hold such a use in reserve? Just something to think about.

~ LAW AND GRACE GO TOGETHER ~

NOW, EVERYTHING IN THE Scriptures goes against spurning the law. Jesus himself identified those who love him as the ones who keep his commandments (John 14:23-24). John said bluntly, "Sin is lawlessness" (1 John 3:4). Paul, equally bluntly, "Abstain from every form of evil" (1 Thessalonians 5:22). And Jesus again, "Why do you call Me, 'Lord, Lord,' and do not do what I say?" (Luke 6:46).

Paul made a major point of explaining that

what the law could not do [namely, secure human conformity to itself by its own power] because of the weakness of human abilities, God brought about by sending his own Son in the likeness of sinful flesh, and by condemning sin in the flesh [showing it up for the imposter it is, on its own turf], in order that what the law requires might be fulfilled in us, who do not walk in terms of the flesh, but in terms of the spirit. (Romans 8:3-4, PAR)

The presence of the Spirit and of grace is not meant to set the law aside, but to enable conformity to it from an inwardly transformed personality. We walk in the spirit of the law and the letter naturally follows as is appropriate. You cannot separate spirit from law, though you must separate spirit *and* law from *legalism*—righteousness in terms of actions.

The law *by itself* kills off any hope of rightness and righteousness through human ability and effort, but it kindles hope in God ever brighter as we walk in the law through Christ *in us* the hope of glory (Colossians 1:27). Grace does not set law aside except on the one point of justification, of acceptance before God. To the contrary, law is itself a primary manifestation of grace and is raised above legalism to a primary instrument of spiritual transformation in union with "the spirit of life in Christ Jesus."

Law comes *with* grace into the renewed soul. There is no such thing as grace without law. Even in human relationships, graciousness must have an order if it is to be graciousness. It is not some formless blob of ecstatic indulgence. Grace has to do with life, not just forgiveness, and life requires order. The order of redeemed life is expressed in the Word of God in the fullest sense of the phrase, including the moral law.

❧ Inner Affinity Between Law and Soul ❧

There is in fact an inner affinity between the law and the soul. That is why rebellion against the law makes the soul sick and distances it from God. That is why love of the law restores the soul. Law is good for the soul, is an indispensable instrument of instruction and a standard of judgment of good and evil. Walking in the law with God restores the soul because the law expresses the order of God's kingdom and of God's own character. That is why it converts and restores the soul. Grace is also essential, but not grace as formless spurts of permissiveness that thrust the law aside.

The correct order that the soul requires for its vitality and proper functioning is found in the "royal law" of love (James 2:8), abundantly spelled out in Jesus and his teaching. That law includes all that was essential in the older law, which he fulfilled and enables us to fulfill through constant discipleship to him. One whose aim is anything less than obedience to the law of God in the Spirit and power of Jesus will never have a soul at rest in God and will never advance significantly in spiritual transformation into Christlikeness.

In summary, then, transformation of our soul requires that we acknowledge its reality and importance, understand scriptural teachings about it, and take it into the yoke of Jesus, learning from him humility and the abandonment of "outcomes" to God. This brings rest to the soul. Then our soul is reempowered in goodness by receiving the law and the Word into it as the structure of our covenant fellowship with God in grace. The law is the structure of a life of grace in the kingdom of God.

Other things may be required for soul recovery in some people: perhaps special acts of deliverance or ministries of inner healing or psychological counseling. Always, the good news of Jesus is presupposed. But the most powerful force for transformation of the soul born "from above" is to walk in righteousness upheld by grace.

Matters for
Thought and Discussion

1. "The soul is deep." What do you understand that to mean? How does it relate to intellectual and cultural tendencies of the twentieth and twenty-first centuries? To biblical teachings?

2. Is "Psalm 1 man" realism? For you? For others you know? What would it look like on the job and in the home?

3. How does "failure of good intentions" relate to disorders of the soul?

4. Why is "meaninglessness" such a problem for modern life? Is it a *soul* problem?

5. Why does *fanaticism* have such an attraction for the broken soul?

6. Do you find the image of the soul as an inward stream of water intelligible? Helpful in understanding the Psalms, and so on?

7. "God has a soul." Explain the meaning of the passages referred to on this point.

8. How did eating affect Isaac's soul and his capacity to bless?

9. What are some ways in which you can *acknowledge* your own soul?

10. How does humility fit in with the "rest of soul" Jesus promises?

11. How do "fleshly lusts . . . wage war against the soul" (1 Peter 2:11)?

12. What is antinomianism and how does it affect one's life and faith today—especially prospects for spiritual formation?

13. How is law and obedience to law an expression of grace? Does the idea of an affinity between law and the soul make sense to you?

THE CHILDREN OF LIGHT AND THE LIGHT OF THE WORLD

*You were formerly darkness, but now you are light in the
Lord; walk as children of light (for the fruit of light consists
in all goodness and righteousness and truth), verifying
what is pleasing to the Lord.*
THE APOSTLE PAUL (EPHESIANS 5:8-11, PAR)

*The simple program of Christ for winning the whole world
is to make each person he touches magnetic enough
with love to draw others.*
FRANK LAUBACH[1]

✎ WHAT IS GAINED BY HUMAN HISTORY ✎

The significance of human life upon the earth must either be very small or very great. Very small from the strictly natural point of view. If we represent earth's history on a twenty-four-hour clock, from midnight to midnight, then according to the evolutionary story, our remotest human ancestors appeared at 11:59 P.M., and what we call the "civilization" of the last several thousand years is represented as the pop of a flashbulb at midnight.[2] By any account, from the merely scientific point of view, the earth will not support human society for any long period of time (in cosmic terms), and if the future of the earth's surface resembles its astonishing past, for a few thousand more years *at most.*

God's purposes for human history, as set forth in the Bible, are of course quite another matter. According to the biblical picture, the function of human history is to bring forth an immense community of people, from "every nation and tribe and tongue and people" (Revelation 14:6), who will be a kingdom of priests under God (Revelation 1:6; 5:10; Exodus 19:6), and who for some period of time in the future will actually govern the earth under him (Revelation 5:10). They will also, beyond that, reign with him in the eternal future of the cosmos, forever and ever (Revelation 22:5).

These people will, together as a living community, form a special dwelling place for God. It will be one that allows his magnificence to be known and gratefully accepted by all of creation through all of the ages (Ephesians 2:7; 3:10; Philippians 2:9-11). What the human heart now vaguely senses *should* be, eventually will be, in the cosmic triumph of Christ and his people. And those who have fully taken on the character of Christ—those "children of light" in Paul's language—will in eternity be empowered by God to do what they want, as free creative agents. And it will always harmonize perfectly with God's own purposes.

Spiritual formation in Christlikeness during our life here on earth is a constant movement toward this eternal appointment God placed upon each of us in our creation—the "kingdom prepared for you from the foundation of the world" (Matthew 25:34; see also Luke 19:17). This movement forward is now carried on through our apprenticeship to Jesus Christ. It is a process of character transformation toward complete trustworthiness before God.

A COMPOSITE PICTURE OF "CHILDREN OF LIGHT"

NOW LET US DRAW together the results of our studies in previous chapters to form a composite picture of "the children of light," drawing on how they have changed in the various essential dimensions of their being. To call them *children* of light is, in biblical terminology, to say that they have the basic nature of light: that light is their parent and has passed on to them *its* nature, as any parent does.

Now, these people are not perfect and do not live in a perfect world—yet. But they are remarkably different. The difference is not one of a pose they strike, either from time to time or constantly, or of things they do or don't do—though their behavior too is very different and distinctive. Where the children of light differ is primarily and most importantly on the "inside" of their life. It lies in what they are in their depths.

Thought life: Perhaps the first thing that comes to our attention when we get to know their inner life is what they think about, or what is on their mind. Simply stated, they think about God. He is never out of their mind. They love to dwell upon God and upon his greatness and loveliness, as brought to light in Jesus Christ. They adore him in nature, in history, in his Son and in his saints. One could even say they are "God-intoxicated" (Acts 2:13; Ephesians 5:18), though no one has a stronger sense of reality and practicality than they do. Their mind is filled with biblical expressions of God's nature, his actions, and his plans for them in his world. They do not dwell upon evil. It is not a big thing in their thoughts. They are sure of its defeat, but they still deal with it appropriately in specific situations.

Because their mind is centered upon God and oriented with reference to him, all other good things are also welcome there: "Whatever is true, whatever is honorable, whatever is right, whatever is pure, whatever is lovely, whatever is of good repute, if there is any excellence and if anything worthy of praise," their mind ponders those things (Philippians 4:8). They are positive, realistically so, based upon the nature of God as they understand it.

Feelings: And then perhaps we notice—and small wonder given what has already been observed—that the emotional life of these children of light is deeply characterized by love. That is how they invest the emotional side of their being. They love lots of good things and they love people. They love their life and who they are. They are thankful for their life—even though it may contain many difficulties, even persecution and martyrdom (Matthew 5:10-12). They receive all of it as God's gift, or at least as his allowance, where they will know his goodness and greatness and go on to live with him forever. And so joy and peace are with them even in the hardest of times—even when suffering unjustly. Because of what they have learned about God, they are confident and hopeful and do not indulge thoughts of rejection, failure, and hopelessness, because *they know better.*

Will (spirit, heart): Looking a little deeper we find that these children of light really are devoted to doing what is good and right. Their will is habitually attuned to it, just as their mind and emotions are habitually homing in on God. They are attentive to rightness, to kindness, to helpfulness, and they are purposefully knowledgeable about life, about what people need, and about how to do what is right and good in appropriate ways.

These are people who do not think first of themselves and what they want, and they really care very little, if at all, about getting their own way. "Let each of you regard one another as more important than himself; do not look out for your own personal interests, but for the interests of others" (Philippians 2:3-4). These are easy and good words to them. They are abandoned to God's will and do not struggle and deliberate as to whether they will do what they know to be wrong. They do not hesitate to do what they know to be right. It is the obvious thing to do.

Body: That, of course, involves their body. Their body has come over to the side of their will to do good. It is constantly *poised* to do what is right and good without thinking. And that also means that it does not automatically move into what is wrong, even contrary to their resolves and intentions, before they can think to *not* do it. It is no longer true of them that their "spirit is willing, but the flesh is weak" (Matthew 26:41). They know by experience that these words of Jesus are not a declaration about the inevitable condition of humans, but a diagnosis of a condition to be corrected. The Spirit has substantially taken over their "members."

Consequently, we do not see them always being trapped by what their tongue, facial expressions, eyes, hands, and so on have *already* done before they can think. For their body and its parts are consecrated to serve God and are habituated to be his holy instruments. They instinctively avoid the paths of temptation. The bodies of these people even *look* different. There is a freshness about them, a kind of quiet strength, and a transparency. They are rested and playful in a bodily strength that is from God. He who raised up Christ Jesus from the dead has given life to their bodies through his Spirit that dwells in them.

Social relations: In their relations to others, they are completely transparent. Because they walk in goodness they have no use for darkness, and they achieve real contact or fellowship with others—especially other apprentices of Jesus. "If we walk in the light as He Himself is in the light, we have fellowship with one another, and the blood of Jesus His Son cleanses us from all sin" (1 John 1:7). And "The one who loves his brother abides in the light and there is no cause of offence in him" (2:10, PAR). They do not conceal their thoughts and feelings (nor do they impose them upon everyone). Because of their confidence in God, they do not try to manipulate and manage others. Needless to say, in their social contexts they do not go on the attack or on the hunt, intending to use or to hurt others.

Moreover, they are completely noncondemning, while at the same time they will not participate in evil. They pay it only the attention absolutely required in any social setting, and beyond that, patient and joyful nonparticipation is the rule. They know how to really "be there" (wherever "there" is) without sharing in evil, as was true of Jesus himself. (Of course, as with him, others may disapprove of their "being there," and there are always *some* occasions where one should just step away.) But they do not reject or distance themselves from the people who may be involved in such situations. They know how to "love the sinner and hate the sin" gracefully and effectively.

Soul: Finally, as you come to know these people—though those who know only the human powers of the flesh will *never* be able to understand them (1 Corinthians 2:14)—you see that all of the above is not just at the surface. It is deep, and in a certain obvious sense, it is effortless. It *flows.* That is, the things we have been describing are not things the children of light are constantly trying hard to do, gritting their teeth and carrying on. Instead, these are features of life that well up out of a soul that is at home in God.

This is the outcome of spiritual formation in Christlikeness. Again, it doesn't mean perfection, but it does mean we have here a person whose soul is whole: a person who, through the internalized integrity of the law of God and the administrations of the gospel and the Spirit, has a restored soul. Such a soul effectively interfaces God and the full person and enables every aspect of the self to function as God intended.

❧ THE SCRIPTURAL HIGH POINTS ☙

NOW, WITH THIS COMPOSITE picture of the inner person of the children of light before us, let us return to some of the New Testament descriptions of what the apprentices of Jesus are to be like. We are now in a position to understand them in a new and, I believe, very encouraging way. Certainly, that is just the opposite of their usual effect, even on very devout people. Usually, I think, these bright passages may inspire longing, but a longing that is tinged with hopelessness and guilt. Now we are in a position to change all of that.

The passages we have in mind are very well known. Of course Matthew 5–7 heads the list, but properly understood it really goes no further than familiar passages in Paul's letters, or in those by Peter, James, and John. And there are similar, though on the whole somewhat less penetrating, passages in the Old Testament. We might cite in this connection Romans 12:1-21, 1 Corinthians 13, 2 Corinthians 3:12–7:1, Galatians 5:22–6:10, Ephesians 4:20–6:20, Philippians 2:3-16 and 4:4-9, Colossians 3:1–4:6, 1 Peter 2:1–3:16, 2 Peter 1:2-10, 1 John 4:7-21, and so on. Perhaps Micah 6:8 could serve well as an Old Testament point of reference. Deuteronomy 10:12-21 would also serve. I urge the reader to plan a full day in silent retreat to read and reread these passages meditatively.

❧ THE CONTRASTING PICTURE OF DARKNESS ☙

THESE PASSAGES PORTRAYING THE children of light are given additional force by contrasting passages on the "unfruitful works of darkness" (Ephesians 5:11, NRSV). In Galatians 5 Paul described "the deeds of the flesh" when natural human impulses and abilities are allowed to be the rule of life. These "deeds" are acts of "[sexual] immorality, impurity, sensuality, idolatry, sorcery, enmities [or grudges], strife, jealously, outbursts of anger, disputes, dissensions, factions, envying, drunkenness, carousing, and things like these" (verses 19-21).

Another of Paul's "dark" passages—we have already examined Romans chapter 1—is 2 Timothy 3:2-5. Speaking of "the last days," apparently when evil on earth will have had time to "'ripen,'" he says that "men will be lovers of self, lovers of money, boastful, arrogant, revilers, disobedient to parents, ungrateful, unholy, unloving, irreconcilable, malicious gossips, without self-control, brutal, [despisers] of good, treacherous, reckless, conceited, lovers of pleasure rather than lovers of God." They will be religious in lifestyle, but will deny all that is genuine in it.

Now, we know from Jesus' teachings that all of these defiling things come out of a sick and rebellious heart (Mark 7:21-23). The trouble lies in the hidden side of the self. Conversely, whatever is good also comes out of what is good in the heart. "No good tree produces bad fruit. . . . The good man out of the good storehouse of his heart brings forth what is good" (Luke 6:43,45, PAR).

✑ *EACH* DIMENSION OF THE HUMAN SELF MUST CHANGE ✑

SO THERE IS NO mystery about all of this. When people live in evil it is because of what is wrong on their "insides." Similarly, the way to a life filled and fruitful with goodness is the transformation of every dimension of the inner or "spiritual" side of the self. You cannot bypass any of those dimensions if the life is to be transformed. Each one must of necessity be a source either of weakness or of strength. The renovation of the heart simply requires that each inner dimension of the human self be rectified and established in righteousness by effectively and thoroughly receiving into it—specifically into *it*, each particular dimension of the self—"the grace of God that brings salvation."

The "grace of God that brings salvation"—Paul's words, once again—*"trains* us (*paideuousa*) in denying ungodliness and worldly desires and in living sensibly, righteously and godly in the present age," expecting the glorious return of the one who saves us, Christ Jesus, "who gave himself for us, that he might buy us back from every lawless deed and cleanse for himself a people peculiarly his own, sold out to good works" (Titus 2:12-15, PAR).

So we now understand what lies back of the "glowing" passages such as Matthew 5 or 1 Corinthians 13 or Colossians 3 or 1 John 4. It is the process of inner transformation, which we here call "spiritual formation."

✑ THE SPIRITUAL GROWTH PROGRESSION AS LAID OUT BY PETER ✑

THIS FACT IS SET out more clearly in some passages than others. Second Peter 1:3-11 is one of the clearest. Here, starting from the bedrock of "God's divine power, that has granted to us everything pertaining to life and godliness"— stop now and think about how much "everything" leaves out—the writer proceeds to point to the "precious and magnificent promises" of God that make it possible for us to "become partakers of the divine nature, having escaped the corruption that is in the world through excessive desire or lust" (verses 3-4, PAR).

And how is this escape to come about? By putting forth *your very best efforts*—"applying all diligence," a good translation says—to add to your faith, your confidence in Christ, moral excellence or *virtue*. That is, train yourself to simply do what is good and right. Obviously, this is something we are to do, which will not be done for us.

And then, in your virtue, add on knowledge or *understanding*. That is, come to know why the good and right you do *is* good and right. Operate from insight into the realities of it all.

And then, in your insight, add on *self-control*. That is, develop the capacity to carry out your intentions and not be thrown off by any turn of events.

And then, in your self-control, add on *perseverance* (endurance, patience). This is the capacity to stick with the course, to stay with it over the long haul, regardless of how you may feel.

And then, in your perseverance add on *godliness*. Perhaps we can best think of this as depth and thoroughness of all the preceding attainments of grace. God is characterized by his inexhaustible resources of goodness.

And then, in your godliness add on the *kindness* and *gentleness of care* which one sees among siblings and true friends. The word here is *"philadelphia."* That is, extend family feeling and action to those in your community. Just think of what that would mean to this wounded world. But it is possible to do this superhuman thing only through the goodness and strength of godliness.

And then, in your brotherly kindness add on *agape* love. This is the kind of love that characterizes God himself, and is spelled out in heart-rending detail on the cross of Jesus and in 1 Corinthians 13. It goes far beyond *philadelphia* and into the very heart of God. We are not just to love as family, but as he loved us (John 13:34). *Agape* love is always presented, in the biblical descriptions of the children of light, as the ultimate move, which completes and solidifies all of the other gains in spiritual progression (see Romans 5:5; 1 Corinthians 13; Galatians 5:14; Ephesians 4:15-16; Colossians 3:14; 1 John 4:16; and so on).

Peter concludes his great progression by telling us that, if we do what he here says, we will "never stumble" and that "entrance into the eternal kingdom of our Lord and Savior Jesus Christ will be *abundantly* supplied to you" (2 Peter 1:10-11, emphasis added).

✒ THE MISUNDERSTANDING MOST COMMON HERE ✒

NOW, WHAT IS THE mistake most commonly made by believers and others today, as they approach these glowing passages about the children of light? Simply this: They do not understand the presupposition of inner transformation into Christlikeness that accompanies all the passages. They assume that we are supposed to "do" all the glowing things mentioned in such passages without loving God with all our heart, soul, mind, and strength. In fact, they think we must do them while our heart, soul, mind, and strength are still strongly inclined in the opposite direction, against God. And of course their despair is totally justified. What *they* are thinking would be completely impossible.

To the person who is not inwardly transformed in each essential dimension, evil and sin still *look good*. They are strongly attractive. That is precisely what Peter calls, "the corruption that is in the world through strong desire or lust" (2 Peter 1:4, PAR). To such people the law is hateful because it denies them what they have their hearts set on; and everything must then be done to evade the law and do what they want. The force of their whole being is set against Christlikeness, even if they do suffer from a bad conscience that tells them they are in the wrong.

As Jesus trains them and "cleanses them for himself," however, all of that begins to reverse. The law begins to appear as a beautiful gift of God, as precious truth about what is really good and right. It becomes, in the language of the psalmist, "sweeter than honey freshly dripping from the honeycomb" (Psalm 19:10, PAR; honey never again tastes as good as when freshly taken). At that point it is sin that looks stupid, ridiculous, as well as repulsive—which it really is. Resistance to sin is then based upon that new and realist vision of what it is, not on fear of punishment. The illusion that sin is really a good thing arbitrarily prohibited by God is dispelled, and we see with gratitude that his prohibitions are among his greatest kindnesses.

✎ UNDERSTANDING SANCTIFICATION ✎

AND NOW WE CAN begin to speak of "sanctification," as a condition of the human soul established in imparted (not just imputed) righteousness. It is the condition of soul in the mature children of light. What are we to make of it? Especially, is it to be taken as a goal for every apprentice of Jesus? Is sanctification sensible, or is it magical?

What exactly is sanctification anyway? This is a matter that used to be much better understood than it is now, and we turn to some older authors. In his *Systematic Theology*, A. H. Strong quotes the famous New Testament scholar, Godet:

> The work of Jesus in the world is twofold. It is a work accomplished *for us,* destined to effect *reconciliation* between God and man; it is a work accomplished *in us,* with the object of effecting our *sanctification.* By the one a right *relation* is established

between God and us; by the other, the *fruit* of the reestablished order is secured. By the former, the condemned sinner is received into the state of grace; by the latter the pardoned sinner is associated with the life of God. . . . How many express themselves as if, when forgiveness with the peace which it procures has been once obtained, all is finished and the work of salvation is complete! They seem to have no suspicion that salvation consists in the health of the soul, and that the health of the soul consists in holiness. Forgiveness is not the reestablishment of health; it is the crisis of convalescence. If God thinks fit to declare the sinner righteous, it is in order that he may by that means restore him to holiness.[3]

Strong goes on to quote a striking illustration from another (now unknown) author: "The steamship whose machinery is broken may be brought into port and made fast to the dock. She is *safe,* but not *sound.* Repairs may last a long time. Christ designs to make us both safe and sound. Justification gives the first—safety; sanctification gives the second—soundness."[4]

And yet another: "Sanctification does not mean perfection reached, but the progress of the divine life toward perfection. Sanctification is the Christianizing of the Christian."[5]

And, finally, A. A. Hodge on the inseparability of accepting forgiveness and accepting sanctification: "Any man who thinks he is a Christian, and that he has accepted Christ for justification, when he did not at the same time accept him for sanctification, is miserably deluded in that very experience."[6]

Strong himself then adds these vital comments:

Not culture, but crucifixion, is what the Holy Spirit prescribes for the natural man. . . . Sanctification is not a matter of course, which will go on whatever we do, or do not do. It requires a direct superintendence and surgery on the one hand, and, on the other hand a practical hatred of evil on our part that cooperates with the husbandry of God. . . . The Holy Spirit enables the Christian, through increasing faith, more fully and consciously to appropriate Christ, and thus progressively to make conquest of the remaining sinfulness of his nature.[7]

These comments fill out the meaning of his own definition of sanctification as "that continuous operation of the Holy Spirit, by which the holy disposition imparted in regeneration is maintained and strengthened."[8]

❧ A CONTEMPORARY INTERPRETATION ❧

AN EXCELLENT CONTEMPORARY WRITER, Wayne Grudem, opens his discussion of sanctification by speaking of

> a part of the application of redemption that is a *progressive* work that continues throughout our earthly lives. It is also a work in which *God and man cooperate,* each playing distinct roles. This part of the application of redemption is called sanctification: *Sanctification is a progressive work of God and man that makes us more and more free from sin and like Christ in our actual lives.*[9]

It may be that only one clarification would be useful here, so far as my own understanding of sanctification is concerned. Although it is certainly true that the work or process of *sanctifying* the apprentice begins immediately in the newly regenerate heart, the "safe" but still "unsound" person, to use language quoted previously, is not in a condition of settled, pervasive righteousness that is appropriately named "sanctification."

Sanctification in this life will always be a matter of degree, to be sure, but there is a point in genuine spiritual growth before which the term "sanctification" simply does not apply—just as "hot" when applied to a cup of coffee is a matter of degree, but there is a point before which it is *not* hot, even if in the process of being heated.

❧ SUMMARY ON SANCTIFICATION ❧

SO WHAT SHALL WE say about sanctification in summary? It is a consciously chosen and sustained relationship of interaction between the Lord and his apprentice, in which the apprentice is able to do, and routinely does, what he or she knows to be right before God because all aspects of his or her person have been substantially transformed. Sanctification applies primarily to the moral and religious life, but extends in some measure to the prudential and practical life (acting wisely) as well.

Sanctification is not an experience, though experiences of various kinds may be involved in it. It is not a status, though a status is maintained by means of it. It is not an outward form and has no essential connection with outward forms. It does, on the other hand, become a "track record" and a system of habits. It comes about through the process of spiritual formation, through which the heart (spirit, will) of the individual and the whole inner life take on the character of Jesus' inner life.

❧ Some Marks of the Children of Light ❧

Several characteristics can serve as marks of those who have become established in their whole being as children of light. One is that whenever they are found to be in the wrong, they will never defend it—neither to themselves nor to others, much less to God. They are thankful to be found out, and they fulfill the proverb, "Reprove a wise man, and he will love you" (9:8). Indeed, when accused of being in the wrong when they are not, they will not defend *themselves,* but will say only as much as is required to prevent misunderstanding of the good and to assist those who truly desire to know the facts of the case. Thus the meaning of being *justified* by grace alone has penetrated to every pore of their being, and they rest there in human relations as well as before God.

Another of their characteristics is that they do not feel they are missing out on something good by not sinning. They are not disappointed and do not feel deprived. They do not fret because evildoers prosper, and they are not envious toward them (Psalm 37:1). They know that "better is the little of the righteous than the abundance of many wicked" (verse 16). This of course is related to the point made earlier that they do not regard sin as something good, but as slop—which is exactly what everyone knows after engaging in it. Why stick your head, your soul, or your body into *that?*

Another characteristic, following upon these mentioned, is that the children of light are mainly governed by the pull of the good. Their energy is not invested in *not* doing what is wrong, but in doing what is good. For example, they are not struggling with "Thou shalt not covet," but rejoicing that others have the good things they do. Whatever desires one might have for what is forbidden by God are regarded as ridiculous, not as something to be seriously thought about. The good is the only thing worth considering.

Finally, here, life in the path of rightness becomes easy and joyous. That is a characteristic of children of light who are well on their way. Good old Walter Marshall, a Puritan stalwart contemporary with Richard Baxter, said,

> I acknowledge that the work of God is easy and pleasant to
> those whom God rightly furnisheth with endowments for it.
> True, those who assert it to be easy to men, in their common
> condition, show their imprudence in contradicting the general
> experience of Heathens and Christians. But the wisdom of God
> hath ever furnished people with a good persuasion of a sufficient
> strength, that they might be enabled both to will and do their
> duty.[10]

❧ VIRTUOUS AND HAPPY ❧

THE GOOD NEWS OF Jesus Christ is that such a life is available to all. A depressed and hopeless man came to John Wesley to inquire what message he gave to the multitudes of hearers he regularly addressed, morning and evening. Wesley replied,

> You ask, what I would do with them: I would make them virtuous and happy, easy in themselves and useful to others. Whither would I lead them? To heaven; to God the Judge, the lover of all, and to Jesus the Mediator of the new covenant. What religion do I preach? The religion of love; the law of kindness brought to light by the Gospel. What is this good for? To make all who receive it enjoy God and themselves: to make them like God; lovers of all; contented in their lives; and crying out at they death, in calm assurance, "O grave, where is they victory! Thanks be unto God, who giveth me the victory, through my Lord Jesus Christ."[11]

No talk here of "the crushing burden of piety," as it has been called, or of religion as a "life sentence" instead of a life. Our walk with Christ, well learned, is a burden only as wings are to a bird or the engines are to an airplane. The mature children of light are like their Master. They know God and his Word, they think straight, and they live in the truth, because every essential dimension of their being has been transformed to serve God: heart, soul, mind, and strength.

The Amplified Bible gives a version of Ephesians 5:15-17 that gets this just right:

> Look carefully then how you walk! Live purposefully and worthily and accurately, not as the unwise and witless, but as wise—sensible, intelligent people; making the very most of the time—buying up each opportunity—because the days are evil. Therefore do not be vague and thoughtless and foolish, but understanding and firmly grasping what the will of the Lord is.

❧ THE LIGHT OF THE WORLD ❧

JESUS STOOD FORTH AMONG humanity as the light of the world (John 8:12; 9:5). What did that mean? "In Him was life," the apostle said, "and the life was the light of men"—a light of such power that the darkness in the world cannot extinguish it (John 1:4-5). Light means both energy and knowledge.

From the person of Christ there uniquely came into the world the energy and knowledge by which human beings could be delivered from evil and enabled to live life as it ought to be lived.

This is why we said in chapter 1 that when Jesus sent out his apprentices to make apprentices of all ethnic groups on earth, what he had in mind was *worldwide moral revolution.* What that would mean can be realized only if we think of the population of the earth being transformed into "the children of light" as we have presented them here—or if there were only a substantial minority of such people. Ordinary human beings in their ordinary positions in life were appointed and empowered by him to be, each in their peculiar place, "the light of the world." It would no more be possible to hide them than it is possible to hide a city set on a hill (Matthew 5:14-16). We can understand the subsequent course of history only if we see it as a combination of the successes *and* the failures of those who became identified with Christ to be the light of their world in the character and power of Christ himself.

✎ DARKNESS DECLARED TO BE LIGHT ✎

NOW, MODERN HUMANITY—SAY since the late 1800s—has lived in a rage of moral self-righteousness. In its intellectual leaders it has lived in an attitude of superiority and condemnation toward the morality of the culture that is, supposedly, "Christian." Its "greatest" prophets—a line of those thought to be among our greatest thinkers—have weighed Jesus in the moral balances and found him wanting.

In fact, they have found ways of treating him as inaccessible and have then concentrated on finding those who profess to be his followers wanting. Fearsome "Christian" types—the Enforcer, the Proper-Above-All, the Propagandist, the Happy Yappy, the Obsequious Self-Promoter, the Cowardly Faithful, the Heartlessly Successful, and on and on—are relentlessly hammered on as proving the moral bankruptcy of the way of Christ, though in fact these are *human* types, found in all cultures. Nevertheless, modern humanity has officially, *in its governing institutions,* forsaken the true light of the world, Jesus himself. In times of desperation they may still turn to him in prayer, but they do not think of him as the only one who knows reality and how the world should go.

Meanwhile, all of the horrendous political movements of the twentieth century, from the Soviet form of Communism to Hitler's Fascist state, from Maoism to Pol Pot—pled moral righteousness on their side and unrighteousness in their opponents as the justification for brutalities that no one would have thought possible before the fact. And the leaders of worldwide terrorism do the same. (The Nazi, for example, saw himself as *morally* superior to the

Jew, the Gypsy, and others. That was the basis of his actions toward them. If there is to be an accurate history written of the nineteenth and twentieth centuries, it will have to give prominence to the fact that the highest ethical teaching the world has ever been given was rejected by the intellectual leaders of humanity in favor of teachings that opened the way to forms of human behavior more degraded than any the world had seen to that point.

It is certainly no justification for all that historical horror to say that it was partly due to *the failure of those who have professed Christ to stand throughout the earth as the manifest children of light*. And yet that is a very essential part of the truth about our modern world. Still today those who are concerned about contemporary culture do not seem to fully realize what has happened—that those identified with Christ, and Christ himself, have come to be seen as morally inferior. They do not realize that the attacks on what we might call traditional Christian morality—or just "traditional values"—is a *moral* attack: an attack from the point of view of (supposed) moral superiority.

∾ DARKNESS NOW PRESENTED AS LIGHT ∾

PEOPLE IN "HOLLYWOOD" WHO are sometimes criticized as pushing immorality do not, in general, see themselves in that way. Rather, they regard themselves as pushing a "higher" and "better" morality. (Hugh Hefner is a most obvious illustration, but just listen to what others there say.) Traditional Christian practice is held up as *morally* inferior to the values sponsored by "Hollywood" presentations and as having been intellectually discredited. Of course the same is true of the Islamic critique of "the West." Can we learn anything from these voices?

At the present time, popular culture and political parties have largely taken over the attack, though government is still involved in various ways—especially in education. Lyrics of popular music before the Beatles and Bob Dylan did not undertake to critique traditional (Christian) teachings. Just look back at the lyrics of Perry Como and Doris Day. Even Elvis—while he was perceived as threatening to Christian behavior—did not critique it. *He* did not find Christian teachings inferior to his own moral insights.

But all of that changes with the Beatles and Bob Dylan. In them all the bitterness of the previous generation's literary writings broke through to the general culture. They profess to have *seen through* "The Establishment." And no doubt they found much there to criticize justly. They promoted by their "art" a "higher" morality to replace what they took to be "The Establishment." This is a major turning point for contemporary life. Darkness was then said to be light and was portrayed as light artistically. Of course this could not have happened but for the work of our "greatest thinkers" of recent centuries. They become the cultural *authorities*, though hardly anyone could claim to understand them.

That shift at the popular level set the trend for the present; and now the vilest and most brutal "music" unleashed upon the popular scene is delivered with an assurance of moral superiority and self-righteousness so palpable and pervasive that most people, I think, cannot recognize it for what it is. And that is now true of all the art forms. Indeed, many of the other forms were a century ahead of popular music in sponsoring darkness as light.

In any case, moral assuredness and self-righteousness in the practice of what, traditionally, would have been regarded as blatant evil is now the single most dominant feature of our common world. "Sex and violence" in the media is but one symptom of this overwhelming fact and is very far from being the central issue. The central issue is the replacement of Jesus Christ as the light of the world by people like Nietzsche and John Lennon, or like Lenin and Mao.

⮞ NOW IS THE TIME TO *BE* CHILDREN OF LIGHT ⮜

THAT IS WERE WE now stand in our world. That is the situation we now have to deal with. We are beyond the point where *mere talk*—no matter how sound—can make an impression. Demonstration is required. We must live what we talk, even in places where we cannot talk what we live. We stand again on Mt. Carmel (1 Kings 18:19 and following). Or perhaps the best comparison is the world of the first century, when children of light first entered it. The test is *reality*. If the bewildering array of spiritualities and ideologies that throng our times really can do what apprenticeship to Christ can do, what more is there to say?

There is no effectual response to our current situation except for the children of light to *be* who and what they were called to be by Christ their head. Mere "reason" and "fact" cannot effectively respond, because they are now under the same sway of public spirit and institutions as are the arts and public life generally—and indeed as much of the "church visible" as well. Only when those who really do know that Jesus Christ is the light of the world take up their stand with him, and fulfill their calling from him to *be* children of light where they are, will there be any realistic hope of stemming the tide of evil and *showing* the way out of that tide for those who really want out.

The call of Christ today is the same as it was when he left us here to serve him "even to the end of the age" (Matthew 28:20). We have not yet come to the "end of the age." That call is to be his apprentices, alive in the power of God, learning to do all he said to do, leading others into apprenticeship to him, and also teaching them how to do everything he said.

231

If we follow *that* call today in our Christian groups, then, as in past times, the most important thing happening in our communities will be what is happening in our churches. And now that we know, from our studies here, what it takes to become mature children of light, how could we possibly be excused from not taking that open path and leading others into it. We will then, once again, see among us the presence of the God who answers by fire. As Moses said to the Lord long ago: "Is it not by Thy going with us, that we, I and Thy people, may be distinguished from all the other people who are upon the face of the earth?" (Exodus 33:16).

Matters for Thought and Discussion

1. What is the outcome of human history from God's point of view, and what is your share in it?

2. Have you known people who fit the composite picture of the children of light drawn in this chapter? Some who were close? Some moving in that direction?

3. Do you take the scriptural descriptions ("high points") of the children of light to be accurate portrayals of what earlier apprentices of Jesus actually became?

4. How do you understand the central thesis of this book, that *spiritual transformation actually happens as each essential dimension of the self is transformed to Christlikeness under the direction of a regenerate will interacting with constant overtures of grace from God*? Do you agree or disagree with this claim?

5. Can people in our churches today put into action the plan for spiritual growth stated by Peter (2 Peter 1:3-11)? Why or why not?

6. How would you go about adding self-control to your knowledge (or any of Peter's other "add-to's")?

7. What do you think of the view of sanctification presented in this chapter? Is it biblical and psychologically correct?

8. Is the list of "characteristics of the children of light" given here adequate? What would you add or take away from it?

9. Is the emphasis placed here on the *ease* of the sanctified life appropriate? Or must we say that the holier you are, the harder life gets?

10. How do you see the relationship between the modern *rejection* of Jesus as authoritative teacher of the world and the present state of the popular arts (music, movies, video)?

13

SPIRITUAL FORMATION IN THE LOCAL CONGREGATION

*In case I am delayed, I write that you may know how people
ought to conduct themselves in the household of God, which
is the church of the living God, the support structure
and foundation of the truth.*
PAUL (1 TIMOTHY 3:15, PAR)

*Christ loved the church and gave Himself up for her; that He
might sanctify her, having cleansed her by the washing of
water with the word, that He might present to Himself the
church radiant, having no stain or wrinkle or any other
blemish; but that she should be holy and blameless.*
PAUL (EPHESIANS 5:25-27)

If what we have said about the spiritual formation of the children of light is true, what would we expect to find in those gatherings of disciples of Jesus into local congregations, which we call "churches"? Of the actual churches around us, what would they do better to omit, and what do they need more of?

A reasonable response might be that these local congregations would be entirely devoted to the spiritual formation of those in attendance—to the "renovation of the heart," as we have explained it here. This seems to have been Paul's idea, and he, more than any other, was given the role of defining the church, this new thing on earth, the non-ethnic people of God. In it there was to be "no . . . Greek and Jew, circumcised and uncircumcised, barbarian, Scythian, slave and freeman, but Christ is all, and in all" (Colossians 3:11). Identification with Christ and the emerging community of Christ obliterated all other identities, not by negation, but by its new and positive reality.

Thus we have Paul's magnificent statement to the Ephesians that Christ, in his triumphant capacity as risen Lord of all (4:11), has given certain people to the "called out ones" or *ecclesia* (that is, the church) "as apostles, prophets, evangelists, pastors, and teachers" (verse 10). And these special, supernatural functions are solely for the purpose of "equipping the holy ones ('saints') for the work of service, for building up the body of Christ, until all of us arrive at a coherent faith and the full knowledge of the Son of God—at a completed human being, as measured in terms of the stature of the fullness of Christ" (verses 12-13, PAR).

As a result of this "building up" we will no longer be like children, swept up in every current of teaching that comes by, or taken in by human trickery and deceitful schemes. (Doesn't that sound all too familiar?) Instead, "speaking the truth in love, we are to grow up in every respect into him who is the head, Christ, from whom the whole body, being adapted and held together by what is supplied through every part functioning properly, grows and builds itself up in love" (verses 14-16, PAR).

❧ A SPIRITUAL "HOSPITAL" ❧

OF COURSE THIS STILL leaves room for some pretty weak and needy people and some distressing events in the process, but no room for doubt concerning where it all is to come out. The local groups of disciples, in the usual case, will certainly have people at all stages of the journey. They can be compared to hospitals, with people at various stages of recovery and progress toward health. Some will be undergoing radical surgery or other strong treatment. Some will be in ICU. Others will be taking their first wobbly steps after a lengthy time bed-ridden. And others will be showing the flush of health and steady strength as they get ready to resume their ordinary life.

Parallels to these stages should be found in every church, and explicitly recognized and treated as such. And in addition, there would be those who are stepping out strongly in a strength of life that far exceeds just not being "sick" (sin-ridden), and there would be old warriors with many battle scars and many victories, with the steady gleam of "a better country" (Hebrews 11:16) in their eyes.

What these local congregations look like is spelled out in more detail in the rest of Ephesians (4:17–6:24). It would be worth the reader's time at this point to step aside and review this brilliant passage. But here, given all the foregoing, we can perhaps just say that these local congregations are made up of the children of light who light up their world. The Ephesians passage makes it starkly clear that the ones described are the ones in whom spiritual formation in Christlikeness has done and is doing its steady, ongoing work. They are the emerging and the mature children of light, and they "shine like lights" in a darkened world, "blameless and innocent, children of God above reproach in the midst of a crooked and perverse population" (Philippians 2:15, PAR).

∾ BEING REALISTIC ABOUT OUR CURRENT CONGREGATIONS ∾

NOW, WE CANDIDLY ADMIT that this represents the church, the people of Christ through the ages, at its best. But what we see here is not an impossible dream, a hopeless idealization. It has been done and can be done now, if we turn our efforts under God in the right direction. And that direction would be one that makes spiritual formation in Christlikeness *the exclusive primary goal of the local congregation*. This is what one would naturally expect after having read what Paul says—and, indeed, after having read what Jesus sent his world revolutionaries out to do (Matthew 28:18-20).

We don't want to spend a lot of time here on what is wrong in the local congregations, leading to distressing failures to routinely produce quantities of "children of light" to be the light of their world. I do take this contemporary failure seriously, as surely must be clear by now, and we must discuss its central cause. But I really do not intend what I shall say in the rest of this chapter as criticism of any individual or group.

I rarely ever meet anyone in a leadership position among Christ's people today who is not doing his or her very best to serve Christ in the best way he or she knows how—usually sacrificially, and frequently with much good effect. But we need to understand how we can do better—and better, I think, by standards with which there will be little disagreement.

∾ THE CENTRAL CAUSE OF OUR CURRENT SITUATION ∾

WHAT CHARACTERIZES MOST OF our local congregations, whether big or little in size, is simple *distraction*. The oft-noted "failures" of many kinds that show up within them and around them are not the fundamental problem of church life today. They are much more a result than a cause.

By contrast, one of the most helpful and profound statements I have read in recent years for the understanding of contemporary church life is by Leith Anderson. He notes,

> While the New Testament speaks often about churches, it is surprisingly silent about many matters that we associate with church structure and life. There is no mention of architecture, pulpits, lengths of typical sermons [or *sermons!*], rules for having a Sunday school. Little is said about style of music, order of worship, or times of church gatherings. There were no Bibles, denominations, camps, pastor's conferences, or board meeting minutes. Those who strive to be New Testament churches must seek to live its principles and absolutes, not reproduce the details.[1]

Those details simply aren't given.

Now you might ask yourself, *Why does the New Testament say nothing about all those matters to which the usual congregation today devotes almost all its thought and effort?* Answer: Because those matters are not primary and will take care of themselves with little attention whenever what is primary is appropriately cared for. Pay attention to the "principles and absolutes" of the New Testament church and, one might suppose, everything else will fall into place—in large part because "everything else" really doesn't matter much one way or the other. To fail to put the focus on those principles and absolutes, on the other hand, is to wander off into a state of distraction, which is where most of our local congregations actually are. They wind up majoring on minors and allowing the majors, from the New Testament point of view, to disappear.

ᴥ THE VESSEL AND THE TREASURE ᴥ

OF COURSE WE DO not think we are distracted. The things we are investing our efforts in seem absolutely primary. These are usually things that make up being a good and proper . . . whatever—Protestant, Catholic, Anglican, Baptist . . . or just a "good Christian" as understood in the particular place. But the people on location have actually mistaken the *vessel* for the *treasure*.

Paul gives us a crucial distinction: "For God, who said, 'Light shall shine out of darkness,' is the One who has shone in our hearts to give the light of the knowledge of the glory of God in the face of Christ. But we have this treasure in earthen vessels, that the surpassing greatness of the power may be of God and not from ourselves" (2 Corinthians 4:6-7).

The primary application of this distinction between treasure and vessel in the context was to Paul's own body and the visible events of his life in the world. Of this he said, "Our outer man is decaying" (verse 16). He was not troubled by this, for he looked to his spiritual side in the spiritual world. And he wanted the faith of his hearers to stand on the "demonstration of the Spirit and of power, that [their] faith should not rest on the wisdom of men, but on the power of God" (1 Corinthians 2:4-5). The weakness of the vessel, Paul's physical reality, was accepted and recognized by him as the occasion for the triumph of the treasure.

But the same principles of "vessel" and "treasure" apply to our local congregations, their traditions, and their higher-level groupings called "denominations." Now, it is worth noting that nearly everything that defines any given denomination is negative—that is, something "we" do not do that "they" do. By far most of our groups were born in negation. Just think of the mass of people of many denominations who are called *Protest*-ants. Our identity is that we *protest?* Against what? And then within both Protestant and Catholic traditions there are the multitudes of groupings that have been defined by what they don't do that others do.

Our various groups become over time nearly 100-percent vessel. That is, what they seem to regard as essential and what they devote almost all their attention and effort to, has to do with human, historical contingencies that have attached themselves to individuals brought up in a certain way. They of course love those contingencies, and they love the dear ones who have shared life with them within the contingent forms. And because the contingencies *are* dear to us—often there is much good associated with their past—we mistake them for the treasure of the real presence of Christ in our midst, and we spend most of our time concerned with the historical accidents or contingencies of our group, even trying to urge them upon others as essential to salvation, or at least as what is *best* for us and for them. No wonder we are distracted from the path of spiritual formation in Christ.

So, what kind of clothes should people wear to meetings, and should they stand still when they sing, and what should they sing? Should there be prayer ministry, and should it be part of the service, after the service, or at a different service? Should we be seeker friendly, or—whatever the alternatives are? Should we expect (permit) miracles to happen in our services, or just sound teaching? How should the Lord's Supper be done? And baptism? Should we use a prayer book, and if so should it be the old one or a new one? How should we raise funds for the church, and how should they be spent? Who should spend them? What should our creed be, and should we have one? What about those people who use incense? Or who don't? Or who wear unusual clothes to do the ministerial things? Or who don't? And on and on.

Now please note: I am not saying that such things are of *no* importance, though for some of them it is a close call. I am saying two things: One is that they are not the starting points or the essential and foundational matters. And that is why the New Testament, as Leith Anderson points out, says nothing about them. And secondly, if you make them out to be essential or even *very* important—even if you do so only practically, in the sense of spending most of your time on them—the local congregation will make little or no progress in terms of the spiritual formation of those in regular attendance. These "vessel" matters do *not* bring anyone into Christlikeness, whichever side of them one stands on. That is a proven fact of life. Look and see.

⟡ RIGHTEOUSLY MEAN CHRISTIANS ⟡

IN FACT, STANDING ON these things as essential is what produces mean and angry Christians. This is an inevitable result of failing to center everything on becoming people who have the character of Christ.

Warren Wiersbe tells how he was approached by an older gentleman at a church where he was to speak. The man expressed awareness that Warren sometimes quoted a certain popular paraphrase version of the Bible. Warren replied, "When I write, I quote whatever translation best says what I want to teach at that point in the book, it doesn't mean I approve of everything in it." To this the man replied, almost shouting, "Well, I'm not going to sit and listen to a man who has no convictions about the Word of God," and he "turned and stormed out of the church in anger, disobeying the very Bible he thought he was defending."[2]

One of our finest Christian-college presidents recently devoted his periodic mail-out to the question "Why are Christians so mean to one another so often?" He quotes numerous well-known Christian leaders on this theme, and says for himself:

> As a leader of a Christian organization, I feel the brunt of just this kind of meanness within the Christian community, a mean-spirited suspicion and judgment that mirrors the broader culture. Every Christian leader I know feels it. . . . It is difficult to be Christian in a secular world. . . . But, you know, it is sometimes more difficult to be a leader in Christian circles. There too you can be vilified for just the slightest move that is displeasing to someone.

And he continues on with the details.

This is one of the most common points of commiseration among our leaders. The leader of one denomination recently said to me, "When I am finished with this job I am going to write a book on the topic, *Why Are Christians So Mean?*"

Well, there actually is an answer to that question. And we must face this answer and effectively deal with it or Satan will sustain his stranglehold on spiritual transformation in local congregations. Christians are routinely taught by example and word that it is more important to be right (always in terms of their beloved vessel, or tradition) than it is to be Christlike. In fact, being right licenses you to be mean, and, indeed, *requires* you to be mean — righteously mean, of course. You must be hard on people who are wrong, and especially if they are in positions of Christian leadership. They deserve nothing better. This is a part of what I have elsewhere called the practice of "condemnation engineering."[3]

Now I must say something you can be mad at *me* about. A fundamental mistake of the conservative side of the American church today, and much of the Western church, is that it takes as its *basic* goal to get as many people as possible ready to die and go to heaven. It aims to get people into heaven rather than to get heaven into people. This of course requires that these people, who are going to be "in," must be *right* on what is basic. You can't really quarrel with that. But it turns out that to be right on "what is basic" is to be *right* in terms of the particular church vessel or tradition in question, not in terms of Christlikeness.

Now, the project thus understood and practiced is self-defeating. It implodes upon itself *because* it creates groups of people who may be ready to die, but clearly are not ready to live. They rarely can get along with one another, much less those "outside." Often their most intimate relations are tangles of reciprocal harm, coldness, and resentment. They have found ways of being "Christian" without being Christlike.

As a result they actually fall far short of getting as many people as possible ready to die, because the lives of the "converted" testify against the reality of "the life that is life indeed" (*ontos zoas,* 1 Timothy 6:19, PAR). The way to get as many people into heaven as you can is to get heaven into as many people as you can—that is, to follow the path of genuine spiritual transformation or full-throttle discipleship to Jesus Christ. When we are counting up results we also need to keep in mind the multitudes of people (surrounded by churches) who will *not* be in heaven because they have never, to their knowledge, seen the reality of Christ in a living human being.

Charles Finney used to say that the Christian minister is frequently in the position of a lawyer who states to the court the case he intends to prove (that would be the biblical picture of life from above), and then calls his witnesses (professing Christians), who contradict in their testimony (their life) every point he said he would prove.

❧ HOW TO AVOID THE "VESSEL" TRAP ☙

BUT IS THERE ANOTHER way for local congregations to go? Can we avoid the vessel trap? Certainly we can't avoid *having* vessels. And we must be tender to them, for that is a part of what it is to be human and finite. Even Jesus had his vessel. It was a Jewish one, and that became the first vessel trap the earliest congregations of disciples faced. The book of Acts and the New Testament letters are a record of how it was transcended.

And so we *can* avoid making the vessel the treasure. We can identify the treasure without reference to any vessel, though the treasure will always have a vessel. Jesus himself has shown the way, and the local congregation can follow that way. It involves the application of our VIM pattern of spiritual growth (see chapter 5) to the group as well as to the individual involved in the group.

Simply stated, the local congregation that would adopt the "principles and absolutes" of the New Testament, with the natural outcome of being and producing children of light, has only to follow Jesus' parting instructions: "As you go throughout the world, make apprentices to me from all kinds of people, immerse them in Trinitarian reality, and teach them to do everything I have commanded you" (Matthew 28:19-20, PAR). These instructions are bookended by categorical statements about the plentiful resources for this undertaking: "I have been given say over everything in heaven and earth" and "Look, I'm with you every moment, until the work is done" (verses 18,20, PAR).

These few words give the principles and absolutes of the New Testament church, and history declares the result. As long as we do what these words say, we can do anything else that is helpful to this end. And the rest doesn't even have to be "right" for God to bless us—though no doubt it is always better it should be so, as long as we don't put our confidence in that rightness. Anyone who thinks God only blesses what is "right" has had a very narrow experience and probably does not really understand what God has done for them.

✍ GOD'S PLAN FOR SPIRITUAL FORMATION ✍

BUT NOW LET US turn away from all of the negatives and just focus upon application of Matthew 28:18-20. This is God's plan for the growth and prospering of local congregations as well as of the church at large. *It is his plan for spiritual formation in the local congregation.* It has three stages:

1. *Making disciples—that is,* apprentices, *of Jesus.* It is these of which the local congregations of the called-out-ones are to consist. The New Testament does not recognize a category of Christians who are not apprentices of Jesus Christ in kingdom living now, though it clearly does recognize "baby" apprentices who are still predominantly preoccupied with and dependent upon natural human abilities (are "carnal").

2. *Immersing the apprentices at all levels of growth in the Trinitarian presence.* This is the single major component of the prospering of the local congregation: the healing and teaching God in the midst.[4]

3. *Transforming disciples* inwardly, *in such a way that doing the words and deeds of Christ is not the focus but is the natural outcome or side effect.* This is what "teaching them to do everything I have commanded you" amounts to. It is clearly the main, ongoing function of the local congregation, so far as human effort is concerned (recall the Ephesians 4–6 passage) and is presumed in the ideal outcome for character development as presented in all the New Testament writings.

◈ STAGE ONE ◈

WE BEGIN WITH THE making of apprentices (disciples, students) of Jesus, because it is presupposed in everything that follows. I have written on this at such lengths elsewhere that I hesitate to take up the topic again.[5] But we must be clear on several points.

Most fundamental, of course, is to be clear on what an apprentice of Jesus is. It is to be one of those who have trusted Jesus with their whole life, so far as they understand it. Because they have done so they want to learn everything he has to teach them about life in the kingdom of God now and forever, and they are constantly with him to learn this.

Disciples of Jesus are those who are with him learning to be like him. That is, they are learning to lead their life, their actual existence, as he would lead their life if he were they. This is what they are learning together in their local gatherings, and with those gatherings a constant part of their life, they are learning how to walk with Jesus and learn from him in every aspect of their individual lives.

◈ TWO INSEPARABLE ASPECTS OF APPRENTICESHIP ◈

TWO DIFFERENT THOUGH INSEPARABLE aspects of discipleship need to be singled out. The first is what we might, in misleading language, describe as the specifically *religious* aspect. Here we are learning to understand and do the things Jesus gave us in specific commandments and teachings. We are studying his words and deeds in the four gospels. This "learning" is primarily developed through the teaching ministry of our church as we gather.

Here, for example, we will be learning what it means to trust ourselves wholly to Christ and then to "not fear those who kill the body, but are unable to kill the soul," to "give a cup of cold water to a little child in the name of Jesus," to "swear not," to "love your enemies and pray for those who persecute you," and so forth. We are learning how to actually do these things. While developed in the gatherings of disciples, this learning is only completed as we take it into all of our life activities, especially at home and work, and increasingly practice there as a matter of course the things that Jesus taught.

But the second aspect of discipleship concerns all the details of what, for lack of a better term, we call our "secular," our "non-churchy" life. How do you run a business? How do you live with your parents or a mate, or raise a family? How do you get along with neighbors, participate in government, get an education, engage in the cultural life of your society? These too are matters in which we are to be constantly learning how Jesus would lead our lives if he were we. He would do those things if he were we. And they are not just matters of keeping his commandments, though they presuppose that. In these matters of ordinary human existence also, Jesus is our constant teacher and we his constant apprentices. "He walks with me and he talks with me," as the old hymn says, about all these matters.

～ ALL THAT IS REQUIRED TO BEGIN ～

NOW, WHEN WE FIRST become disciples, we have very little understanding of all this. We simply believe that Jesus is the one who really is in charge of everything—"The Lord," in other words—and that he is good and trustworthy. We earnestly want not to be left out of what he is and what he is doing, for we sense, perhaps dimly, that his work is all that really matters and that our life is nothing outside of it. We must make our work his work. So we cast our whole being upon him, so far as we understand it at the time.

We *in one move* find forgiveness for our sins and "take his yoke upon us and learn of him" (Matthew 11:29, PAR). The idea that these can be separated is, as A. W. Tozer pointed out years ago, simply a modern heresy. It is based upon many levels of misunderstanding and has attained the status of dogma. It is choking the life out of the contemporary Western church.[6]

When setting out as his apprentices, we will sharply encounter all of the harmful things that are "in" us: false thoughts and feelings, self-will, bodily inclinations to evil, ungodly social relationships and patterns, and soul wounds and misconnections. These our Savior and Teacher will help us remove as we strive forward through the many-sided ministries of himself, his kingdom, and his people. All will be bathed in the Holy Spirit. The process of spiritual formation in Christlikeness is a process through which all the dimensions of our life are transformed as they increasingly take on the character of our Teacher. That process is the natural condition of the disciple of Jesus, and the natural outcome is that we will increasingly do what he says.

～ FLAWED VERSIONS OF FAITH NEGATE SPIRITUAL FORMATION ～

ON THE OTHER HAND, spiritual transformation is *unnatural* to the condition of one who has not become an apprentice of Jesus. It cannot happen to such a one, and it is treated as an astonishing irregularity in church contexts where apprenticeship is not assumed—that is, by and large, our present condition in our local congregations. We must recognize, sadly, that those congregations are not based on discipleship and that they assume one can be a Christian forever and never become a disciple in any New Testament sense. This is because of a flawed view of what it is to have faith in Christ.

Most professing Christians today have "prayed to receive Christ" because they felt a need and would like him to help them deal with it. Now, one cannot lay a satisfactory foundation for spiritual formation or growth in grace by approaching people in terms of "the trouble they are in." I do not say that "felt needs" are to be disregarded, but in human affairs the "presenting problem"—the thing that needs to be *fixed now*—is rarely the real problem. One should of course be sympathetic with people who are lonely, guilt-ridden, and incapable of dealing with life, and so on, but these are not their problem.

Their problem is that they have rejected God, for whatever reason, and have chosen to live life on their own. They have not surrendered their will to him. They do not want to do what God says to do, but what *they* think is best. And they are lost because of that, in the sense explained in an earlier chapter. They do not know what their real needs are and do not think of themselves as rebels and outlaws who must radically change because they are not acceptable to God. They do not think they need the grace of God for radical transformation of who they are, but that they just need a little help. They are good people. Or so it seems to them.[7]

✎ Giving Up Your Life ✎

Now, becoming a disciple or apprentice of Jesus cannot be negotiated on this basis. Rather, becoming a disciple is a matter of *giving up* your life as you have understood it to that point. Jesus made this starkly clear in Luke 14 and elsewhere. And without that "giving up," you cannot be his disciple, because you will still think you are in charge and just in need of a little help from Jesus for your project of a successful life. But our idea of a "successful life" is precisely our problem.

The groups and times where individual and social transformation unto Christlikeness have manifestly taken place and have shaken the human order to its foundations all verify this completely: the early Christians, the early monastics, the early Franciscans or Dominicans, the early Quakers and early Methodists, for example. Note how in all these cases the word "early" has to be used. This is because the "vessel" that emerges in the course of a particular outbreak of radical discipleship gradually overwhelms the heavenly "treasure" it initially served to convey. *That is a primary satanic strategy in defeating the cause of Christ on earth.* Then we have yet another tradition on exhibit in the museum of Christian history.

Usually that means an institution of some sort, perhaps a local church or a denomination, whose perpetuation and survival becomes the main concern of the people associated with it. Discipleship to Christ is either dropped altogether from the basic objectives or is redefined as devotion to the institution.

Spiritual formation then in some cases is actually and explicitly understood as the process of conforming to the tradition. Being disciples and making disciples in the obvious sense of the New Testament is omitted from the local congregations and their higher groupings.

Clearly, then, the first stage of Jesus' plan for spiritual formation in local congregations, as stated in Matthew 28:18-20, has to do with the vision and the intention sections in our VIM pattern of spiritual growth. If spiritual formation is to be the central focus of the local congregation, the group must be possessed by the vision of apprenticeship to Jesus in kingdom living as the central reality of salvation and as the basic good news, and they must have formed the clear intention to be disciples and to make disciples, as the central project of their group.

❧ DISCIPLES ARE US ❧

TO ACHIEVE THIS, THE leadership of the local congregation, the ministering elders and overseers, must recognize that the primary candidates for discipleship are the people who are already there. And they must recognize that the first step in leading the people who are there to become apprentices of Jesus is for the ministering elders and overseers to *be* apprentices of Jesus.

It is, I gently suggest, a serious error to make "outreach" a *primary* goal of the local congregation, and especially so when those who are already "with us" have not become clear-headed and devoted apprentices of Jesus, and are not, for the most part, solidly progressing along the path. Outreach is one essential task of Christ's people, and among them there will always be those especially gifted for evangelism. But the most successful work of outreach would be the work of *inreach* that turns people, wherever they are, into lights in the darkened world.

A simple goal for the leaders of a particular group would be to bring all those in attendance to understand clearly what it means to be a disciple of Jesus and to be solidly committed to discipleship in their whole life. That is, when asked who they are, the first words out of their mouth would be, "I am an apprentice of Jesus Christ." This goal would have to be approached very gently and lovingly and patiently with existing groups, where the people involved have not understood this to be a part of their membership commitment.

And of course it need not be assumed that every person in the local congregation has fully moved to this position. But the goal would be for them to be clearly in motion *toward* it, at least, and that goal should be constantly and gently held before the group by example, teaching, and ritual. We don't want to be picky over the details of how this is done. It just needs to be done, and pastoral care must constantly help the people along. A too-detailed *technique* for being and making disciples should be regarded with considerable wariness, because it will certainly presume to take too much into human hands.

Another point should be added here, because it has been so commonly misunderstood. We are not talking about *purifying* the church, by getting all the "tares" out (Matthew 13). Even tares, real or apparent, are to be loved and served—and called to apprenticeship to Jesus. "Purifying" the church, on the other hand, has always been a part of the illusion of being perfectly "right." Instead of pursuing that illusion, we are trying to *clarify* the local congregation to itself in the light of Christ's call to it. We are trying to make clear what it is that even a false professor must profess in order to participate fully in the congregation. They would, namely, have to profess to be disciples or apprentices of Jesus. But the Lord is the only purifier of groups, and he has his own schedule for it. Our task is to be fruitful wheat and to cultivate others to be so.

Who we are in our inmost depths is the most basic issue. Ray Stedman wrote some years ago:

> God's first concern is not what the church does, it is what the church *is*. Being must always precede doing, for what we do will be according to what we are. To understand the moral character of God's people is a primary essential in understanding the nature of the church. As Christians we are to be a moral example to the world, reflecting the character of Jesus Christ.[8]

In our present context, to be sure, serious work will have to be done, and there is a strong likelihood of failure. Here is a true story: A lady came to a pastor who had been emphasizing discipleship and said, "I just want to be a Christian. I don't want to be a disciple. I like my life the way it is. I believe that Jesus died for my sins, and I will be with him when I die. Why do I have to be a disciple?" How would you answer that question? Would you say, "You don't"?

❧ STAGE TWO ❧

BUT NOW LET US turn to the last two stages in Jesus' pattern for spiritual formation in the local congregation. These concern the M in our VIM. They concern *means*. And the second stage has to do with immersing the avowed apprentices into the Trinitarian presence inhabiting and enclosing the group. Once we have a group of apprentices to Jesus, this is the single major component of a local congregation's prospering in spiritual formation: the teaching God—Father, Son, and Holy Spirit—in the midst. It is not human work, though it constantly is in interaction with the human work of stage three.

The presence of God in the midst is the only sure mark of the true *ecclesia*.

Of course there are conditions under which God will not be present in a group, and biblical and church history painfully illustrate this over and over. But every condition that omits his presence as the essential redeeming factor is just another effort at substituting a vessel for the treasure. Spiritual transformation will not occur, in that case, for it is a work of God. God's intent is to be present among his people and to heal them, teach them, and provide for them.

In Leviticus 26:11-12 we read, "I will place my dwelling in your midst, and I shall not abhor you. And I will walk among you, and will be your God, and you shall be my people" (NRSV). In Exodus 29:44-46: "I will consecrate the tent of meeting and the altar; I will also consecrate Aaron and his sons to minister as priests to Me. And I will dwell among the sons of Israel and will be their God. And they shall know that I am the LORD their God who brought them out of the land of Egypt, that I might dwell among them; I am the LORD their God."

The psalmist cried out, "The nearness of God is my good" (73:28). Deuteronomy 7:21 says, with regard to surrounding enemies, "You shall not dread them, for the LORD your God is in your midst, a great and awesome God." Jesus committed to his disciples: "For where two or three have gathered together in My name, there I am in their midst" (Matthew 18:20). And speaking specifically of meetings of the *ecclesia,* Paul described how the outsider coming into the presence of the prophetic word is "convicted by all, he is called to account by all; the secrets of his heart are disclosed; and so he will fall on his face and worship God, declaring that God is certainly among you" (1 Corinthians 14:24-25).

So what should we expect of a local congregation of disciples of Jesus. If we come at it from the viewpoint of New Testament realities—"principles and absolutes"—and the highest ideals of historic Christianity, we should expect it to be *a place where divine life and power is manifestly present to glorify God and meet the needs of repentant human beings.* This would imply an atmosphere of honesty, openness, indiscriminate acceptance of all, supernatural caring, with utter admiration for and confidence in Jesus.

✎ ELIMINATING PERFORMANCE ✎

PERFORMANCE IS WHERE WE try to make an impression rather than just be what we are. The element of performance would be absent in the Trinitarian gathering, as would constant solicitude concerning "How did the service go?" God is the primary agent in the gathering. The truth is, from the only point of view that matters—God's—it is very likely no human knows how the service went; and in any case that cannot be judged by reading overt responses of the attendees.

The sufficiency of Christ to all is the basis of our efforts in gathering and service. His "I have been given authority over all things," and "Look, I'm with you every moment," is our only hope. The ministers—pastors, teachers, and others—should, with time and experience, expect to receive from the Christ-with-them profundity of insight, sweetness and strength of character, and abundance of power to carry out their role in the local group. The minister does not need tricks and techniques, but need only speak Christ's word from Christ's character, standing within the manifest presence of God. Of course we are talking about a steady course of life, not a momentary inspiration, and for such a life in its leaders the church languishes.

When we gather in our meetings, however, we do not come to see how the speaker and other leaders do. We are not checking their performance. We come to encounter the Trinitarian presence and to hold them up within it. That is our expectation. In Paul's language, we are "determined to know nothing among you except Jesus Christ, and Him crucified" (1 Corinthians 2:2). We expect to find Christ in others and that is *all* we are looking for. We don't worship "worship" or a fine service or impeccable teaching or fine-looking people.

Far too often we approach our gathering together all prepared to major on minors. Our attitude is captured by the children's rhyme:

Pussy cat, pussy cat, where have you been?
I've been to London, to see the great Queen.
Pussy cat, pussy cat, what saw you there?
I saw a wee mouse under her chair.

Why consider the wee mouse, when your eyes could be on the Queen, whom, supposedly, you went to see anyway? Why look at some aspect of per-formance—some "vessel" matter, no doubt—when you could come to Jesus in the midst?

Stage Three

THE THIRD STAGE IN God's plan for the growth and prospering of local con-gregations, as well as of the church at large, is intending and arranging for the inner transformation of disciples. Again, this deals with means, but now, unlike stage two, they are means to be implemented by human action. This is what Jesus described as teaching the disciples to do all he commanded. But, we reemphasize, the *doing* of what he commanded is not the focus of our activities at this point. Rather, it is the "natural" outcome or side effect. The focus is, of course, inner transformation of the six essential aspects of human personality, which we have been studying. Human implementation of the *means* for this inner transformation (of course such means will be of no use in the absence of stages one and two) is the third stage of the divine plan, and it should be the local congregation's constant preoccupation.

Once the spirit or will has been quickened with new life from above, then *the priority of the mind (thought and feeling)* in inner transformation must be respected. This is true whether we are thinking of what we can do for ourselves to grow in grace and in knowledge of Christ, or of how we can help others among whom we serve. The ideas and images and the "information" and ways of thinking that occupy our mind must be changed to godly ones, as is also true of the feeling tones that make up our emotional life.

❧ WE DO NOT *CHOOSE* TO BELIEVE OR NOT ❧

OUR BELIEFS AND FEELINGS cannot be changed by choice. We cannot just choose to have different beliefs and feelings. But we do have some liberty to take in different ideas and information and to think about things in different ways. We can choose to take in the Word of God, and when we do that, beliefs and feelings will be steadily pulled in a godly direction.

One of the worst mistakes that can be made in practical ministry is to think that people can choose to believe and feel differently. Following that, we will mistakenly try to generate faith by going through the will—possibly trying to move the will by playing on emotion. Rather, the will must be moved by insight into truth and reality. Such insight will evoke emotion appropriate to a new set of the will. That is the order of real inward change.

My father was a two-pack-a-day smoker until he was in his seventies. Then one day, in the Veterans' Hospital where he went for health care, he saw a man smoking with the aid of a special machine that enabled him to smoke even though his lips had been eaten away by cancer caused by smoking. He *saw* the foolishness of smoking, and he *believed* it. He never smoked another cigarette. That is what belief does, though merely professed belief does not. Belief is when your whole being is set to act as if something is so. And that is how the commands of Jesus finally come to us as we grow. We see them to be reality.

C. S. Lewis tells how one day he got into the sidecar of his brother's motorcycle to travel a short distance. When he got in, he was an unbeliever still, though much had been happening in him. When he got out, he was a believer. He did not make this change. He discovered it after it had happened. Then he could "confess" it, and it held him, not he it.

So we do not, in general, control our beliefs or those of others. We never *choose* to believe, and we must not try to get ourselves or others to choose to believe. That is God's work. We can try to understand and try to help others to understand. And beyond that—God must work. Once we understand this and stop trying to get people to choose to believe or to do things they really don't believe, he will certainly work as we do our part. People *will* progressively learn to do the things Jesus commanded us. We will begin to see real changes in belief and emotion, and the actions will follow.

We seek to know truth and we teach others: *There is a God. This is his world, and we with it. This God is totally good and totally competent. He comes to us in Jesus Christ, whom we can totally trust. He gives us a book and a history, through which his Spirit will lead us to all we need to know about him and about us.*

Respecting the priority of the mind in spiritual formation means that we seek to understand these things and to help others understand them. We work in depth. We *can* choose to turn our minds toward these truths. Belief will come as God's gift within the hidden depths of our life and will grow under the nurturing of the Word and the Spirit. That is what is going on in a local congregation that is following God's plan for spiritual formation.

◈ AND BEYOND TEACHING ◈

BUT SOMETIMES THE WAY to this is blocked—even among people who have genuinely become apprentices of Jesus and have the best of intentions. They are not capable of receiving truth. Their body, soul, feelings, thoughts, and their social atmosphere are in such turmoil, or so badly inclined, that their mind cannot be reached just by periods of teaching.

They cannot be significantly helped by "regular church services." They may need ministries of deliverance, drawn from the healing God in our midst, and that must be provided. Or they may need to be taken out of their ordinary routine and given lengthy periods of time in retreat, under careful direction. We must be Spirit led, Bible informed, intelligent, experimental, and persistent. The Christian past holds a huge store of information on spiritual formation. It is a treasure—a God deposit—in Christ's people. We must take the trouble to know it and to own it in ways suitable to today.

We should never forget that this sort of intensive training away from "ordinary life" is exactly what Jesus did in the spiritual formation of the selected few who were to be his shock troops, his "green berets" in world revolution. He gave them almost three years of special training away from their ordinary life. Only after that were they led through his death and resurrection to the Upper Room and the endowment with power from on high. We well might ask ourselves, *What have we actually gone through in the process of spiritual formation?*

We must flatly say that one of the greatest contemporary barriers to meaningful spiritual formation in Christlikeness is overconfidence in the spiritual efficacy of "regular church services," of whatever kind they may be. Though they are vital, they are not enough. It is that simple.

Individuals and local congregations of disciples must discover and effectively implement whatever is required to bring about the inner transformations of those who have really become apprentices of Jesus and who really do gather in immersion in the Trinitarian presence. In doing so they will have put in place the principles and absolutes of the New Testament churches, and they will certainly see the corresponding fruits and effects. Jesus did not give us a plan for spiritual formation that will fail, and he has the resources to see to it that it does not.

❦ TWO STEPS OF CONFIDENCE ❧

SET UPON THIS PATH of "teaching them to do everything he said," the local congregation will be stabilized and drawn onward if it will explicitly do two things. These are actually very simple things, but, as you will see, they also are great acts of confidence in Jesus.

First, openly *expect* the apprentices to learn to do the various things that Jesus taught us to do. At present, there is no such expectation—no matter how elaborate our religious programs may be. We know, in general, that students respond to expectations—and the lack of expectations—to learn by doing what is expected of them. A dismaying amount of "stuff" would have to be worked through with "already Christians" to get them to do this. But that could be done, and there is no hope for real progress without expectations, realistic instruction, and recognition of progress.

Start with simple things like being genuinely kind to hostile people or returning blessing for cursing. Often we have plenty of opportunity to practice and refine these in our own families. Develop understanding of such situations, role-play them, take testimonies of successes and failures, and give further teaching and practical suggestions. Keep going. Disciples might be invited to keep a journal of which things they have learned to do. (What would my journal look like? Have I actually learned to *do* a single thing Jesus commanded? Which ones? Which ones have I not, and what am I doing about them?)

Second, *announce* that you teach people to do the things that Jesus said to do. Put it out in front of your meeting place on a sign, declare it in local print media and on your Web page. Publicize and run training programs designed to develop specific points of the character of Christ as given in the New Testament. Put the whole weight of the staff and the congregation back of this.

Who you and your congregation will have to be, and what you will have to do to back this up and carry it out, will concretize and make utterly real God's plan for the spiritual transformation of human existence on earth.

In bringing this chapter to a close, we want to emphasize once again that all of the other details of church activities will matter little, one way or the other, so long as all is *organized around* God's plan for spiritual formation in the local congregation, as given in Matthew 28:18-20. So far as they do matter, they will sort themselves out and fall easily into place, so long as we have our eyes on what really counts before God.

And, again, if all is *not* organized around that plan, what difference does it really make if we regard some churches and ways of "doing church" as more "successful" than others. Biblical and historical "Christianity" has brought forth children of light to be, with Jesus Christ, the light of the world only in those times and places where it has steadily drawn people into his "kingdom not of this world" and taught them to live increasingly in the character and power of God.

No special talents, personal skills, educational programs, money, or possessions are required to bring this to pass. We do not have to purify and enforce some legalistic system. Just ordinary people who are his apprentices, gathered in the name of Jesus and immersed in his presence, and taking steps of inward transformation as they put on the character of Christ: that is all that is required.

Let that be our only aim, and the triumph of God in our individual lives and our times is ensured. The renovation of the heart, putting on the character of Christ, is the unfailing key. It will provide for human life all the blessing that money, talent, education, and good fortune in this world cannot begin to supply, and will strongly anticipate, within this present life, a glorious entry in the full presence of God.

Matters for Thought and Discussion

1. Is the "reasonable response" of our churches to the call to spiritual formation (see second paragraph) really a reasonable response?

2. Is that response compatible with the picture of the church as a "spiritual hospital"?

3. Do you agree with the claim that *distraction* is the central cause of our current situation in our churches? Reflect on Leith Anderson's statement on page 235.

4. Does the distinction between the "vessel" and the "treasure" make sense to you? As applied to Paul? To you? To religious traditions, denominations, and local groups of Christians?

5. What effects of vessel-importance have you personally seen in Christian practices and endeavors?

6. Does "righteous meanness" actually happen? If so, do you agree with the explanation given in this chapter of why it is acceptable behavior? How would you explain it?

7. As simply as possible, explain how we can avoid "the vessel trap." We can't avoid having a vessel, can we?

8. What is Christ's plan for spiritual formation in the local congregation—and worldwide?

9. Describe a disciple, and how one becomes a disciple.

10. How do misunderstandings of what faith in Christ is disconnect it from spiritual transformation?

11. Could it really be true that "outreach" should *not* be a *primary* goal of church life? What should be primary goals? (See the Ray Stedman quotation on page 245.)

12. Could we really eliminate "performance" from our church gatherings? What would our meetings be like if we did?

13. How does the priority of the mind in spiritual formation affect the *means* employed to advance spiritual formation in the local congregation?

14. What things could your local congregation do beyond "regular church services" to advance spiritual transformation in its members?

15. Could we really publicly announce that we teach people how to actually do the things Jesus said for us to do? What would have to change around the church house if we were to do that?

16. "It really matters little what else you do or don't do in the local congregation, so long as all is organized around God's plan for spiritual formation as given in Matthew 28:18-20." Could this possibly be true? If so, what should we do about it?

POSTLUDE

Now it is time to look back and to look forward: back to what we have studied in this book, and forward to our life, which lies ahead of us, where we will move onward in time to become the persons we will ever be, for eternity.

In this book I have tried to clearly present the path of spiritual formation, the authentic formation of the human person, as seen in the people of Jesus Christ through the ages. I have tried to gently ignore the many *vessels* of spiritual formation that litter the historical and contemporary landscapes and concentrate on the *treasure:* Jesus Christ himself, living with increasing fullness in every essential dimension of the personality of the individual devoted to him as Savior and Teacher.

The renovation of the heart in Christlikeness—that is, in humanity as God always intended it—is not something that concerns the heart (spirit, will) alone. The heart cannot be renovated if the other aspects of the person remain in the grip of evil. "Willpower"—even inspired willpower—is not the key to personal transformation. Rather, the will and character only progress in effectual well-being and well-doing as *all other essential aspects of the person* come into line with the intent of a will brought to newness of life "from above" by the Word and the Spirit.

The path of renovation of the heart is therefore one in which the revitalized will takes grace-provided measures to change the content of the thought life, the dominant feeling tones, what the body is ready to do, the prevailing social atmosphere, and the deep currents of the soul. These all are to be progressively transformed *toward* the character they each have in Jesus Christ. This is what we call "putting on the character of Christ"—or in Paul's language, "putting off the old man and putting on the new man." And as it transpires, the individual or group more and more effectively acts for the good things they intend; and the will itself evermore broadens and deepens its devotion to good and the God of the good.

Of course this is, in reality, the great race of mortal life, run before the

253

"great cloud of witnesses." We are come as spiritually alive beings "to the city of the living God, the heavenly Jerusalem, and to myriads of angels in festal assembly, and to the church of the first-born who are enrolled in heaven, and to God, the Judge of all, and to the spirits of righteous men made perfect, and to Jesus the mediator of a new covenant" (Hebrews 12:1,22-24, PAR). To run this race well—to hear at the end, "Well done, good slave, because you have been faithful in a very little thing, be in authority over ten cities," (Luke 19:17)—is to become the kind of person whom God will welcome to participate with him in his future governance of all creation (Revelation 22:5). "You were faithful over few things, I will put you in charge of many things, enter into the joy of your Lord" (Matthew 25:21, PAR). The joy of our Lord is the use of power for good. He loves to create and sustain everything that is good. That is to be our joy as well.

To run the race well, to be faithful over few things, is our part. And as we look at the road ahead, we must deal with details. That is, we must take the particular things that slow us down and the sins that entangle us, and put them aside in a sensible, methodical way (Hebrews 12:1). We remove their roots from our minds, feelings, and so forth. We are neither hysterical nor hopeless about them. We find out what needs to be done and how to do it, and then we act. We know God will help us with every problem as we take appropriate steps.

So our running is also with *patience*. We take the long view of the race that is set before us. We don't try to accomplish everything at once, and we don't force things. If we don't immediately succeed in removing a weight or a sin, we just keep running—steadily, patiently—while we find out how it can be removed in God's way.

All the while, we keep looking up at our Teacher, who we know gave us faith to run in the first place and who will bring us safely to the end (Hebrews 12:2). We concentrate on his thoughts, feelings, character, body, social bearing, and soul. We are constantly learning from him, and he shows us how to let the weights and sins drop off so we can run better.

As we run we sense divine assistance making our steps lighter. We realize truth more strongly, see things more clearly. We find greater joy in those running with us, our companions in Christ and those who went before and are coming after. His yoke *is* easy, we find, his burden *is* light. As our "outer man" perishes, our "inner man" is renewed on a daily basis (2 Corinthians 4:16). And no matter what the difficulty, we sing as we run, "Deliverance will come!"

But, as we look forward, now is the time for specific planning. Individually we must ask ourselves what are the particular things we need to do in order to bring the triumph of Christ's life more fully into the various dimensions of our being. Are there areas where my will is not abandoned to where old segments of fallen character remain unchallenged? Do some of my thoughts, images, or patterns of thinking show more of my kingdom or the kingdom of evil than they do God's kingdom—for example, as they relate to money, or social practices, or efforts to bring the world to Christ? Is my body still my master in some area? Am I its servant rather than it mine.

And if I have some role in leadership among Christ's people, am I doing all that I reasonably can to aid and direct their progress in inward transformation into Christlikeness? Is that progress the true aim of our life together, and are there ways in which our activities might be more supportive of that aim? Is the teaching that goes out from me appropriate to the condition of the people, and is my example one that gives clear assurance and direction? Is "my progress evident to all"? (1 Timothy 4:15, PAR).

Whatever my situation is, now is the time to make the changes and undertake the initiatives that are indicated by the studies we have made in this book. Spiritual formation in Christlikeness is the sure outcome of well-directed activities that are under the personal supervision of Christ and are sustained by all of the instrumentalities of his grace. This aching world is waiting for the people explicitly identified with Christ to be, through and through, the people he intends them to be. Whether it realizes it or not. There is no other hope on earth.

And that, of course, is where we stand: *on earth*. Strangely, perhaps, it is only spiritual formation in Christ that makes us at home on earth. We are pilgrims, of course, and we look for a better city (Hebrews 11:16). But we are content that this is not yet. Christ brings me to the place where I am able to walk beside my neighbor, whoever he or she may be. I am not above them. I am beside them: their servant, living with them through the events common to all of us.

I am not called to judge them, but to serve them as best I can by the light I have, humbly and patiently, with the strength I have and the strength God supplies. If it is true that our ways will at some point part for eternity, I shall love them none the less for it. And the best gift *I* can give them is always *the character and power of Christ in me and in others who really trust him.* Beyond that I look to God for the renovation of their heart as well. I know that, no matter what comes, he is over all.

NOTES

CHAPTER 1: INTRODUCING SPIRITUAL FORMATION

1. In the midst of much misunderstanding of Jesus, the historian Will Durant still correctly grasped the role of Jesus as world revolutionary: "He is not concerned to attack existing economic or political institutions. . . . The revolution he sought was a far deeper one, without which reforms could only be superficial and transitory. If he could cleanse the human heart of selfish desire, cruelty, and lust, utopia would come of itself, and all those institutions that rise out of human greed and violence, and the consequent need for law, would disappear. Since this would be the profoundest of all revolutions, beside which all others would be mere *coups d'etat* of class ousting class and exploiting in its turn, Christ was in this spiritual sense the greatest revolutionist in history." Will Durant, *Caesar and Christ* (New York: Simon and Schuster, 1944), p. 566.

2. The former statement has a long scholarly background at this point, but is mainly associated with the thought of Paul Tillich. (See pp. 3 and 9 of Paul Bjorklund, *What Is Spirituality?* [Plymouth, MN: Hazelden Foundation, 1983]). The second statement is by Leo Booth, *When God Becomes a Drug* (Los Angeles: Tarcher Inc., 1991), p. 20. What is at work here is the relentless drive of human beings to be "spiritual" without God. Even explicit atheism will not protect you from the gnawing need to come to terms with your spiritual side. At a popular level, the presence of this drive constantly manifests itself in the amazing magazines at the checkout in the supermarket, and in people like Oprah and Shirley MacLaine. But it runs much deeper than this would make one think. This and the threat it poses to genuine discipleship to Christ will be discussed at greater lengths in chap. 6.

3. On these matters see, for example, Pierre Hadot, *Philosophy as a Way of Life: Spiritual Exercises from Socrates to Foucault,* Arnold I. Davidson, ed., and Michael Chase, trans. (Cambridge, MA: Blackwell, 1995), and

Martha C. Nussbaum, *The Therapy of Desire: Theory and Practice in Hellenistic Ethics* (Princeton, NY: Princeton University Press, 1994). There is, of course, an ocean of literature from Eastern thought on the formation of the human spirit.

4. According to *Newsweek,* April 16, 2001, p. 49. The irony is that each one of the 33,800 groups is "right."

5. Although we do not intend a scholarly treatment in this book, it may be helpful to compare such statements as this about spiritual formation and spirituality to some other authors; for example, Richard P. McBrien, *Lives of the Saints* (San Francisco: HarperSanFrancisco, 2001), especially pp. 18-19, and Francis A. Schaeffer, *True Spirituality* (Wheaton, IL: Tyndale, 1971), especially pp. 16-17. Understanding of many deep problems concerning spirituality and spiritual formation can be gained by comparing these and other authors with what I say in this book.

6. Please see my book *The Divine Conspiracy* (San Francisco: HarperSanFrancisco, 1998), chap. 5, for a more detailed explanation of Jesus' teachings on these and related matters.

7. The well-known hymn from which these lines were taken, "Rock of Ages" by Augustus Toplady, captures what has been the understanding of Christ's people through most of their past: that Christian redemption involves, in seamless unity, both the remission of guilt for sins and the deliverance of our lives from domination by sin. Though these are *distinct,* they were not, in our past, generally thought of as *separable,* and of course they aren't separable—ever. Recall also the words of Charles Wesley's hymn, "O for a Thousand Tongues": "He breaks the power of canceled sin, / He sets the pris'ner free; / His blood can make the foulest clean; / His blood availed for me."

CHAPTER 2: THE HEART IN THE SYSTEM OF HUMAN LIFE

1. On this and on points immediately following concerning the body and its role in life and in the spiritual life, see my book *The Spirit of the Disciplines* (San Francisco: HarperSanFrancisco, 1988), chaps. 5–7.

2. On this point nothing more helpful has been written than Dietrich Bonhoeffer's excellent study of the texture of the church, *The Communion of Saints: A Dogmatic Inquiry into the Sociology of the Church* (New York: Harper & Row, 1963), especially chap. 2.

3. Quoted from Aylmer Maude, *Tolstoy and His Problems* (New York: Grant Richards, 1901), p. 64.

4. An overly cynical but still painfully instructive parody of the hymn "Onward Christian Soldiers" reads,"Like a mighty tortoise / Moves the

church of God. / Brethren we are treading / Where we've always trod."
We may be, but for sure God is not.

CHAPTER 3: RADICAL EVIL IN THE RUINED SOUL

1. C. S. Lewis, *The Weight of Glory* (Grand Rapids, MI: Eerdmans, 1973), p. 15.
2. *Christianity Today,* July 10, 2000, p. 2. It is one of the all-time greatest ironies of human history that the founding insights and practices of the most successful "recovery" program ever known—insights and practices almost 100-percent borrowed from bright spots in the Christian movement, if not outright gifts of God—are not routinely taught and practiced by churches. What possible justification or explanation could there be for this fact?
3. Edith Schaeffer, *Affliction* (Old Tappan, NJ: 1978), p. 212.
4. John Calvin, *Institutes of the Christian Religion*, vol. 2 (Grand Rapids, MI: Eerdmans, 1975), p. 7.
5. Calvin, p. 9.
6. Dietrich Bonhoeffer, *The Communion of Saints* (New York: Harper & Row, 1963), p. 71.
7. The proposal regarding Evil Studies was made by Paul Shore in "The Time Has Come to Study the Face of Evil," *The Humanist*, November/December 1995, pp. 37-38. Shore is a professor of education and American studies at Saint Louis University. There are some indications that the inability of the "learned" world to deal with evil may be changing. Recent publications such as Iris Chang's *The Rape of Nanking* (New York: Penguin Putnam, 1997), and especially, Jonathan Glover's *Humanity: A Moral History of the Twentieth Century* (London: Jonathan Cape, 1999), are promising of enhanced realism about evil. But we are still far removed from any realistic and widely understood conceptualization of evil that would begin to allow us to deal with it in ourselves and in our world.
8. This theme is powerfully presented in C. S. Lewis's *The Great Divorce* (New York: Macmillan, 1975) and numerous other editions. See also John Finnis, *Fundamentals of Ethics* (Washington, D.C.: Georgetown University Press, 1983), p. 152, and also Bonhoeffer, p. 201.

CHAPTER 4: RADICAL GOODNESS RESTORED TO THE SOUL

1. For a study of the deep roots of Calvin's spirituality in the Christian past, see Lucien Joseph Richard, *The Spirituality of John Calvin* (Atlanta: John Knox Press, 1974).
2. John Calvin, *Institutes of the Christian Religion*, vol. 2 (Grand Rapids, MI: Eerdmans, 1975), p. 7.

3. See Calvin, chap. 7, bk. 3.

4. Erich Fromm, *The Art of Loving* (New York: Harper, 1974), pp. 18-19.

5. Fromm, pp. 18-19.

6. B. McCall Barbour, "If It Die . . ," no. 3 of the Deeper Life Series (Edinburgh, Scotland: B. M'Call Barbour, n.d.), p. 24. For many other testimonies, see the remainder of this little booklet and the others in the same series.

7. Thomas à Kempis, *The Imitation of Christ*, pt. 3, chap. 25 (many editions).

8. *The Works of John Wesley*, vol. 8, 3rd ed. (Peabody, MA: Hendrickson Publishers, 1986), p. 344.

9. For further discussion of the roots and centrality of anger in life apart from God, see chap. 5 of my *The Divine Conspiracy* (San Francisco: HarperSanFrancisco, 1998).

CHAPTER 5: SPIRITUAL CHANGE

1. For further discussion see chaps. 6–7 of my *The Spirit of the Disciplines* (San Francisco, Harper & Row, 1988), as well as the chapter on the body to follow.

2. Erich Przywara, ed., *An Augustine Synthesis* (Gloucester, MA: Peter Smith, 1970), p. 89.

3. For development of this understanding please see chaps. 1–2 of my *The Divine Conspiracy* (San Francisco: HarperSanFrancisco, 1998).

4. In his "On the Improvement of the Understanding," the Jewish philosopher Spinoza (1632-1677) wrote of his decision "to inquire whether there might be some real good having power to communicate itself, which would affect the mind singly, to the exclusion of all else: whether, in fact, there might be anything of which the discovery and attainment would enable me to enjoy continuous, supreme, and unending happiness." This is the universal human desideratum, for all who think and have not in some measure despaired.

5. Adequate treatment of inner hindrances and positive steps against them used to be fairly standard among Christian teachers. As a case in point, see the many writings of Richard Baxter (died 1691).

CHAPTER 6: TRANSFORMING THE MIND, 1

1. In an extremely important book published in 1952, J. V. Langmead Casserley stated, "The redemption of religion is indeed perhaps the most gigantic of the tasks with which Christianity finds itself confronted, for the natural tendency of religion left to itself is not to bring men to God, however sincerely and wisely religious leaders may

endeavour to do so, but rather to immerse them in some kind of idolatry." *The Retreat from Christianity in the Modern World* (London: Longmans, Green and Co., 1952), p. 7.

According to him we can now "see and distinguish between two broad ways or avenues of retreat from Christianity: the retreat from Christianity into irreligion, and the retreat from Christianity into religion" (pp. 4-5). He argues very convincingly that the period of retreat into irreligion (secularism) is now drawing to a close, after 250 years, and "that the retreat from Christianity into some alternative form of religion is the more profoundly and enduringly important form of the retreat. . . . The retreat from Christianity into irreligion does no more than create a spiritual vacuum, but the retreat from Christianity into religion may do something far more terrible and menacing to the future of mankind: it may fill that vacuum, fill it with reborn superstitions and mythologies, giving new life to the paganisms and idolatries, so recklessly sacrificial of human life and energy, from which the gospel once delivered us, and may now have to deliver us all over again" (p. 5).

What Casserley foresaw so clearly fifty years ago has now substantially come to pass and continues on the *increase*. As François Mauriac pointed out, "Paganism, apparently conquered (and even at that, only in one part of the planet), survives in its lowest forms in every living heart." *Holy Thursday: An Intimate Remembrance* (Manchester, NH: Sophia Institute Press, 1991), p. 46.

2. A. W. Tozer, *The Knowledge of the Holy* (New York: Harper and Brothers, 1961), p. 10. See also his *Worship: The Missing Jewel* (Harrisburg, PA: Christian Publications, 1992).

3. Henri J. M. Nouwen, *Life of the Beloved* (New York: Crossroad, 1992), p. 21.

4. Roland H. Bainton, *Here I Stand: A Life of Martin Luther* (New York: The New American Library, 1955), p. 144.

5. On these matters see further, J. P. Moreland, *Love Your God with All Your Mind* (Colorado Springs, CO: NavPress, 1997), and James W. Sire, *Habits of the Mind: Intellectual Life as a Christian Calling* (Downers Grove, IL: InterVarsity, 2000).

6. For more on this see my "Jesus the Logician," *Christian Scholar's Review*, 1999, vol. 28, no. 4, pp. 605-614 (reprinted in *The Best of Christian Writing 2000* [San Francisco: HarperSanFrancisco, 2000]), and chap. 3 of my *The Divine Conspiracy* (San Francisco: HarperSanFrancisco, 1998).

7. Isaac Watts, *Logic: The Right Use of Reason in the Inquiry after Truth* (1724; reprint, Morgan, PA: Soli Deo Gloria Publications, 1996), pp. iii-iv.

8. Thomas Watson, *All Things for Good* (1663; reprint, Carlisle, PA: The Banner of Truth Trust, 1986), p. 74.

9. Immanuel Kant, "Idea for a Universal History," Proposition 6, p. 62, in *German Idealist Philosophy,* Rüdiger Bubner, ed. (New York: Penguin Books, 1997).

10. One of the best places to begin in understanding disciplines, what they are and how they work, is Richard Foster's *Celebration of Discipline: The Path to Spiritual Growth* (San Francisco: HarperSanFrancisco, 1978, 1998). This understanding is absolutely crucial to the renovation of the heart. It is a primary part of the *means* in the VIM structure.

11. To come to know many of these people of the past, study Richard Foster's *Streams of Living Water* (San Francisco: HarperSanFrancisco, 1998) and James Gilchrist Lawson's *Deeper Experiences of Famous Christians* (Uhrichsville, OH: Barbour Publishing, 2000).

CHAPTER 7: TRANSFORMING THE MIND, 2

1. Baruch Spinoza, "Of Human Bondage," *Ethics*, bk. 3, and Somerset Maugham's novel *Of Human Bondage,* the title of which is taken from Spinoza. Both books have appeared in numerous editions.

2. Jeff Imbach's *The River Within* (Colorado Springs, CO.: NavPress, 1998) is very helpful in clearing up the importance of feeling to human life and spirituality.

3. One of the best introductions to modernity and what it means for life today is Anthony Giddens' *The Consequences of Modernity* (Stanford, CA.: Stanford University Press, 1990).

4. Leo Tolstoy, *A Confession, etc.,* Aylmer Maude, trans. (London: Oxford University Press, 1958), p. 17.

5. Thomas Hibbs has done a masterful study of what is really presented in such so-called "sitcoms." See his *Shows About Nothing: Nihilism in Popular Culture from* The Exorcist *to* Seinfeld (Dallas, TX: Spence Publishing Company, 1999).

6. Tolstoy, p. 57.

7. Robert Reich, who served as Secretary of Labor under the Clinton administration, has written a very useful analysis of "The Age of the Terrific Deal," in which we now live, and of the human toll it takes, in his *The Future of Success* (New York: Knopf, 2001). See the excellent summary on pp. 221-223. His suggestions as to what might be done to help are, I think, profoundly misguided. For a very different and deeper approach to essentially the same problems, one might consult F. H. Bradley's *Ethical Studies* or John Ruskin's *Unto This Last,* both in numerous editions.

8. Quoted in Amy Carmichael, *Gold Cord* (Ft. Washington, PA: Christian Literature Crusade, 1996), p. 41.

9. For a full treatment of this subject see chaps. 5–7 in my *The Divine Conspiracy* (San Francisco: HarperSanFrancisco, 1998).

CHAPTER 8: TRANSFORMING THE WILL (HEART OR SPIRIT) AND CHARACTER

1. William James, *The Principles of Psychology,* vol. 2 (London: Macmillan, 1918), pp. 578-579.

2. Kant is still the best expositor of this point. See his *Foundations of the Metaphysics of Morals*, sect. 2 (many editions), as well as his other writings in ethics.

3. On this and the matters referred to in the previous paragraph, see the writings contained in Walter Kaufmann, ed., *Existentialism from Dostoevsky to Sartre* (New York: Meridian Books, 1968).

4. Quoted from Frederick Buechner, *Speak What We Feel* (San Francisco: HarperSanFrancisco, 2001), p. 40.

5. See Jonathan Glover, *Humanity: A Moral History of the Twentieth Century* (London: Jonathan Cape, 1999), and Philip Hallie, *Tales of Good and Evil, Help and Harm* (New York: HarperCollins, 1997), for the shocking realities of twentieth-century history.

6. Edith Schaeffer, *Affliction* (Old Tappan, NJ: Revell, 1978), p. 126-127.

7. Andrew Murray, *Absolute Surrender* (Chicago: Moody, n.d.), p. 124.

8. From Margaret Magdalen, *A Spiritual Check-up: Avoiding Mediocrity in the Christian Life* (East Sussex, UK: Highland Books, 1990), p. 101.

9. The picture of the life crushed by a "master passion" in Plato's *Republic,* bks. 8 and 9, teaches us one of the all-time greatest essential lessons in moral and spiritual psychology ever given.

CHAPTER 9: TRANSFORMING THE BODY

1. Disagreements about the nature of the body abound in the fields of health care and medicine today. For an older but very illuminating treatment of the body see Walter B. Cannon, *The Wisdom of the Body* (New York: Norton, 1932), as well as, more recently, Paul Brand's *Fearfully and Wonderfully Made* (Zondervan, 1997).

2. For further discussion on these matters, see chap. 7 ("St. Paul's Psychology of Redemption") in my *The Spirit of the Disciplines* (San Francisco: HarperSanFrancisco, 1988).

3. On the spiritual nature and calling of the body, see chaps. 4–6 of *The Spirit of the Disciplines.*

4. Karen R. Norton, *Frank C. Laubach: One Burning Heart* (Syracuse, NY: Laubach Literacy International, 1990), p. 11.

5. For the remarkable story of Laubach's recovery and further spiritual growth, see the rest of Norton's biography and the writings by Laubach himself in *Frank C. Laubach: Man of Prayer* (Syracuse, NY: Laubach Literacy International, 1990).

6. This can be found, for example, as no. 335 in *Worship and Service Hymnal* (Chicago: Hope Publishing Company, 1957), and in many other standard hymnals.

7. Frances Ridley Havergal, *Kept for the Master's Use* (London: James Nisbet & Company, Ltd., 1897).

8. Margaret Magdalen, *A Spiritual Check-up: Avoiding Mediocrity in the Christian Life* (East Sussex, UK: Highland Books, 1990).

9. This is from the section headed "Diversion," subsection 135, in Pascal's *Pensées*. This appears, among many other publications, in Richard H. Popkin, ed., *Pascal: Selections* (New York: Macmillan, 1989), p. 214.

CHAPTER 10: TRANSFORMING OUR SOCIAL DIMENSION

1. Origen, *Against Celsus*, III, 29, quoted in John Hardon, *The Catholic Catechism* (Garden City, NJ: Doubleday, 1975), p. 215.

2. See C. S. Lewis's discussion of "The Inner Ring" and the desire to be in it as "one of the great permanent mainsprings of human action." *The Weight of Glory* (Grand Rapids, MI: Eerdmans, 1973), p. 61.

3. The finest exposition of the biblical and moral concept of love I know of is in Charles Finney, *Lectures on Systematic Theology*, lectures 12–15 (Grand Rapids, MI: Eerdmans, 1953). In particular Finney strongly shows that love is not a *feeling*.

   Today in "Western culture" there are two broadly different ways of thinking about love. Hardly anyone today rejects love as some kind of ultimate value and guide to life. But to most people, to love someone now means to be prepared to approve of their desires and decisions and to help them fulfill them. "If you love me you'll do what I want" is the cry here. On the biblical (and any sane) view, to love people means to favor *what is good for them* and to be prepared to help them toward that, even if that means disapproving of their desires and decisions and attempting, as appropriate, to prevent their fulfillment.

   A serious problem is created today by the identification of the *good* and the *desired*. If there is no point of reference for good other than desire, then the identification (confusion) of these two things naturally follows. And there is then no way to distinguish the desired from the desir*able*. Of course from the biblical point of view we have ample resources for distinguishing them.

4. A surprising reemergence on the contemporary scene of the primacy of

"the other" in human obligation has occurred in the work of the Jewish thinker Emmanuel Levinas. See for example the papers in *The Levinas Reader,* edited by Sean Hand (Oxford: Blackwell, 1997), and especially the paper, "Substitution," pp. 88-119.

5. Aristotle, *Politics,* bk. 1, chap. 2 (many editions).
6. John Donne, *Meditation XVII* (many editions).
7. Larry Crabb, *Connecting* (Nashville: Word, 1997), p. xi.
8. C. S. Lewis, *The Screwtape Letters,* Letter II (New York: MacMillan, 1962, p. 12).
9. Dietrich Bonhoeffer, *The Communion of Saints* (New York: Harper and Row, 1963), p. 137.
10. Robert Reich, *The Future of Success* (New York: Knopf, 2001). This entire book needs to be carefully studied for understanding of where we stand today with regard to matter dealt with in this chapter. Reich does not seem to realize the deeper moral roots and consequences of the approach to life he is evaluating, and even less so the spiritual significance. His book is actually a profound study in "spiritual formation" in the broad human sense explained in chapter 1 of this book.

CHAPTER 11: TRANSFORMING THE SOUL

1. The one thing most approaches to the human being take for granted is that there is *something* "deep" in it, from depth psychology to deep structures of myth and language. Some of the popular writers of our time really never give any other idea of the soul than that it is what is "deep."
2. Robert L. Wise, *Quest for the Soul* (Nashville: Nelson, 1996), p. 88.
3. One of the most realistic and instructive testimonies of the soul's response to grace in tragedy is Gerald L. Sittser's *A Grace Disguised: How the Soul Grows Through Loss* (Grand Rapids, MI: Zondervan, 1995). The final pages, 178-181, say pretty much all that needs to be said on this point.
4. A good starting point for study of biblical terms and teachings on the soul might be §§70-71 of Gustave F. Oehler, *Theology of the Old Testament* (Grand Rapids, Mich: Zondervan, n.d.). A. B. Davidson's *The Theology of the Old Testament,* chap. 6 (Edinburgh: T. & T. Clark, 1955) is very helpful. Franz Delitzsch, *A System of Biblical Psychology,* 2nd English ed. (Edinburgh: T & T. Clarke, 1869), is a classic in the field. A. H. Strong's *Systematic Theology* (Valley Forge, PA: Judson Press, 1993), pp. 483-497, is useful on the "Essential Elements of Human Nature," as is chap. 3 of Wayne Grudem, *Systematic Theology* (Grand Rapids, MI: Zondervan, 1994).

For more philosophical approaches, the "Treatise on Man,"

questions 75–89, in the first part of St. Thomas Aquinas's *Summa Theologica* (many editions) is indispensable. I also recommend F. R. Tennant, *Philosophical Theology*, vol. 1, "The Soul and Its Faculties" (Cambridge: At The University Press, 1956); S. L. Frank's *Man's Soul: An Introductory Essay in Philosophical Psychology* (Athens, OH: Ohio University Press, 1993); and Richard Swinburne, *The Evolution of the Soul*, rev. ed. (Oxford: Oxford University Press, 1997).

Finally, I recommend Kees Waaijman, "The Soul as Spiritual Core Concept: A Scriptural Viewpoint," in *Studies in Spirituality*, published in The Netherlands, June 1996, pp. 5-19; and, especially, the entire no. 1 of vol. 26 (1998) of *Journal of Psychology and Theology*, which is on the soul and ably grapples with most of the contemporary issues.

5. Viktor Frankl has tried to make *meaning* and *soul* fundamental concepts in the field of clinical psychology. See his *Man's Search for Meaning*, 3rd ed. (New York: Simon and Schuster, 1948), and *The Doctor and the Soul*, 2nd ed. (New York: Bantam Books, 1969). Other psychologists, such as Carl Jung, have also tried to take these concepts seriously, often with astounding outcomes, especially in the direction of so-called "transpersonal psychology."

6. This language and conceptualization, due to the sociologist David Riesman, *The Lonely Crowd* (New Haven, CT.: Yale University Press, 1961), is vital for understanding the spiritual life of contemporary Christians and others.

7. On this great and essential tradition, see John T. McNeill's wonderful study, *A History of the Cure of Souls* (New York: Harper & Brothers, 1951). This is a thorough and careful study of what we today have forfeited by our neglect of the soul.

8. Ann Stafford, "Angela of Foligno," in *Spirituality Through the Centuries: Ascetics and Mystics of the Western Church*, James Walsh, ed. (New York: P. J. Kenedy & Sons, n.d.), p. 191.

9. From the excellent article "Antinomians" in *Cyclopaedia of Biblical, Theological and Ecclesiastical Literature*, vol. 1, John M'Clintock and James Strong, eds. (New York: Harper & Brothers, 1895), pp. 264-266.

10. Much, not all, of the anti-government sentiment in the United States today is thinly veiled hatred of law and exaltation of brutal self-will. Thus it easily slips over into "righteous wrongdoing."

CHAPTER 12: THE CHILDREN OF LIGHT AND THE LIGHT OF THE WORLD

1. Frank Laubach, *Man of Prayer* (Syracuse, NY: Laubach Literacy International, 1990), p. 154.

2. William K. Hartmann and Ron Miller, *The History of Earth* (New York: Workman Publishing, 1991), p. 195.

3. Augustus H. Strong, *Systematic Theology* (1907; reprint, Valley Forge, PA: Judson Press, 1993), p. 869.

4. Quoted in Strong, p. 869.

5. Quoted in Strong, p. 869.

6. Quoted in Strong, p. 869.

7. Strong, p. 870.

8. Strong, p. 869.

9. Wayne Grudem, *Systematic Theology: An Introduction to Biblical Doctrine* (Grand Rapids, MI: Zondervan, 1994), p. 746. See the remainder of Grudem's helpful discussion in the following pages.

10. Walter Marshall, *The Gospel Mystery of Sanctification* (1692; reprint, Grand Rapids, MI: Zondervan, 1954), pp. 25-26.

11. John Wesley, *Selections from the Writings of the Rev. John Wesley* (New York: Eaton & Mains, 1901), p. 138. This quotation is taken from Wesley's tract, "An Earnest Appeal to Men of Reason and Religion," published in many editions of his writings.

CHAPTER 13: SPIRITUAL FORMATION IN THE LOCAL CONGREGATION

1. Quoted in R. Daniel Reeves and Thomas Tumblin, "Council on Ecclesiology: Preparation and Summaries," for Councils II and III, at Beeson Divinity School (Birmingham, AL) and Westminister Theological Seminary (Escondido, CA). Unpublished notes.

2. This is from an article, "We Grow in an Atmosphere of Love," excerpted from chap. 10 of Warren Wiersbe's *Being a Child of God*.

3. See chap. 7 of my *The Divine Conspiracy* (San Francisco: HarperSanFrancisco, 1998).

4. If anyone actually believes that the last part of Matthew 28:19 is only a command to get willing people wet, in some way deemed appropriate, while saying the words, "I baptize you in the name of the Father and the Son and the Holy Spirit," we can only ask them to ponder the matter. The *name*, in the biblical world, is never just words, but involves the thing named. The ritual should be a special moment of entry into the reality, and that was certainly how it was understood in biblical times. The presence of God in the midst was tangible and dangerous. People *died* of taking the Lord's Supper in the wrong attitude (1 Corinthians 11:30) or of misleading others in the fellowship (Acts 5:1-12).

5. Especially in chap. 8 of my *The Divine Conspiracy*, and in chap. 1 and

app. 2 of my *The Spirit of the Disciplines* (San Francisco: HarperSanFrancisco, 1988).

6. A. W. Tozer, *I Call It Heresy* (Harrisburg, PA: Christian Publications, 1974), p. 5.

7. As these words are written, the American public has just been treated once again to a leader in government involved in disgraceful affairs. Pretty clearly he is at least a long-standing adulterer and liar. He was asked on a nationally viewed interview, after stonewalling on what he had done, if he is a moral person. He replied—these were his exact words—"I *am* a moral person." Pretty clearly he believed it.

8. Ray C. Stedman, *Body Life: The Church Comes Alive* (Glendale, CA.: Regal, 1972), p. 13.

ABOUT THE
AUTHOR

DALLAS WILLARD IS A professor and former director of the School of Philosophy at the University of Southern California. He received his Ph.D. from the University of Wisconsin. Dallas is the author of more than thirty publications, including *The Divine Conspiracy*, *The Spirit of the Disciplines* (both Harper San Francisco), and *Hearing God* (InterVarsity). He and his wife, Jane, live in Chatsworth, California. They have two children and one grandchild. Many of his writings in philosophy and religion are available from his webpage: www.dwillard.org.